ETHICS FOR PSYCHOLOGISTS
A Commentary on the APA Ethics Code

Mathilda B. Canter
Bruce E. Bennett
Stanley E. Jones
Thomas F. Nagy

American Psychological Association • Washington, DC

Fifth printing February 1999

Published by
American Psychological Association
750 First Street, NE
Washington, DC 20002

Copies may be ordered from
APA Order Department
P.O. Box 92984
Washington, DC 20090-2984

In the United Kingdom, Europe, North Africa, and the Middle East, copies may be ordered from
American Psychological Association
3 Henrietta Street
Covent Garden
London WC2E 8LU
England

Typeset in Century by EPS Group Inc., Easton, MD

Printer: Data Reproductions Corporation, Auburn Hills, MI
Cover designer: Berg Design, Albany, NY
Technical/production editor: Valerie Montenegro

Library of Congress Cataloging-in-Publication Data
Ethics for psychologists : a commentary on the APA ethics code / Mathilda B. Canter
    . . . [et al.].
        p.   cm.
    Includes bibliographical references and index.
    ISBN 1-55798-259-7 (acid-free paper)
    1. Psychologists—Professional ethics. 2. American Psychological Association—
By-laws. I. Canter, Mathilda B.
    BF76.4E82   1994
    174′.915—dc20   94-36224
                                                                            CIP

British Library Cataloguing-in-Publication Data
A CIP record is available from the British Library.

Printed in the United States of America

To our parents, who taught us and enabled us,
and to our spouses and children,
who, in addition, encouraged us to produce this book
and sustained us while it was being written.

Contents

APA Ethical Standards

Preface

In the evolution of scientific and professional organizations there comes, usually, a point at which developing formal standards are codified, in order to delineate behaviors that are in keeping with those standards and behaviors that violate them. Such codes may be as concise as the Hippocratic Oath or as complex as that of the American Psychological Association (APA).

The first formal ethical standards of the APA were published in 1953, following a long process of solicitation from the membership of descriptions of situations psychologists faced involving ethical decisions. The material that was collected and analyzed revealed and reflected the values, problems, and concerns of psychologists then engaged in the science and practice of psychology and determined the ultimate scope of that ethical code. Many revisions of varying comprehensiveness were undertaken over the years. The latest revision, the APA Ethical Principles of Psychologists and Code of Conduct (1992), hereinafter called the Ethics Code, was adopted in August 1992 and went into effect on December 1, 1992. This current Ethics Code, although incorporating the general aspirational values of earlier documents, reflects a major revision in terms of its format, which separates aspirational principles from mandatory standards and includes detailed specification of those standards. It reflects the changes in our culture, in our professional and scientific data and beliefs, in our professional practices, in our workplaces, and in the state-of-the-art technologies now available to psychologists. In summary, it reflects the learning that has taken place, over time, as psychologists have developed and experienced their discipline.

In the course of processing the many comments addressed to it in response to various earlier drafts of this Ethics Code, the Revision Comments Subcommittee (RCS) of the APA Ethics Committee made changes reflecting many of the thousands of comments that were received. In that way the Ethics Code was improved through input drawn from the tremendous practical experience of the profession. Naturally, however, it was not possible—or sensible—to include many proposed changes, qualifications, or added provisions. The RCS directed its efforts toward keeping the Ethics Code standards, to the extent possible, as simple statements, behaviorally focused, and expressed as unitary concepts, in order to facilitate their application. To have done otherwise could have resulted in a code of such length and complexity as to diminish its usefulness. It would have become unwieldy as an educative guide and impractical for ethics committees to apply. It was frequently necessary to reject inclusion (in the Ethics Code) of an idea, a caution, an elaboration, or the like, even while understanding and agreeing with the content and potential utility value of the comments received. Generally, the decision to exclude was based on the inappropriateness of including in a document such as the Ethics Code a detailed commentary on any standard.

During the process of the revision, people often expressed eagerness for a casebook to be written and provided as a resource for increased understanding of the Ethics Code. Although such a casebook is likely to be written by the APA Ethics Committee, it must await the resolution of a sufficient number and variety of cases under the 1992 Ethics Code in order to provide the contents of a pertinent casebook.

All four of us were involved in the work of the RCS, and played a significant role in the crafting of the current Ethics Code. We began to consider the possibility of a book such as this one as a vehicle for providing some helpful commentary, in a timely fashion, to assist psychologists in learning and understanding the Ethics Code.

Many of the Ethics Code's standards address problems with which some psychologists may not have personal experience, and the commentary is designed to help ensure that the focal issues are made more accessible to the psychologist, whether experienced in addressing those ethical concerns or not. Although many of the cogent aspects of individual provisions may be apparent to ethics experts and to the governance groups that adopt them, they are not always apparent to the psychologist applying the Ethics Code's provisions in his or her unique circumstances. It is also true that there are many areas in which no rule has been adopted, because a clear consensus about an enforceable rule has not been reached. In such areas, too, educational guidance regarding the concerns is helpful.

In writing this book, we have, of course, been communicating our best understanding of what the 1992 Ethics Code was designed to communicate and the spirit in which it was written. It is our hope that it will serve the science and profession of psychology, as well as the public, by providing additional educational material to assist in ethical decision making and to facilitate a high level of ethical behavior by psychologists.

We are indebted to many for their roles in facilitating our writing of this book. First, we would like to acknowledge the contributions of Clifford D. Stromberg and Betsy K. Ranslow. They played significant roles in broadening our understanding of the legal aspects and implications of the ethical codes, their enforcement, and their impact on the profession and the public. They have our respect, our friendship, and our thanks. We would also like to acknowledge our debt to the many colleagues who have, over the years, taught us so much by sharing their views regarding ethical issues and dilemmas. The following people took time out of busy schedules to read all or part of our manuscript and share their extensive knowledge and various perspectives with us: Peter C. Appleby, Rosie P. Bingham, Sionag M. Black, Wayne J. Camara, Susan B. Cave, Charles R. Clark, Celia B. Fisher, Gwendolyn P. Keita, John C. Linton, A. John McSweeney, Esteban L. Olmedo, Ralph E. Packard, Randolph B. Pipes, Sherry L. Skidmore, Martha Storandt, and Jeffrey N. Younggren. We are grateful to all of them for their interest, their expertise, and their important contributions.

Debbie Felder was of great help in providing us with responsible and capable support services early in our work. It was also our good fortune to have the excellence of APA's publications staff to guide and minister to us. Patricia Harding-Clark kept our manuscripts and disks circulating and set up countless telephone conference calls for us, graciously and efficiently. We are grateful, too, to Gary VandenBos for his consultation and advice throughout the process of preparing the manuscript. Our editors, Mary Lynn Skutley and Peggy Schlegel, and Kevin Scully, editorial assistant, were extremely skillful and fulfilled their roles with sensitivity and good humor despite the difficulty of working with manuscripts from four people with four different writing styles! They have our deepest appreciation and respect.

Introduction

For more than four decades the American Psychological Association (APA) has expressed its interest in the professional ethics of its members, as manifested through a formal ethics code. The code has functioned essentially as an educational tool for psychologists, informing and instructing them about behaviors and values that are considered important in teaching, carrying out research, and providing psychological services. To address the many changes that have occurred in recent years as the profession of psychology has evolved, the APA, with much input from its membership, developed a new code of ethics, titled Ethical Principles of Psychologists and Code of Conduct (American Psychological Association [APA], 1992a; see also Appendix A). It was formally adopted by a vote of the APA Council of Representatives in August 1992, and it became operational in December of that year.

In a document with as many changes as the 1992 version, there is a possibility that misunderstandings or omissions in reading will occur, resulting in a desultory knowledge of the standards. Also, unfortunately, psychologists may tend to avoid studying a code of ethics very carefully until they encounter a state board of psychology investigation or a dissatisfied student or consumer of their services who initiates an ethics complaint, civil suit, or some other grievance procedure. At that hapless moment, these psychologists would learn that ignorance of the code does not constitute a defense of their actions; moreover, they would learn that such ignorance is a violation in and of itself.

This book is intended to be a resource for psychologists as they consider ethical issues. They are encouraged to seek assistance as well from other resources and documents, such as the APA Ethics Office; the state board of psychology; state and local psychological association ethics committees; and publications, guidelines, and other standards that might help resolve ethical questions. Also explored in this book is the relation between the APA and the state psychology boards, and other regulatory agencies that may cite the APA Ethics Code. It is likely that the guidance provided in the chapters that follow may well be pertinent under state law, as many state boards of psychology reference the APA Ethics Code. It should be noted, however, that these and other bodies, which may choose to enforce some or all of the standards of the Ethics Code, may apply them in their own way and will not necessarily be guided or regulated by the APA or its rules and procedures.

In a sense this book may function as providing general and specific answers, as relevant to the readers' concerns. However, it is not necessarily intended to be a substitute for a casebook or a personal consultation where there is significant doubt about professional conduct. The vignettes included in these pages are *illustrative* of a variety of likely scenarios encountered by psychologists; however, they are not based on actual opinions rendered by ethics committees. Nor is the commentary on each standard, or the illustrations provided, intended to be exhaustive. By contrast, a casebook is written by ethics committee members after enough time has passed to allow them to have experience resolving complaints involving most or all of the standards. It should be noted that individual situations may vary, and neither the Ethics Code nor this book will always adequately address the specifics of a situation faced by a psychologist or a consumer. Also, readers must keep in mind that it is the Ethics Code itself, and not this guidebook, that must be complied with.

As the work of psychologists continues to evolve, reflecting the changes in society, it is doubtless true that the Ethics Code will undergo further revisions. These revisions are what make the Ethics Code relevant and vital to psychologists, by keeping pace with the changing needs of students, patients, consumers, and society at large. Although it is impossible to always anticipate which areas will need further revision, it is likely that some of the newer standards will be modified in future revisions (e.g., barter and forensic activities).

Furthermore, it should be noted that our observations about the content and structure of earlier codes are offered in the context of meeting the current needs of psychologists and those who consume their services. It is not our intent to cast aspersions on earlier versions of ethics codes. Rather, we wish to point out where earlier versions may no longer have the same degree of clarity or cultural relevance as they once did, given the natural changes inherent in the evolution of our social structure. At the same time, it is important to note and acknowledge the importance of the work that preceded this (or any) revision as well as the debt we all owe to those who worked on earlier versions.

This book is divided into three sections—Part 1: Foundations, Part 2: Interpreting the Ethics Code, and Part 3: Conclusion. The Foundations section consists of two chapters that lay the groundwork for studying the Ethics Code. The first chapter describes the structure of the new Ethics Code and explores the process of ethical decision making through which psychologists proceed in their normal day-to-day work. The next chapter explores the historical perspective of the APA Ethics Code—its growth, development, and birth in 1953, as well as its revisions over the years. The revision process for the 1992 major revision is described, along with the 1989 limited revision associated with the challenges by the Federal Trade Commission and the Consent Agreement that ultimately ensued. Also, some of the thinking that went into the standards representing the culmination of 6 laborious years of processing thousands of proposals for change is explored.

The middle section of the book, Interpreting the Ethics Code, is the largest section, consisting of commentary on and analysis of each ethical standard. We have presented the standards and their implications from our perspectives as members of ethics committees, state psychology boards, APA boards or committees, and other professional bodies within the APA or state psychological associations. Both professional and legal implications of the standards are examined, with occasional presentations of minivignettes that illustrate the concept being discussed.

Some of the standards are essentially self-evident or uncomplicated. An example of this would be Standard 6.19, Honoring Commitments, which requires psychologists to honor commitments they have made to research participants. Other standards require extended analysis, however, as they are new concepts or quite complex. An example of this would be Standard 1.18, Barter (With Patients or Clients), which addresses the new rules permitting bartering for services or goods in return for psychological services.

In the final section of the book, the Conclusion, we have attempted to place ethics in a broader context and view the Ethics Code as a living document. The effects of legal, societal, and cultural values and trends are presented along with their impact on the evolving Ethics Code. Also, other means of regulating psychologists in the workplace are discussed. These include publications, such as guidelines, standards, policy statements, and other relevant ethical codes. Also included are the disciplinary functions of governmental agencies, such as state and provincial psychology boards. We have also attempted to examine the civil and criminal consequences of noncompliance and why psychologists should know and obey the laws and ethical standards that pertain to their work.

It is our hope that this book can be used in conjunction with the Ethics Code and can inform psychologists about pitfalls and dilemmas in the work setting before they are encountered. It will have served a useful purpose if it inspires a thorough study of the document, thereby filling in the gaps that would inevitably result from a cursory examination of the Ethics Code. By consistently implementing the "musts" and "must nots" of the Ethics Code, psychologists can generally assume that the risk of doing harm to another in the course of carrying out their professional responsibilities will be minimized.

It is also our hope that this book will be helpful to members of the public who interact with psychologists. It may provide them with an idea of what to expect in dealing with psychologists, whether in the role of student, research participant, client, or patient, to name a few.

Part I

Foundations

Chapter 1 _____

Learning the Process of Ethical Decision Making

Sound ethical decision making is based on a process that involves multiple steps, some of which are preventive and taken in advance, and some of which are taken at the time the ethical dilemma presents itself. These steps are as follows: (1) Know the Ethics Code, (2) know the applicable state and federal laws and regulations, (3) know the rules and regulations of the institution where you work, (4) engage in continuing education in ethics, (5) identify when there is a potential ethical problem, (6) learn the skills needed to analyze ethical obligations in often complex situations, and (7) consult with senior professionals knowledgeable about ethics. Each of the steps in ethical decision making is addressed in turn.

1. *Know the Ethics Code.* In order to understand and apply the Ethics Code, one should read, digest, and periodically review every section of it: the Introduction, the Preamble, the six aspirational General Principles, and the 102 mandatory Ethical Standards. It is also important to be alert to any revisions that may occur in parts of the Ethics Code over time. A synopsis of the major parts of the Ethics Code is presented in chapter 2 as a prelude to examining it in depth.

2. *Know the applicable state laws and federal regulations.* Psychologists must be well informed about current, relevant state and federal laws and regulations and should keep abreast of changes that may occur at any time, independent of changes that may occur in the Ethics Code itself. This is important in matters such as confidentiality, record keeping, testing and assessment, malpractice, research activities, and other professional and business areas. Also, state licensure laws and state boards of psychology may reference parts of the Ethics Code or adopt it in its entirety; this effectively invests the standards with the force of law and opens up an array of sanctions that are independent of the APA or any state psychological association. Psychologists who conduct research would be well advised to be familiar with relevant publications in their areas of work, such as the regulations of the U.S. Department of Health and Human Services and its National Institutes of Health, the National Science Foundation, more specialized centers such as the Department of Agriculture's Animal Welfare Information Center (AWIC), and so forth. Those involved in employment testing and human resources work should likewise be knowledgeable about

pertinent federal legislation, such as statutes and the regulations that implement them, concerning employee selection procedures, rights of persons with disabilities, employee rights, and rights concerning health records, to name a few.

3. *Know the rules and regulations of the institution where you work.* It is essential to be familiar with the current rules and regulations of the institution, organization, or group in which one works or practices. For example, when practicing as a clinician in a military setting, a psychologist will encounter significantly different regulations about confidentiality than is commonly the case in a civilian setting. Also, research activities that take place in a certain hospital or school must conform to that institution's rules and regulations governing such activities and the welfare of research participants. Generally, researchers will be required to receive approval from the appropriate institutional review board (IRB) before proceeding with their investigation; they should be familiar with the requirements of the IRB and be prepared to cooperate fully with them by submitting all appropriate documentation and responding to all questions about the research.

4. *Engage in continuing education in ethics.* There are many ways of becoming familiar with the Ethics Code, and psychologists should regularly make efforts to broaden their knowledge of the Ethical Principles and their implications. It is important for psychologists to learn the skills needed to analyze ethical obligations in often complex situations. This can be accomplished by such actions as taking a course or workshop in ethics, subscribing to a journal that focuses on ethics and professional issues, or reading books on ethics as they pertain to one's particular area of practice. Reading professional publications that pertain to ethics and attending seminars or workshops should be an ongoing activity of psychologists that extends throughout their professional life. In these days of rapidly expanding databases, innovative services, new health care delivery systems, new research interests, novel education and training experiences, ubiquitous lawyers, litigious consumers, and ever changing ethical rules, there is much opportunity to lose sight of the rules and the subtleties of ethics unless one persists with ongoing efforts at continuing education. Some resources are listed in the footnote of the Introduction to the Ethics Code and throughout this book and are available on request from most professional organizations.

It might be wise to bear in mind that as psychologists we have an obligation not only to follow the Ethics Code ourselves but to expect our colleagues to do likewise (see Standard 8.04). Therefore, in order to make a judgment about the ethical conduct of a psychologist who has a different role from one's own (e.g., teacher or clinician), it is essential to know the entire Ethics Code. For example, if a researcher learns of a psychotherapist who routinely hands out business cards at funeral homes, he or she might not be confident in judging the ethical propriety of this behavior without first being familiar with Principle 3.06 (In-Person Solicitation). Obviously, it is not sufficient to learn only parts of the Ethics Code that directly pertain to one's work.

It should be noted that APA documents, such as *General Guidelines for Providers of Psychological Services* (APA, 1987a), *Guidelines for Providers of Psychological Services to Ethnic, Linguistic, and Culturally Diverse Populations* (APA, 1993b), or *Guidelines for Child Custody Evaluations in Divorce Proceedings* (APA, 1994) are not to be construed as providing enforceable standards. Rather, they offer a wealth of information on a broad variety of subjects pertaining to competent and ethical conduct in psychology. However, these documents change over time, can be revised, or can even be rescinded; it is the responsibility of psychologists to be familiar with the most current versions, as needed, and their applicability. Many of these documents can be ordered directly from the Order Department of the APA.

5. *Identify when there is a potential ethical problem.* Obviously the process of identifying that an ethical dilemma might exist is of crucial importance in taking steps to address it. Sometimes this may require developing insight or knowledge about one's own blindspots, prejudices, weaknesses, or ignorance. This insight or knowledge may also require that a psychologist be able to admit that he or she does not know all of the answers and that what was presumed to be a relatively simple or even routine psychological innovative professional activity could have a harmful effect on a particular consumer. Certainly it is important to be familiar with the relevant research literature, including ethical issues, as it affects the activity at hand.

Framing the right question is a large part of addressing an ethical issue, and a response to the question that indicates concern does not necessarily mean that the intended behavior is unethical. It should be noted that questions that are answered in the direction of increased risk for harm would prompt the psychologist be more vigilant, to act decisively, and to thoroughly address the issues at hand. Some of the important questions to be asked that might help uncover the relevant ethical, professional, and legal issues are as follows: (a) Are you practicing within your boundaries of competence, according to your formal training, supervision, or experience? (b) Are you about to engage in a new activity, research project, or intervention that has little or no referent in your training or professional experience? (c) What type of harm might result from your actions to an individual, group, or organization? (d) Can you be sufficiently assured of an individual's diagnosis, history, or psychological makeup so as to proceed ahead with reasonable certainty that no adverse reactions will occur? (e) Will you be entering into a business or personal relationship with a recipient of your services in addition to the professional one? (f) Does the proposed activity involve a real or apparent conflict of interest, exploi-

tation, loss of objectivity, or impaired judgment? (g) Are you system-
atically avoiding or refusing to address certain topics or situations
that you normally would embrace? (h) Do you find yourself changing
your usual and customary practices in dealing with a particular individual or situation? (i) Are you changing your customary boundaries
or limits by either engaging the individual in a secondary role or
attempting to increase or decrease your social distance? (j) Do you
have something to gain by *using* the other for his or her knowledge,
expertise, money, status, or some other attribute for your own personal
or professional gain? (k) Are your statements accurate, or are they
misleading with the intent of serving some secondary purpose for your
own gain? (l) Are you familiar with the laws and regulations that
pertain to your area of work?

In the press of day-to-day professional activities, it is certainly easy
to avoid scrutinizing the ethical aspects as reflected in the aforementioned questions. Part of the importance of training in ethics is to
develop an "automatic monitor" that will appropriately cue the psychologist that a situation requires a careful review of the ethical issues.
As noted earlier, the training can, and should be, through formal
graduate work, continuing education, informal work with colleagues,
and self-study. It should also involve "practice" through active thinking about the ethics of situations, whether or not an ethical issue is
apparent. Psychologists should also be aware of the unlikely combi-
nations of events that may cause harm to an individual who has a
formal relationship with a psychologist, because such events are more
common than they appear. For example, a therapist married to an
alcoholic, philandering husband may be treating a depressed male
patient, whom she finds attractive, when the patient reports that his
wife of 25 years has just left him for another man. Her objectivity and
competence to work with *this type of patient* may be impaired, given
her life situation, and her vulnerability to act inappropriately with
him may increase as she overidentifies with him. It is important to
consider the possible scenarios addressing the likelihood of harm resulting from an intended psychological intervention, even though these
might not be apparent at the outset. By continuously posing the question, What could happen next?, one can achieve a sense of the range
of possible negative outcomes and be guided by them in ethical decision
making. Although this might appear to be focusing too much on the
negative or the potential "downside," it is an important exercise that
ultimately will lead to better judgment, resulting in more appropriate
preventive measures being taken.

6. *Learn a method for analyzing ethical obligations in often complex sit-
    uations.* There are numerous systems for formal analysis and reso-
    lution of ethical problems and dilemmas. Such models may be difficult
    to apply when an immediate decision is required, but many situations
    do allow time for such review. Detailed discussion of these systems is

beyond the scope of this book, so interested psychologists should consult other sources. Examples of such models can be found by consulting the following authors: Haas and Malouf (1989, pp. 5–14), Keith-Spiegel and Koocher (1985, pp. 18–25), Kitchener (1984), and Tymchuk (1982, 1986).

7. *Consult with professionals knowledgeable about ethics.* At times, psychologists engaged in ethical decision making for a particular set of circumstances may find insufficient guidance from either the Ethics Code, the law, or other guidelines, documents, or published materials on the subject. In these cases it is best to seek professional consultation with others. Even those in rural areas, with few professional resources immediately available, can make use of telephone consultations in resolving difficult issues concerning their professional work. Some of the resources available are official ethics bodies (e.g., state, regional, or APA divisional ethics committees, the APA Ethics Office, or hospital ethics committees), ethics instructors in universities and professional schools of psychology, and psychologists in the community who have published and lectured in the area of ethics. Qualified lawyers who are familiar with issues in mental health and health care services may also be helpful. It is important to note that although it may be a useful practice to consult with attorneys, child protection agencies, boards of psychology, or other regulatory agencies, this should not necessarily be considered a substitute for consulting with a senior psychologist experienced in ethics. It should also be noted that APA divisions that have ethics guidelines or committees may be useful in an advisory capacity; however, they do not resolve formal ethics complaints, nor do they relieve psychologists of the responsibility to adhere to the APA Ethics Code.

In this chapter we have presented a series of steps for psychologists to follow to assist in ethical compliance. As a part of taking these steps, psychologists should bear in mind that they are responsible for keeping themselves informed of the standards and relevant guidelines, as well as any changes to those standards and guidelines that may affect their work. It is important to remember that in matters of professional ethics, ignorance is not bliss. Sound ethical behavior is ultimately based on a solid knowledge of pertinent codes and regulations, sharpened by a clear understanding of the consequences of one's actions.

Chapter 2 _____

Changing the Rules That Govern Psychologists: The Evolution of the APA Ethics Code

Ethics codes generate great passion, both in the importance of the guidance they provide and in the intensity with which their provisions are debated. Consistent features of the APA Ethics Code have been the importance of aspiring to high ethical standards and the intensity of debate over controversial aspects. The history that follows provides examples of changes motivated by factors such as the evolution of society and the inevitable and continuing tension between science and practice.

A less recognized factor in the reasons for changes, however, has been the balance between the Ethics Code as clear and useful guidance on the one hand and the Ethics Code as a standard with which to challenge psychologists on the other. Psychologists working primarily in research and academic settings have complained that some provisions are infringements on, or at least unnecessary irritants in, academic freedom and pursuit of research interests, whereas psychologists working primarily in practice settings complain that the Ethics Code is a sword to be used against them in malpractice, licensing board, and ethics committee actions. Psychologists do not argue that they should not be ethical; rather, some argue that detailed provisions in ethics codes contribute to harassment or reduce reasonable psychological judgment in maximizing the welfare of those with whom they work. Those forces were at work in the development of the original Ethics Code and continue to shape today's code.

In this chapter, we explore the history of the ethical regulation of psychologists. We begin by describing the first APA Ethics Code and the empirical, critical-incident methodology that made it unique. The nature of subsequent revisions to the Ethics Code is discussed next, and the evolution, through various revisions, of selected content areas is summarized. Finally, we present a description of the 1992 revision (see Appendix A), with a focus on the salient changes in both structure and content.

The Prelude

A major historical factor that led to the creation of the first formal APA Ethics Code was the increasing professional activity of psychologists, both in mental health treatment and in industrial consulting (Hobbs, 1948). This led to (a) an increased need for a formal code as a necessary component of a "profession"; (b) increased instances of psychologists advertising and otherwise representing their services and credentials, with inevitable concerns about misrepresentations and inappropriate practices; and (c) a need for regulation of the profession. As psychologists sought licensure in various states, there were calls for a code of ethics to establish a disciplinary standard. The question became, What kind of code should it be and how should it be developed?

The stage had been set in 1938 with the formation of a temporary Committee on Scientific and Professional Ethics (CSPE).[1] That group recommended that the time was not right for the creation of a formal code, but recommended the formation of a continuing committee because "complaints of unethical conduct . . . have been referred to the [temporary] Committee and have been handled privately and informally, with apparently good results" (Olson, 1940, pp. 718–719). In 1940, the continuing committee was formed with the charge to "investigate complaints of unethical conduct . . . and to formulate from time to time rules or principles of ethics for adoption by the Association" (Olson, 1940, p. 721).

The new committee that settled most of the cases referred to it "informally," but found much of its task increasingly complicated. Its 1947 report to the Council of Representatives recognized that "it will never be practical or desirable to devise a 'complete' or a 'rigid' code. Yet in view of the rapid growth of professional psychology, the time is clearly ripe to formulate certain guiding principles" (American Psychological Association [APA], 1947, p. 489). The committee indicated that it advised "somewhat arbitrarily" in response to member requests for guidance, and "in dealing with [an] offender, the Chairman had no authoritative statement to support him. The present unwritten code is tenuous, elusive, and unsatisfactory" (APA, 1947, p. 489).

The First Ethics Code

The first Committee on Ethical Standards for Psychologists (CESP) was formed in 1947, with Edward C. Tolman as its chairperson (Peak, 1947, p. 483). This committee determined that psychology should develop its code using the critical-incident method. This involved asking the APA's 7,500 members (in 1948) "to describe a situation they knew of first-hand, in which a psychologist made a decision having ethical implications, and to indicate . . . the ethical issues involved" (APA, 1953a, p. vi). The method and its rationale was articulated in an *American Psychologist* article (Hobbs, 1948).[2]

The critical-incident method has been cited as a distinctive feature that

---

[1] The committee names and abbreviations may become confusing: the Committee on Scientific and Professional Ethics (CSPE) was later named the Committee on Scientific and Professional Ethics and Conduct (CSPEC) in 1951, before being given the current name, Ethics Committee, in 1984. The original Ethics Code development, and most revisions, have been done by groups called the Committee on Ethical Standards for Psychologists (CESP).

[2] The author of this document, Nicholas Hobbs, was a member of the Committee on Ethical Standards for Psychologists and the chairperson of the subsequent working committee from 1948 to completion.

sets the APA Ethics Code apart from other professional codes developed by more a priori methods. The APA Ethics Code, although not apparently the method of its development, was used as the model for the development of many other associations' codes (Holtzman, 1979).

In addition to the decision to use an empirical approach, two less cited characteristics were also important. The Introduction of the 1953 Ethics Code notes that there was a conscious decision that "the risks of open discussion of specific ethical issues are considerably outweighed by the advantages" (APA, 1953a, p. viii). Without this openness, the data from the incident method would not have been available to be used openly in active development of standards. Another important feature of the Ethics Code's early development was the formation of a committee separate from the Ethics Committee to coordinate its inception and refinement. This committee, chaired by Nicholas Hobbs, was formally christened the Committee on Ethical Standards for Psychologists.[3]

The Hobbs committee, using several subcommittees and many members, worked through more than a thousand incidents and developed drafts with review and revisions by various groups. Drafts were published in *American Psychologist* for comment by the membership. The final version was adopted in 1952 and published in 1953. That version of the Ethics Code, at 171 pages, is still the longest of all APA Ethics Codes. It was structured into six broad categories that contained a total of 310 rule elements (162 "principles" and an additional 148 numbered "subprinciples").

The 1953 Ethics Code with which most psychologists are now familiar, however, is the summary version, *Ethical Standards of Psychologists: A Summary of Ethical Principles* (APA, 1953b). This was a 19-page document planned to be a "succinct statement of ethical principles, without the incidents and the detailed elaboration contained" in the full code (Adkins, 1952, p. 647). The detailed version was planned only for distribution within the profession, whereas the summary version was intended to be made available "to other professional workers, to legislators, and to the public" (Adkins, 1952, p. 647). In fact, the summary was revised "with the assistance of the APA's Public Information Officer" (Adkins, 1952, p. 647), and some of the principles were modified, some principles were not included, and many subprinciples were included.

Revisions

The first revision of the Ethics Code was planned at the time of the Council of Representatives' adoption in 1952, when it instructed that the adoption was for a trial period of 3 years (Adkins, 1952, p. 647).[4] However, a revised draft

---

[3] The CSPE (APA, 1947), in its report recommending the Ethics Code's development, indicated that "the five members of the [Ethics] Committee themselves provided too narrow a group to undertake the formulation" and noted that "a representative body of psychologists . . . should be formed" (p. 489).

[4] After an extension of the time for revision in 1954 (Hobbs, 1954, p. 724), the Council of Representatives voted in 1955 "that the *Ethical Standards of Psychologists* . . . be continued on an indeterminate basis" and initiated a new Committee on Ethical Standards of Psychologists (Anastasi, 1955, p. 708), chaired by Wayne H. Holtzman.

was not published for comment until 1958. A 2-page introduction to the draft described criticism of the 1953 Ethics Code for its length, codifying etiquette, and overlap of principles as well as the decision to modify the original, detailed structure to "preserve the major strengths of the present [1953] code while changing its form to a more useful, readable one" (APA, 1958, p. 266).[5]

The 1959 Ethics Code consisted of 19 principles "general enough to weather considerable growth of psychology" with "specificity of each principle . . . maintained by the use of short explanatory paragraphs" (APA, 1958, p. 267). The 1959 Ethics Code was adopted provisionally for 3 years by the Board of Directors in 1958 and published in 1959 in the *American Psychologist* (APA, 1959). The full version of the 1953 Ethics Code was "continued in force . . . while the new code is demonstrating itself in [ethics] committee practice" (Carter, 1958, p. 697).[6]

All Ethics Codes subsequent to the original 1953 Ethics Code have been structured in the 1959 code's format (principles without incidents), and, except for 1972, the revisions have been accomplished by the process of a committee presenting drafts for comment. Revisions were adopted in 1958 (APA, 1959), 1962 (APA, 1963), 1965 (APA, 1968), 1972 (APA, 1972), January 1977 ("Ethical Standards," 1977), August 1977 (Conger, 1978), 1979 (APA, 1979), 1981 (APA, 1981), 1989 (APA, 1990), and 1992 (APA, 1992a). These revisions brought changes in content that varied from minor to moderately major. Some of these changes are summarized later in this chapter.

In 1972, significant principles were incorporated that affected science when the Council of Representatives adopted the *Ethical Principles in the Conduct of Research with Human Participants* and published the full document in 1973 (APA, 1973). At adoption, however, the principles themselves became a new component of the *Ethical Standards of Psychologists* (McKeachie, 1973, p. 320).[7] The new Ethics Code was printed as a separate monograph dated 1972 but did not appear in the *American Psychologist* (APA, 1972).

Significant revision activity occurred throughout the late 1970s through

---

[5]The 1990 and 1992 Ethics Codes publication histories incorrectly show the 1958 publication as an official version. The 1958 publication was a draft, published for comment by the CESP. The 1992 Ethics Code does not reference the 1959 version.

[6]The Ethics Committee, then called the Committee on Scientific and Professional Ethics and Conduct (CSPEC), was also encouraged to develop a casebook, part of the overall plan to provide more detailed guidance in the eventual absence of the original incidents in the Ethics Code itself. Although the original plan was for further critical incidents to assist in future revisions, the critical-incident method was formally used again only in the development of the *Ethical Principles in the Conduct of Research with Human Participants* (APA, 1973).

[7]As early as the 1958 CESP report, criticism of the 1953 Ethics Code noted that it was "too heavily focused upon ethical issues involved in the practice of clinical psychology or in other special fields of psychology" (APA, 1958, p. 267). In 1957, the Board of Professional Afffairs (BPA) and the Board of Scientific Affairs (BSA) were formed, and CESP actually reported through the BPA. The perception appears to have been that the regular Ethics Code revision process was a practitioner process, and in 1966 the Board of Directors appointed a Committee on Ethical Standards in Research. The 1969 CESP group was in fact named the Committee on Ethical Standards for Professional Psychology and was seen as the parallel to the Committee on Ethical Standards in Research. The CSPEC, as a standing committee, reported to the Board of Directors and the Council of Representatives.

1981, and the Council of Representatives adopted changes to the Ethics Code in 1977, 1978, 1979, and 1981. The Ethics Code adopted in January 1977 had many changes and was published only in the *APA Monitor*, as was the minor 1978 change. The 1979 Ethics Code was printed as a separate monograph. The 1981 Ethics Code, published in the *American Psychologist* (APA, 1981), made many changes from the 1979 version, including the name change from "Standards" to "Principles" and adding Principle 10, Care and Use of Animals.

In the next section, we consider how the content of selected areas of the Ethics Code evolved from the original version to the 1981 version.

Evolution of Selected Areas

As a "living document," the Ethics Code can be examined as a gauge of both societal changes and changes in our profession. These changes are apparent in the content of various revisions. For example, the drug culture of the 1960s is reflected in the September 1965 adoption of two principles regarding the "use of accepted drugs for therapeutic purposes" (7i) and research "using experimental drugs (for example, hallucinogenic . . . or similar substances)" (16e; Newman, 1965, p. 1034). Several areas have shown important changes in content over the years. Among those are sexual misconduct, dual relationships, advertising, and research.

Sexual Misconduct

There is no reference in the 1953 Ethics Code to "sexual intimacies with clients," which appears for the first time in the 1977 Ethics Code. However, several principles and rules make it clear that such behavior would be unacceptable if brought before an ethics committee. For example, in the 1953 summary code, there is reference to an "appropriate time and place for clinical work to protect both client and clinician from actual or imputed harm and the profession from censure" (APA, 1953b, p. 4). This was continued in the 1959 Ethics Code as Paragraph h under Principle 7 (Client Welfare).

The clearest example, however, occurs in the full-length 1953 Ethics Code as Principle 2.63, Item 1, which follows an incident in which a psychologist became sexually involved with a student client: "The psychologist in the practice of his profession should show sensible regard for the social codes and moral expectations of the people of the community in which he works, recognizing that violations of accepted moral standards may involve his clients in damaging personal conflicts, and impugn his own name and the reputation of his profession" (APA, 1953a, pp. 84–85). This principle did *not* appear in the 1953 summary version but was included in the 1959 revision as Principle 3, Moral and Legal Standards.

In the 1977 and subsequent codes, Principle 6a includes the statement that "Sexual intimacies with clients are unethical." With that explicit rule, the previous Principle 7h (appropriate time and place) was deleted and Moral and Legal Standards was revised and continued to be addressed under General Principle 3.

Dual Relationships

The term *dual relationship* appeared first in the 1953 Ethics Code but applied in 1953 only to "clinical relationships with members of his own family, with intimate friends, or with persons so close that their welfare might be jeopardized by the dual relationship" (APA, 1953b, p. 4). In addition, there was a provision for "an emergency decision . . . to work with [such] a person" (APA, 1953b, p. 4). The 1959 Ethics Code (Principle 8c under Client Relationship) broadens the prohibition with the change to "intimate friends, close associates, or others whose welfare might be jeopardized by such a dual relationship" (APA, 1959, p. 281). The 1963 Ethics Code makes the limited change of "professional relationship" instead of "clinical relationship."

The 1977 Ethics Code places dual relationship in a broader context by adding the concept of "psychologists['] . . . inherently powerful position vis-à-vis clients" and expands the nonexclusive list to include "treating employees, supervisees, close friends or relatives." In 1981 several additional changes were made that also appear to have broadened the prohibition: (a) "inherently powerful" was changed to "potentially influential"; (b) "*vis-a-vis* clients" was broadened to "vis-à-vis persons such as," making the provision more general and then specifically adding students and subordinates to clients; (c) "dual relationships which *might* [emphasis added] impair" was changed to "that *could* [emphasis added] impair"; (d) the list of examples of prohibited dual relationships was expanded, adding research with or treatment of students to employees, supervisees, close friends and relatives; and (e) dual relationship regarding research was moved from 1979 Principle 9e to 6a, resulting in its now being prohibited rather than requiring "special vigilance to protect" freedom to decline to participate in or withdraw from research.

Advertising

Until the adoption of the 1977 Ethics Code, APA's Ethics Code required "adhering to professional rather than to commercial standards" (APA, 1972, p. 3). The 1953 Ethics Code also contained specific advertising prohibitions, describing activities such as direct mail, repeated press ads, and radio announcements as unacceptable. Advertising and promotional issues have been some of the most "volatile" in terms of changes in the code. Comparison of subsequent revisions indicates that relatively major changes occurred in the advertising sections in 1963, 1977, and 1979. The 1963 changes included major restructuring of Principle 10, with a title change from Advertising to Announcement of Services and the addition of a new Principle 19, Promotional Activities. Principle 19 focused on the "promotion of psychological devices, books, or other products" (APA, 1963, p. 60).

The 1977 Ethics Code, although it dropped the "professional rather than commercial" phrase, still prohibited many practices by stating in Principle 4a that "when announcing professional services, psychologists *limit* [emphasis added] the information to" ("Ethical Standards," 1977, p. 22). The 1979 standard continued a liberalizing of advertising provisions by stating that "psychologists *may* [emphasis added] list the following information" and adding that "additional relevant or important consumer information may be included if not prohibited by other sections of the Ethical Standards" (APA, 1979, p. 3).

Federal Trade Commission (FTC) History

An important change historically involved several prohibitions in the 1981 Ethics Code that were the subject of an investigation by the Bureau of Competition of the FTC beginning in 1986. Despite the liberalized advertising provisions, there were sections that the FTC believed posed impermissible restrictions on methods of competition. The FTC had pursued changes in the ethics codes of the American Medical Association (AMA), the American Dental Association, and other groups. After the U.S. Supreme Court upheld action by the FTC against the AMA in 1982, a number of other groups were investigated, even if the provisions in their codes were not as restrictive as those of the professional associations involved in the original actions brought by the FTC.

The provisions at issue included parts of 1981 Principle 4b (APA, 1981) that prohibited "a testimonial from a patient regarding the quality of . . . psychologists' services"; "a statement implying . . . one-of-a-kind abilities"; "a statement . . . likely to appeal to a client's fears . . . concerning the possible results of failure to obtain the offered services"; "a statement concerning the comparative desirability of offered services"; and "a statement of direct solicitation of individual clients" (p. 635). Also addressed were parts of Principle 6d prohibiting the giving or receiving "any remuneration for referring clients for professional services" (APA, 1981, p. 636) and of Principle 7b prohibiting psychologists from offering "their own services directly to" persons "receiving similar services from another professional" (APA, 1981, p. 636).

In 1986, the APA voluntarily suspended taking ethics actions based on these provisions, and in 1989, the provisions were formally rescinded, resulting in the June 2, 1989, amended version of the Ethics Code (APA, 1990). The changes were simply the elimination of the provisions described earlier. The 1992 Ethics Code included new and modified provisions designed to embody the APA's ethics policies and to be acceptable to the FTC (see the discussion later in this chapter).

Although the APA signed the consent agreement in 1989, the FTC did not sign and issue the consent order until 1992. Some confusion occurred because the order required mailing a copy of the order to all APA members after the order was final in late December. Many members assumed that the order meant that the 1992 Ethics Code would need to be changed, whereas required changes had already been completed.

The order itself should be consulted for a complete understanding of its scope and requirements, but it basically provides that that APA may not prohibit, by formal rule or otherwise, certain advertising, solicitation, and referral practices. It also, however, provides explicit exceptions, allowing the APA to adopt and enforce rules with respect to the following:

> 1. representations that [APA] reasonably believes would be false or deceptive; 2. uninvited, in-person solicitation of business from persons who, because of their particular circumstances, are vulnerable to undue influence; or 3. solicitation of testimonial endorsements (including solicitation of consent to use the person's prior statement as a testimonial endorsement) from current psychotherapy patients, or from other persons who, because of their particular circumstances, are vulnerable to undue influence. ("FTC Consent Order," 1993).

The consent agreement between the APA and the FTC defines some terms for purposes of that agreement. These definitions do not apply to the APA Ethics Code generally, but are relevant to consider when applying those portions of the Ethics Code covered by the FTC agreement. The definitions include "psychotherapy" and "current psychotherapy patient," and are included in the commentary on Standard 3.05.

Research

The tension between science and practice has affected the historical development of the Ethics Code. Although the empirical method and broad representation used in developing the first Ethics Code ensured that there was no bias for or against any constituency, the problems encountered by psychology's applied specialties had produced a significant part of the motivation leading to the decision to develop the first Ethics Code and inevitably resulted in more standards and more detailed coverage in the code. Nevertheless, from the beginning, the APA Ethics Code addressed the broad range of research issues, both in terms of human participants and animal subjects. The first animal use guidelines were adopted by APA in 1925, shortly after the formation of the animal experimentation committee, and the 1953 Ethics Code summary version, with a similar statement in the full version, contained the statement that "psychologists using animals in research should abide by the Rules Regarding Animals, drawn up by the Committee on Precautions in Animal Experimentation and adopted by the American Psychological Association in 1949" (APA, 1953b, p. 13).

When the 1959 Ethics Code changed to the principle and subprinciple form from the detailed 1953 format, the code contained a major section called Harmful Aftereffects and several miscellaneous provisions related to research. One subsection continued to reference the Rules Regarding Animals. A significant change occurred with the addition in the 1963 Ethics Code of an introductory sentence to Section 16, which was renamed Research Precautions. The introduction stated that "the psychologist assumes obligations for the welfare of his research subjects, both animal and human" (APA, 1963, p. 59).

As noted earlier, the 1972 Ethics Code added an additional preamble and replaced three of the subsections of Section 16 with the principles provided in the *Ethical Principles in the Conduct of Research with Human Participants*. Holtzman (1979) cited those principles as a "major step forward" and indicated that "although principles [in the 1953 Ethics Code and revisions] were also formulated dealing with research, it wasn't until more recently that ethics for human research received the same amount of attention as did the earlier professional psychologist-client relationship" (p. 107). The development of the *Ethical Principles in the Conduct of Research with Human Participants* began in 1966 when the Board of Directors appointed the Committee on Ethical Standards in Research. This project used the 1953 Ethics Code's critical-incident approach used in developing the research principles, the only formal use of the critical-incident method in the APA Ethics Code since the 1953 Ethics Code.

The 1977 Ethics Code was a major reorganization of numbers and content in many areas of the code, but the research provisions remain similar, with renaming of the primary research principle to Pursuit of Research Activities (Principle 9a–1). However, a reference list was added with the statement, "psychologists are responsible for knowing about and acting in accord with the standards and positions of the APA, as represented in official documents such as the following" ("Ethical Standards," 1977, p. 23): The list includes Ethical Principles in the Conduct of Research with Human Participants (1973) and Principles for the Care and Use of Animals (1971; McKeachie, 1972, pp. 292–293). (The text in 9k still referred to the Rules Regarding Animals.) There were also significant changes in Principle 9 (with 10 subsections), which was renamed Research with Human Participants. New Principle 9b addresses the concept of "minimal risk."

A major change in 1981 was the addition of Principle 10 titled Care and Use of Animals, adding into the code itself the primary principles from the Principles for the Care and Use of Animals (1971). The reference list added in only 1977 was deleted, and the APA policy was changed to enforcement of only the Ethics Code and no other APA documents.

The 1992 Revision Process

As the science and practice of psychology has expanded over the years, there has been a marked shift in the type and frequency of ethics complaints that were brought against psychologists. This can be accounted for partly by the increasing numbers of APA members and affiliates, which approached the 100,000 mark in 1990, and partly by the climate of American society, consisting of consumers who were becoming more knowledgeable about mental health services and more litigious as well.

In 1986 there were a total of 91 active cases at the end of the year, contrasted with only 54 one year earlier (APA, 1987b). There were 69% more ethics cases brought before the APA Ethics Committee than 1 year previously. This trend appeared to continue, with a 56% increase in 1987, as well as an increase of 76% in the number of people contacting the Ethics Office expressing an intent to bring a complaint against a psychologist, over a 2-year period

(APA, 1988). It was increasingly clear that ethics complaints and inquiries were significantly on the rise.

A major revision was needed, many felt, partly because of changes in the professional work of psychologists and changes in American society. Also, 5 years had elapsed since the last revision, and it was timely to implement a thorough review in order to maintain current ethical guidance for psychologists and good protection for those who had professional dealings with them. Psychologists were being asked to conduct forensic evaluations and engage in litigation work more than ever before. Yet, there was little guidance that would assist psychologists in these activities. Also, with an increase in sophistication of consumers of psychological services, there was a concomitant increase in the risk of ethics complaints and malpractice lawsuits faced by psychologists. The broad and lofty language of some of the principles, reflecting the times of the previous revision as well as the will of the APA Council of Representatives, may have increased the perception of vulnerability of psychologists to unjustified complaints from consumers.

An example of some of the problems encountered was the ruling of the North Carolina Court of Appeals, resulting from a 6-year investigatory and adjudication process in the case of *White v. the North Carolina State Board of Examiners of Practicing Psychologists* (1990). The court found that the preambles to the Ethical Principles of Psychologists were "unconstitutionally vague for purposes of being cited for specific violations." It was clear, for a variety of reasons, that the 1981 Ethics Code needed revising and that failure to do so might create problems for both psychologists and recipients of their services.

The Ethics Committee began the revision process by asking state ethics committee chairpeople to submit proposed changes to the existing Ethics Code. In 1986, the Ethics Committee appointed a task force. The six-person task force, chaired initially by Karen S. Kitchener and shortly thereafter by Thomas F. Nagy, consisted of five senior psychologists, all of whom were members of the APA Ethics Committee and experienced in using the ethics code regularly in responding to inquiries and resolving complaints. These five members— Robyn M. Dawes, Karen S. Kitchener, Thomas F. Nagy, Phillip S. Pierce, and Melba J. Vasquez—represented different areas of expertise, including research, clinical and counseling psychology, academia, consulting, and administration (Nagy, 1988). It was decided that they would remain on the task force after their terms on the Ethics Committee expired. They were assisted by Ethics Office Director David H. Mills and Administrative Director Betsy K. Ranslow, who helped in coordinating the activities of the subcommittee.

The original goals of the task force, largely realized in the most current document, were to create a code that would be easily taught, would be easily learned, would contain one concept or idea in each standard instead of multiple ones, and would continue to address the broad variety of problems and dilemmas encountered by psychologists in various aspects of their work (Nagy, 1989). With these changes, the Ethics Code would be easier to read and use for psychologists, students, consumers, and ethics committees.

One consideration in crafting the standards was the past history of ethics complaints, civil suits, or other actions that were brought against psychologists who had engaged in certain behaviors. Standards were created that would minimize the likelihood that those who had professional dealings with psychologists would misunderstand the professional obligations of psychologists. Hence, the code is quite pragmatic in its construction. Given that certain goals constitute the domain of psychological work, this Ethics Code attempts to show the way to meet those goals so that the risk of damaging someone or of being harmed by them is minimized. Generally, its principles were designed with the results or the outcome of an action as the criteria for developing the decision rules. The mandatory standards reflect beliefs about professional conduct that would essentially increase the quality of service provided while simultaneously reducing the risk of harm.

The task force solicited input from APA members and completed its work with publication of a draft in the *APA Monitor* ("Ethical Principles Revised," 1990). In order to address the many comments received, three individuals were appointed by the Ethics Committee to constitute the new Revision Comments Subcommittee. This was chaired by Mathilda B. Canter, then chairperson of the Ethics Committee, and included Bruce E. Bennett, Board of Directors liaison to the Ethics Committee, and Thomas F. Nagy, former chairperson of the revision task force. The subcommittee was assisted by Stanley E. Jones, director of APA's Ethics Office, Betsy K. Ranslow, director of Ethics Investigations, and outside legal counsel Clifford D. Stromberg. The subcommittee reported to the APA Ethics Committee, whose members scrutinized the document at various stages of development and proposed revisions based on their extensive experience resolving current ethics cases. The work of the subcommittee consisted of revising the format of the original task force draft, developing new standards, assembling and reviewing proposals for change to the content of the Ethics Code draft version, and then generating new drafts, which ultimately were printed in the *APA Monitor* ("APA Continues to Refine," 1992; "APA Ethics Code," 1991). The subcommittee then shepherded the final draft version through the APA Council of Representatives at the centennial convention meeting in August 1992, where, after much discussion, debate, and formal amendment making, it was finally formally accepted.

The entire revision process spanned 6 years, from 1986 to 1992. All APA members, associate members, and student members of the APA were invited to be a part of the process. Thousands of comments, amendments, and proposals for change were received from many state association ethics committees, APA divisions and coalitions, various APA boards and committees, and many individuals, representing virtually every subspecialty area and interest group in psychology. The process of considering both the materials received and the ideas generated by the task force, the Revisions Comments Subcommittee, the Ethics Committee, and the Council of Representatives, was highly labor intensive and tremendous in scope.

1992 Ethics Code

At the end of this process, both structure and content were radically altered in the 1992 Ethics Code. Clear distinctions were made between ideal ethical goals toward which all psychologists should aspire and minimal standards of professional conduct, with which every psychologist must comply (Nagy, 1994). In this section of the chapter, these changes are discussed after a brief synopsis of the Ethics Code in its final form.

The Introduction

The Introduction describes the overall organization, applicability, and jurisdiction of the Ethics Code. Here, psychologists are exhorted to rely on both the aspirational and the enforceable sections of the code in making informed decisions and regulating their professional conduct. The Introduction also notes that the Ethics Code does not address every situation that might be encountered during the course of one's work. Therefore, psychologists would do well to read this Ethics Code with an eye for both its letter and its spirit. By interpreting the deeper meanings or implications behind each standard, rather than simply reading it as a "thou shalt" or "thou shalt not," one develops a fuller understanding of the intent or value of the standard. In addition, if a particular situation or dilemma is not specifically addressed by the Ethics Code it can more likely be resolved satisfactorily if the psychologist develops such a deeper understanding of the principle at work.

The Preamble

The Preamble sets the general context for the Ethics Code and touches on the dominant themes of both the General Principles and the Ethical Standards. The Preamble itself contains no enforceable rules. Instead, it describes the ethical considerations of psychologists' work, their goals, and the multiplicity of roles they play, and highlights some of the more important ethical values that are operationally defined later. This includes as its primary goal the welfare and protection of the individuals and groups with whom psychologists work. The Preamble also exhorts psychologists to aspire to the highest possible standards of conduct and to develop a lifelong commitment to not only act ethically oneself but also encourage ethical conduct in one's colleagues.

The General Principles

The six General Principles are broad and comprehensive and form the guiding spirit of the document: Competence, Integrity, Professional and Scientific Responsibility, Respect for People's Rights and Dignity, Concern for Others' Welfare, and Social Responsibility. These overarching paragraphs grew, in part, from the brief introductory paragraphs that preceded each ethical principle of the 1981 Ethics Code. The General Principles address most of the key ethical concepts that are operationally defined in the Ethical Standards. They are written in a generic fashion and use language that is aspirational, exhorting psychologists to aim for the highest goals in their work. For example, psychologists are encouraged to "strive," "promote," and "uphold" various professional standards, but these paragraphs do not specifically define or describe any particular standard adequately to dictate the mode of compliance.

Although the General Principles are considered to be aspirational, and therefore not directly enforceable or directly applicable in resolving formal complaints, they may be considered by ethics committees in interpreting aspects of the enforceable standards. Therefore, psychologists should be conversant with the General Principles as well as the Ethical Standards.

The Ethical Standards

If the General Principles make up the soul of the document, then the Ethical Standards certainly could be considered its heart. These 102 standards are mandatory in nature and are divided into eight sections listing specific, enforceable rules of conduct to which every psychologist must adhere. The eight sections are (a) General Standards (27 standards that are potentially applicable to the professional and scientific activities of all psychologists); (b) Evaluation, Assessment, or Intervention (10 standards); (c) Advertising and Other Public Statements (6 standards); (d) Therapy (9 standards); (e) Privacy and Confidentiality (11 standards); (f) Teaching, Training Supervision, Research, and Publishing (26 standards); (g) Forensic Activities (6 standards); and (h) Resolving Ethical Issues (7 standards).

The Ethical Standards are written in clear and concrete language, with as much specificity as possible, and constitute the list of "musts" and "must nots" that apply to all psychologists. They inform psychologists of their obligations to "provide," "inform," "document," "create," or "take reasonable steps" on one hand, or to "avoid," "reject," or "refrain from" negative actions on the other. The standards essentially educate psychologists about sound ethical conduct and they must be obeyed. This part of the Ethics Code delineates the standards, which are, in effect, decision-making rules for psychologists that are unambiguous, easily taught, and easily learned. These rules also address newly emerging areas and concerns that were not included in earlier versions. The standards have something of a legalistic tone, that, effectively, will serve to minimize misconceptions in understanding and application.

All psychologists, regardless of their specialty area, should thoroughly study Section 1, the General Standards, and Section 5, Privacy and Confidentiality. The Ethics Code states that these standards "are potentially applicable to the professional and scientific activities of all psychologists" (APA, 1992a, pp. 1600, 1606). These standards address issues that are encountered by psychologists in a variety of settings and address problems that have broad application, such as incompetence, sexual harassment, personal problems and conflicts, avoiding harm, multiple relationships, exploitative relationships, barter, confidentiality, and record keeping, to name a few. Also, psychologists should devote extra attention to those standards and parts of the Ethics Code that address their particular area of work. For example, although researchers and forensic psychologists should know the entire Ethics Code, they should devote more time to the standards in Section 6 (Research) and Section 7 (Forensic Activities), respectively. Clinicians who also do research should be especially well acquainted with both Sections 4 and 6, in addition to the rest of the code.

Changes in Structure

As was noted throughout the synopsis, the 1992 Ethics Code includes the Preamble and General Principles, which are aspirational in nature and therefore *not* enforceable, and the Ethical Standards, which include the minimal standards of behavior and *are* enforceable. As a reflection of some of the fundamental differences inherent in this version of the Ethics Code, its very title is novel; never before had psychologists developed an ethics code titled Ethical Principles of Psychologists and Code of Conduct.

Other structural changes included an innovative indexing system. For the first time ever each individual ethical standard has its own title and number, making it easy for a reader to locate a particular topic. A table of contents and cross-referencing within the document helps the Ethics Code to be even more "user-friendly" for both psychologists and the general public.

Examples of Major Changes in Content

The changes in content are particularly significant and include many different areas in research, teaching, and practice. Overall, there is a greater emphasis on psychologists' using understandable language, commensurate with the age and level of education and comprehension of the consumer, client, or patient. "There is also an emphasis upon avoiding unfair discrimination; although this was present in the 1981 version, it is given greater visibility here, citing the variables to consider—age, gender, race, ethnicity, national origin, religion, sexual orientation, disability, socioeconomic status, or any basis proscribed by law" (Nagy, 1994). Examples of other significant changes in content are as follows.

Forensic Activities

For the first time an entire section of the document has been devoted to forensic activities. It is important to note that this section is not designed exclusively for those psychologists who specialize in forensic psychology but addresses the needs of any psychologist who could be deposed or called to testify in court.

Sexual Relationships With Consumers

This code addresses the issues of sexual relationships with students, trainees, patients at various stages of therapy (beginning through posttermination), and other consumers of psychological services.

For the first time ever in an ethics code, psychologists are prohibited from engaging in sex with their own students or training supervisees. In previous codes they were precluded from exploiting students, sexually or otherwise. In this Ethics Code the language clearly states that sexual contact of any sort, even with the willing consent or instigation of the student, is prohibited.

Although sexual harassment was prohibited in the previous Ethics Code, it is defined in a far more detailed way in this version, creating broader obligations than the published policies of the Equal Employment Opportunity Commission.

Other Multiple Relationships

Whereas the 1989 version was frequently interpreted as having a blanket restriction against maintaining more than one concurrent role with a patient or student, the 1992 revision has taken a more practical view. It raises the threshold for a proscription of multiple relationships and thereby acknowledges the inherent difficulties of avoiding some multiple relationships in certain settings. It provides more guidance for the psychologist who is confronted with a sometimes bewildering array of pressures and motivations. Although there is implicit acknowledgment of the acceptability of certain multiple relationships, there is still a basic proscription against participating in multiple roles when there is the likelihood of harm or chance of crossing the threshold of exploiting another.

Advertising and Public Statements

There have been major changes in the area of advertising and public statements that must be understood in the context of the changes to the 1989 Ethics Code that were related to the FTC's investigation discussed earlier in this chapter. For example, the 1981 rule prohibited the use of testimonials from current and former clients and was declared by the FTC to be too limiting. The 1989 Ethics Code rescinded the provision entirely, providing no rule regarding testimonials. The 1992 Ethics Code basically prohibits only *solicitation* of testimonials and only from "current psychotherapy clients or patients or other persons because of their particular circumstances are vulnerable to undue influence" (Standard 3.05).

Another example is the 1981 Ethics Code's prohibition of directly soliciting for treatment individuals already receiving similar services. The 1989 revision removed this prohibition, leaving only the guidance provided in the 1981 code regarding how to handle such clients who themselves request treatment. The 1992 Ethics Code provides guidance regarding client welfare, regardless of whether the psychologist has solicited the client already receiving services or the client has contacted the psychologist; a separate standard provides the prohibition allowed by the FTC order against uninvited in-person solicitation of business from individuals who, because of their particular circumstances, are vulnerable to undue influence.

The 1992 Ethics Code also reintroduces guidance on referral fees, following rescinding in the 1989 code of the 1981 code's general prohibition against any referral fees. The new provision clarifies that this prohibits payments between professionals that are not based on services provided.

Psychologists also have more guidance in the 1992 Ethics Code in dealing with advertising agencies or others who carry out promotional activities for their services. Their personal and professional responsibilities regarding the promotional statements made by others and ultimate accountability and options are delineated. This is particularly important in hospital or large group practices, as well as in the media, or other public presentations, where psychologists may be introduced or promoted in a sensational fashion.

Barter

For the first time barter for payment of psychological services has been formally addressed by the Ethics Code. Although barter is generally discouraged, the Ethics Code acknowledges that there may be compelling arguments for allowing the barter of goods or services under certain circumstances, as long as it is not clinically contraindicated or exploitative.

Fees

There are several changes in the area of fees and their possible impact on psychological services. Included is guidance about the timing and content of fee discussions, informing patients about anticipated limitations of services due to restricted financial resources, and the implications of managed health care policies that may limit the number of treatment sessions and thereby reduce therapy expectations.

Third-Party Requests for Services

Another area of change concerns the provision of psychological services at the request of a third party, such as a court in a custody evaluation or a human resources department in hiring new employees. These standards present more detailed information for psychologists, requiring them to clarify the nature and direction of responsibilities to all parties.

Teaching

The activities of teachers and academic colleagues are also addressed more specifically in the new Ethics Code. It addresses the design of educational programs, teaching, assessment, and issues related to promotion.

Research

In carrying out research, psychologists now have a stipulated responsibility to consult as needed with those who are knowledgeable about the individuals and groups most likely to be affected by the research. The rules pertaining to research participants have also been changed, and in academic settings there is now more explicit guidance for students about the alternatives to research participation. Psychologists also have more guidance concerning the sharing of their data, after their research results are in the public domain.

Publication

The changes in assigning publication credit are also quite specific. Psychologists now have clearer guidelines than ever concerning the listing of coauthors, including student authors who have completed a thesis or dissertation that is being submitted for publication. Plagiarism is addressed in greater detail, including the presenting of information from one's own previous work as though it were innovative.

Psychotherapy

Informed consent about therapy experiences has become an important part of the new Ethics Code. Psychologists must now pay more attention to informing patients and documenting consent at the outset of therapy concerning areas such as capacity to provide consent, fees, confidentiality and its limitations, and significant information about procedures. This reflects an increase in consumer awareness and helps patients to avoid unrealistic expectations about the therapy process by being better prepared for what is to come.

Changes in the mental health care delivery system, including the vicissitudes of group practices and managed health care, have raised some important ethical issues concerning the quality and continuity of long-term treatment. An example of this is the new standard that requires psychologists to formally prepare for any significant interruption of services, such as might occur with their own departure from a group practice or managed health care panel or their own illness or death. This rule also has direct bearing on employment contracts, such as might be found in certain group practices, where new employees are obliged to sign employment contracts with "noncompete" clauses, setting conditions on further contact with patients after psychologists leave a practice. The Ethics Code places paramount importance on client welfare and indicates that these issues must be addressed at the outset of the business contract.

Supervisory responsibilities are addressed more thoroughly in this Ethics Code than any of its predecessors. If formal supervision is to occur, then psychologists must inform the client of that fact as well as the name of the supervisor who has legal responsibility. Also, whenever engaging in professional consultations, psychologists are urged to respect the privacy of their patients by not disclosing their names or identifying information, unless they have the patient's consent to do so. This new rule may have implications for staff meetings as well as formal supervision settings.

Continuity and Confidentiality of Records and Data

The requirements concerning the continuity and confidentiality of records and data have become more stringent in the new Ethics Code. Psychologists who do research or provide psychological services must now make plans to preserve records and data in the event of their withdrawal from a position or practice, incapacity, or death. In addition, those who engage in research are obliged to observe the confidentiality of those records before placing information into a database.

Assessment

Contributing factors in the revision of this section of the Ethics Code were a proliferation in the use of testing and assessment, an increase in the weight accorded tests in making decisions about individuals, and the greater availability of tests due to computer administration and direct sales. These resulted in the development of new rules that are more specific about improper assessment procedures and unsubstantiated statements by psychologists. As a general rule, psychologists must not make formal statements about persons whom they have not evaluated in a defined professional relationship without clarifying the impact of their limited information on the validity of their statements. This has implications for the practice of school psychology, child custody and mental competency assessments, or other complex evaluations in which the psychologist's statements potentially carry great weight and profoundly influence the lives of others.

A new rule provides greater detail about the obligations of psychologists who assess individuals from special populations, defined by factors such as gender, age, race, ethnicity, national origin, religion, sexual orientation, disability, language, or socioeconomic status. They also should acknowledge any limits to the certainty of diagnoses, judgments, or predictions based on assessments. Furthermore, they should consider the characteristics of individuals being assessed and the assessment technique that could affect their interpretations.

Another new rule addresses the improper use of assessment techniques, requiring psychologists to refrain from the misuse of assessment techniques and prevent others from misuse as well. This represents an elaboration of the old rule, pertaining to test misuse, and includes releasing raw test results or raw data to persons who are not competent to use the information (excluding patients or clients, as appropriate). The new rule is also more specific about the required knowledge base before using tests regarding validity, reliability, and standardization or outcome studies.

In these days of expanded use of automated test-scoring services, psychologists are obliged to carefully select vendors with whom they do business. They must consider the validity of the program and procedures offered by the automated scoring services in making their selection, as well as other relevant considerations (e.g., telephone availability for consultation, turnaround time for test scoring).

Ethics Complaints

A separate section has been devoted to the application of the Ethics Code by the filing of ethics complaints. This section helps psychologists, consumers, and others in deciding how to proceed in the filing of a complaint, as well as whether to confront the psychologist with his or her actions or to go directly to an ethics committee or psychology board with a complaint. It also defines and discusses the filing of frivolous complaints.

Summary

The 1992 Ethics Code is significantly different from every previous version in both format and content. It addresses issues that had never before been included in prior codes. It puts psychologists on notice to take preventive action, and frequently it is the failure to take such action that would result in an ethics violation. Preventive action would hopefully minimize the likelihood of harm to students, consumers, and anyone else who has professional interactions with psychologists. As one reads the commentary and analyses of the standards that follow, it may be useful to continually assess one's own customary practices and to make needed changes, if any, in light of the requirements of the new Ethics Code.

Part II

Interpreting the Ethics Code

Chapter 3 _____

General Standards

1. General Standards

These General Standards are potentially applicable to the professional and scientific activities of all psychologists.

The first section of the enforceable standards deals with General Standards. The 1989 code does not contain a section similar to the General Standards, which were written to apply broadly to all psychologists (i.e., the standards address situations and activities that are considered to be a generic part of the day-to-day functioning of all psychologists). The standards cover the vast scope of services and functions performed by psychologists, independent of specialty or setting. Some of the standards provide guidance related to broad issues such as applicability of the Ethics Code and the interface between the Ethics Code and the law. The standards were also written to apply to a broad range of psychological activities, including diagnostic or therapeutic services and teaching, research, supervisory, consultative, or other services and activities engaged in by psychologists. The standards deal with relationships that psychologists have with students, research participants, and recipients of psychological services, and responsibilities that psychologists have to the general public.

Because the General Standards may not anticipate or encompass all of the roles psychologists may be called on to play in a changing world, they may not apply to all psychologists all of the time and in all situations. Hence, the word *potentially* is used to describe their applicability. These standards, however, should be broadly noted and all psychologists need to be familiar with them. The remaining sections (2 through 8), although somewhat more specific in their applicability, may also apply to general situations and to psychologists working in various aspects of psychology.

1.01 Applicability of the Ethics Code

The activity of a psychologist subject to the Ethics Code may be reviewed under these Ethical Standards only if the activity is part of his or her work-related functions or the activity is psychological in nature. Personal activities having no connection to or effect on psychological roles are not subject to the Ethics Code.

This standard recognizes that psychologists, in addition to being professionals, are also private citizens and that they engage in a wide variety of nonprofessional and social behaviors. This clearly states that the Ethics Code applies only to psychologists' activities as psychologists. The Ethics Code is not applicable to a psychologist's personal conduct insofar as such conduct is not construed to be related or to have an effect on the psychologist's professional or scientific work.

A psychologist who delivers health care services, engages in teaching psychology courses, or conducts psychological research, for example, is clearly acting as a psychologist and subject to the Ethics Code with respect to any conduct that is connected to or affects these activities. A psychologist who teaches a course in scuba diving, shops at the local grocery store, operates a nonpsychology business, or serves on the board of a local bank would not be reasonably deemed to be functioning as a psychologist and therefore is not subject to the Ethics Code when engaged in such activities, except to the extent the psychologist's conduct is connected to or affected functioning as a psychologist in other contexts.

On the other hand, certain behaviors that the psychologist might not define as work-related functions may well be construed by others as being a part of the practice of psychology (e.g., citizens of the community may view a psychologist's statements regarding the effect of certain kinds of books on children, made while serving on the library board, as constituting behavior that is "psychological in nature"). In this type of situation, the applicability of the Ethics Code may be in dispute because "the interpretation of" or "the meaning of" the behavior in question is determined by each individual's personal viewpoint (i.e., it resides in the "eye of the beholder"). Some may view it as being related to professional conduct, whereas others may see it as purely private. Likewise, a psychologist who is in an administrative position (e.g., dean of the graduate school or chairperson of the department) might not construe administrative tasks as being "psychological in nature," but such activity may well be a part of "his or her work-related functions" in that role. The psychologist needs to be sensitive to the fact that some activities may be perceived by others as being psychological in nature, even though the psychologist believes that they are not. When disputes arise as to whether complaints regarding "personal activities" may be subject to the Ethics Code, the role of the Ethics Committee would be to review the allegations along with the specific circumstances in order to render a decision as to applicability of the Ethics Code to the specific situation.

1.02 Relationship of Ethics and Law

If psychologists' ethical responsibilities conflict with law, psychologists make known their commitment to the Ethics Code and take steps to resolve the conflict in a responsible manner.

Standard 1.02 deals with the sensitive relationship between the Ethics Code and the law. Standard 8.03, Conflicts Between Ethics and Organizational Demands, should be consulted when the Ethics Code is in conflict with institutional rules, requirements, guidelines, or regulations.

It is recognized that there will be situations in which the requirements of the law may be in conflict with the requirements of the Ethics Code. For example, the Ethics Code may require that the psychologist obtain consent to reveal confidential material, whereas the state law may require, under certain circumstances, that the psychologist reveal confidential information even without such consent. This type of conflict may be very troublesome for the psychologist. The standard addresses conflicts between the Ethics Code and the law but does not always require conformity with the law.

It is further recognized that the psychologist will not always be able to resolve such conflicts. The standard requires the psychologist to take action in order to inform the proper authorities of the ethical issues involved. It is only through such information sharing that improper laws will be changed. There are four elements to this standard:

1. In order for this standard to apply, a standard of the Ethics Code must be in conflict with some known aspect of the law.
2. When such conflict occurs, the psychologist must make his or her commitment to the Ethics Code known. This can be accomplished by, for example, letter or memo to the proper authority (e.g., employer, supervisor) or by informing the proper authority and documenting such conversation in the file, chart, research protocol, and so on.
3. The Ethics Code requires that the psychologist act proactively, (i.e., take steps). In fact, taking no action may be an ethical violation.
4. The psychologist must attempt to resolve such conflicts in a responsible manner. Doing nothing, absent a logical, well-thought-out decision to do so, would not appear to meet these criteria. On the other hand, in a forensic matter in which records are ordered to be released without consent, the psychologist may consider requesting the judge to review the material in private and make a determination if any information should be released, commonly known as an *in camera hearing*. The procedure may result in a limited release of relevant information rather than a blanket release.

1.03 Professional and Scientific Relationship

Psychologists provide diagnostic, therapeutic, teaching, research, supervisory, consultative, or other psychological services only in the context of a defined professional or scientific relationship or role (See also Standards 2.01, Evaluation, Diagnosis, and Interventions in Professional Context, and 7.02, Forensic Assessments.)

When psychologists act in a professional capacity, they restrict their professional activities to a time and place and conduct themselves in such a manner that all concerned will clearly understand that the services are provided in the context of a professional relationship. It should be noted that a written contract, exchange of fees, or a billing statement are not always necessary for the establishment of a defined professional or scientific role. For example, a psychologist who consults with employees of a corporation (the client) has established a defined professional relationship with both the employer client and the employee being evaluated. The fact that an individual has requested an appointment at the psychologist's office to discuss personal problems may, depending on the specific circumstances, be sufficient to establish a defined professional relationship. The exchange of fees is not always the benchmark because many psychologists provide pro bono services in times of emergencies or for those without resources. On the other hand, a psychologist who attempts to gain power over others by providing unsolicited psychotherapy or offers uninvited observations about another's "psychopathology" in social settings may well be in violation of this standard.

1.04 Boundaries of Competence

Standard 1.04a relates to competence in current areas of practice, teaching, or research. Recognizing that psychologists are not competent in every aspect of psychology, Standard 1.04b addresses the requirements necessary when a psychologist expands his or her area of practice or service. Standard 1.04c relates to new areas of practice, teaching, or research in which there are no generally recognized standards for training.

> **(a) Psychologists provide services, teach, and conduct research only within the boundaries of their competence, based on their education, training, supervised experience, or appropriate professional experience.**

In delivering services to clients or patients, psychologists must always be mindful that a primary obligation is to function competently. When providing services outside of one's area of competence, the risk of harm increases significantly. A psychologist who has had no experience or training in custody evaluations, in treating borderline patients or those with addiction problems, or in conducting employment testing in accordance with federal laws and professional standards should not undertake these types of activities without obtaining the proper supervision or training. Similarly, if a psychologist provides professional services to members of ethnic or minority groups, he or she should have the necessary skills or expertise to work with these populations, (see Standard 1.08). A primary goal of this standard is to protect others from harm by restricting practice to one's area of competence. It should be noted that merely having an "interest" in a particular area does not necessarily qualify one to practice in that area.

The same requirements apply to psychologists engaging in teaching or research activities. A psychologist should not conduct research using procedures or instruments unless he or she is familiar with the procedures or instruments, nor should psychologists engage in research with ethnic or minority populations unless the psychologist is competent to work with these populations (see Standard 1.08).

Competence to teach, provide services, and conduct research may be gained through education, training, *or* supervised experience. *Supervised experience* refers to being supervised by one who is already competent in the specified area. A friend or close associate who does not have the requisite skills and training would not meet this requirement. The "or" indicates that competence may be obtained through one or more of these modalities (i.e., "education, training, or supervised experience"). In addition, competence may also be obtained by "appropriate professional experience" (e.g., experience in working with individuals with a particular type of problem or disability).

> **(b) Psychologists provide services, teach, or conduct research in new areas or involving new techniques only after first undertaking appropriate study, training, supervision, and/or consultation from persons who are competent in those areas or techniques.**

The requirement of this standard can be met by any or all of the following: appropriate study, training, supervision, and/or consultation. The burden of demonstrating that the psychologist has obtained the skills to work in areas new to him or her rests with the psychologist (see Standard 1.06). This standard does not mandate competence (that subject is governed by Standard 1.04a and others); rather, it requires that the psychologist get the training, supervision, or consultation necessary from those who do have demonstrated competence in the area or techniques. Additional training or study might be obtained by attending workshops or seminars offered by the national or state psychological association, by taking additional courses offered by graduate programs, or by keeping abreast of changes in the field by reading current literature and books. In each of these cases, it is incumbent on the psychologist to be sure that the program or reading material is presented by an individual with specific expertise in the area under consideration. Peer supervision from another psychologist who does not possess the requisite skills or expertise would fail the test, as would attending a workshop whose presenter clearly has no real expertise in the area. Psychologists undertaking research in new areas or with new populations may satisfy this standard by becoming familiar with the literature in the area, working collaboratively with researchers already familiar with the area, or undertaking additional training.

> **(c) In those emerging areas in which generally recognized standards for preparatory training do not yet exist, psychologists nevertheless take reasonable steps to ensure the competence of their work and to protect patients, clients, students, research participants, and others from harm.**

This standard recognizes the fact that psychology is a rapidly expanding field of study and application and that, as professionals, psychologists are constantly challenged by issues and problems that are unique and uncharted. The fact that there are emerging areas of scientific inquiry and practice, however, does not relieve the psychologist from the responsibility to address the problems in a competent manner and to protect patients, clients, students, research participants, and others from harm when engaging in emerging areas of practice. The requirements of this standard can be met by applying known and acceptable methods of scientific inquiry and professional practice and by taking proper and acceptable precautions in consultation, teaching, and clinical work.

When a new technique is to be used, the recipient should be made aware that the technique is new or experimental, and precautions should be in place to protect the individual from harm (see Standard 1.07). In providing direct services or conducting research, the use of informed consent, especially when working in "emerging areas," may help protect patients and others from harm.

In addition, acceptable research protocols should be implemented to avoid harm to research participants and students participating in a research project. Patients' welfare can be enhanced by use of ongoing consultation with knowledgeable professionals, including medical professionals when treating patients with unusual conditions that may have medical components or consequences. Reasonable steps might also include careful consideration of the data on which the new hypotheses or treatment are based and consultation with experts regarding unique populations when indicated.

1.05 Maintaining Expertise

Psychologists who engage in assessment, therapy, teaching, research, organizational consulting, or other professional activities maintain a reasonable level of awareness of current scientific and professional information in their fields of activity, and undertake ongoing efforts to maintain competence in the skills they use.

Standard 1.05 requires that psychologists keep reasonably up to date on current developments in their specific field without requiring either that every practicing psychologist become an exhaustive scholar or that they necessarily change their preferred methods every time new findings are reported. What *is* required is simply a reasonable awareness of ongoing developments in the field. In addition, however, it requires that psychologists make efforts to assure competency in the skills they personally use. This standard can be met by a variety of activities (e.g., reading appropriate journals and books on relevant subject matter, attending or presenting at workshops or conventions, obtaining continuing education credits, seeking peer consultation or supervision on difficult projects or cases, attending peer study groups).

1.06 Basis for Scientific and Professional Judgments

Psychologists rely on scientifically and professionally derived knowledge when making scientific or professional judgments or when engaging in scholarly or professional endeavors.

It would be improper for psychologists, in their professional capacity, to say or do something merely because it "felt right," "seemed logical," or they were curious about the impact of an untried approach in a specific case (e.g., telling a spouse abuser to take his or her aggression out on the family pet in hopes that the cathartic experience would reduce the risk of additional abuse). The standard acknowledges that psychologists make judgments in areas in which there is no or limited scientific evidence, but such judgments must be based on professionally derived knowledge. As professionals, psychologists have a responsibility to act in ways that are consistent with sound scientific principles and professionally derived knowledge (e.g., knowledge from course work, appropriate seminars and workshops, refereed journals, interventions based on hypothesis derived from recognized and accepted theoretical orientations, research conducted by the psychologist or others, or from the psychologist's own experiences over time).

1.07 Describing the Nature and Results of Psychological Services

(a) When psychologists provide assessment, evaluation, treatment, counseling, supervision, teaching, consultation, research, or other psychological services to an individual, a group, or an organization, they provide, using language that is reasonably understandable to the recipient of those services, appropriate information beforehand about the nature of such services and appropriate information later about results and conclusions. (See also Standard 2.09, Explaining Assessment Results.)

This standard covers all aspects of psychology and provides a nonexhaustive list of areas. Other standards throughout the Ethics Code provide more specific information where appropriate (e.g., Standards 4.01 and 4.02 regarding therapy and Standard 6.11 regarding informed consent to research).

The reasonable language requirement in 1.07a means, for example, speaking in the recipient's native tongue, using sign language with hearing impaired individuals, or when appropriate, using trained interpreters, as well as using vocabulary understandable to cognitively impaired persons. It may also mean using vocabulary appropriate to the educational level of the person. Whether reporting orally or in writing, the psychologist should use language that can be reasonably understood by the individual intended to receive the information. For example, psychologists should avoid generating reports for clients that are written at a 12th-grade reading level if the client is functioning at a 6th-grade level. The psychologist who relies on skilled interpreters must also be cognizant of the confidentiality limitations involved. This standard does *not* mean that a psychologist is "unethical" if a patient misunderstands, or fails to understand, something that is said. It simply requires reasonable efforts to convey an appropriate range of information.

The standard requires that information regarding the nature of the services be provided before the services are rendered and that the results and conclusions be provided after the services are completed.

Appropriate information about the nature of professional services may include information such as a description of the procedures to be used, their purpose, alternative approaches that might affect the individuals' participation, the projected time involved, the anticipated cost of the services, billing procedures, confidentiality limits, policies related to handling phone calls, billing for phone calls and missed sessions, coverage while on vacation, and perhaps any negative reactions that are foreseeable. Although many practitioners have developed brochures to describe the nature of their practice, the use of such brochures is not mandated by the standard.

If the psychologist is providing industrial/organizational services, it is important to determine who the client is and to determine in advance what, if any, limitations will restrict the types of information that may be shared with individuals to whom the services are rendered (see also Standards 1.23, 1.25, 4.01, and 5.01).

Appropriate information about the results might include a review of the results of any testing or evaluation completed, recommendations regarding any additional services needed, or conclusions reached as a result of the procedures used. In determining what information is appropriate to share, one must consider the context of the service provision; the needs, rights, and capacities of the client; and the rights of others. Young children or persons with significant brain impairments may not be able to appreciate or understand the feedback or may be unnecessarily disturbed by an explanation of the results.

> **(b) If psychologists will be precluded by law or by organizational roles from providing such information to particular individuals or groups, they so inform those individuals or groups at the outset of the service.**

The psychologist should have a clear understanding with the organization or agency of what the psychologist's role is and any limitations that are imposed with regard to informing recipients of services of results or conclusions of the work. Situations that involve such preclusions are most likely to occur in industrial/organizational or forensic settings but may occur elsewhere as well. For example, a psychologist in a hospital setting who performs psychological testing at the request of a patient's physician may be required by institutional policy to provide the results to the physician rather than directly to the patient. Under these circumstances the psychologist must inform the recipient of the limitations on providing feedback before providing services.

In some circumstances the psychologist may not be able to provide information about the results of the services to specific individuals due to the employment agreement with the sponsoring organization (e.g., a corporation may have a policy not to share the results of personality assessments for security purposes when the assessments were completed at the request of the corporation). It is also possible that sharing information about the nature of the services may be prohibited due to the nature of the specific research design being implemented. In such situations the psychologist must still inform the individuals of these limitations at the outset of the services. When employed by or consulting with an organization, the psychologist must be clear about her or his own role within the organization and the limits placed on her or his functioning.

1.08 Human Differences

Where differences of age, gender, race, ethnicity, national origin, religion, sexual orientation, disability, language, or socioeconomic status significantly affect psychologists' work concerning particular individuals or groups, psychologists obtain the training, experience, consultation, or supervision necessary to ensure the competence of their services, or they make appropriate referrals.

Psychologists should always be sensitive to how human differences may significantly affect their work. The required competence may be gained or ensured through training, experience, consultation, or supervision. The standard requires that the psychologist obtain the necessary competence through any or all of the listed mechanisms. If this is not feasible, the psychologist should make a proper referral. It should be noted that this standard does not posit an impossibly high standard of omniscience and objectivity. It simply says that the psychologist must have or obtain that degree of awareness of these special issues that is needed to ensure the basic competence of services.

At the initiation of services the psychologist may not be aware that one of these issues may interfere with the adequacy of services. If the psychologist cannot ensure the competence of the services at the time he or she becomes aware of the potential interference, a proper referral must be made in an appropriate and timely manner. The psychologist may wish to refer to the APA Guidelines for Services to Ethnic and Minority Populations, which, although not enforceable, may provide important guidance.

1.09 Respecting Others

In their work-related activities, psychologists respect the rights of others to hold values, attitudes, and opinions that differ from their own.

Psychologists recognize that many factors, including but not limited to, an individual's religion, ethnic or cultural background, or political beliefs, play a significant role in determining the person's values, attitudes, and opinions on different subjects. Psychologists respect others' right to hold differing values by not imposing their personal beliefs, values, or attitudes on persons with whom they work. Likewise, a psychologist does not degrade individuals who hold differing opinions, values, or beliefs, based, for example, on their dress, religious values, cultural or ethnic background, or politics. This standard should not be interpreted, for example, to imply that professors must not challenge a student's opinion, or correct erroneous beliefs, or that a therapist may not challenge a client's attitudes or distorted thinking processes that are the subject of professional services.

1.10 Nondiscrimination

In their work-related activities, psychologists do not engage in unfair discrimination based on age, gender, race, ethnicity, national origin, religion, sexual orientation, disability, socio-economic status, or any basis proscribed by law.

It is well-known that psychologists, in the course of their professional and scientific work, routinely use procedures that differentiate among various categories of individuals. In a linguistic (but not legal) sense, this may be viewed as a type of "discrimination." Therefore, the standard uses the phrase "unfair discrimination" to permit appropriate scientific and professional differentiations (e.g., placing children in special classes or categorizing subjects for research purposes), but to prohibit unlawful or invidious discrimination based on the listed criteria.

Unfair discrimination may take many forms (e.g., it may result from the use of test or assessment procedures that are widely known to be culturally biased). Likewise, psychologists should take special care that their personal biases not interfere with their work-related activities. It should also be recognized, however, that not all psychologists are skilled to work with the same clientele. The standard should not be interpreted to require that a psychologist must offer services to all individuals regardless of the psychologist's training, experience, background, and so forth, because doing so would be harmful to some patients and violate other ethical rules.

1.11 Sexual Harassment

(a) Psychologists do not engage in sexual harassment. Sexual harassment is sexual solicitation, physical advances, or verbal or nonverbal conduct that is sexual in nature, that occurs in connection with the psychologist's activities or roles as a psychologist, and that either: (1) is unwelcome, is offensive, or creates a hostile workplace environment, and the psychologist knows or is told this; or (2) is sufficiently severe or intense to be abusive to a reasonable person in the context. Sexual harassment can consist of a single intense or severe act or of multiple persistent or pervasive acts.

Standard 1.11a prohibits sexual harassment without qualification. The definition of the scope of harassment has been carefully delineated and specified, so that people can be educated about the kinds of conduct that are proscribed. Sexual harassment is related to gender discrimination, but the elements of proof for gender discrimination are quite different from those for sexual harassment. Gender discrimination is covered in Standard 1.10, Nondiscrimination.

The purpose of this standard is flatly to prohibit sexual harassment and to define it clearly enough that innocent parties are not subjected to claims for conversations or other conduct that they have no reasonable way of knowing would be regarded as sexual harassment. It is designed to notify potential victims of sexual harassment of their rights to be free of such harassment and to notify potential subjects of claims as to what conduct is prohibited, as well as what conduct will not violate the standard.

In this standard, verbal sexual harassment is defined as unwelcome or offensive remarks or remarks that create a hostile workplace environment if the psychologist knows this. It should be noted that a psychologist risks being found in violation of this standard if the subject of the harassment tells the psychologist that the behavior is unwelcome and offensive and the psychologist subsequently repeats the unwelcome behavior. Psychologists should not always assume that others may appreciate their type of humor or conduct in the workplace. A joke that is funny to one person may be offensive to another, especially if it has sexual overtones. A pattern of such sexually offensive behavior after requests that it stop can constitute harassment. In addition, if the verbal behavior, potentially even a single act, is of such severity that a reasonable person would agree that it is personally abusive, then it may be an ethical violation.

Finally, there are certain behaviors that are so offensive that no notice need be provided the psychologist in order for the psychologist to be expected to know that the conduct is improper. Such behaviors include extremely offensive language, inappropriate touching or fondling, and offers of special attention or advancement in return for sexual favors. Other behavior that is known by the psychologist to be offensive, or to create a hostile work environment, may also constitute an ethical violation even in the absence of specific notice.

The law generally protects individuals from sexual harassment in the workplace. This standard, however, also covers many other situations in which psychologists function, including teaching, research, providing continuing education seminars or workshops, and in daily professional interactions with others, including colleagues. It applies only to conduct that occurs in connection with psychologists' activities or roles as psychologists, not to their social behavior in a club, bar, or restaurant late on a Saturday night, as long as the behavior is not related to the psychologists' roles or functions as psychologists (see Standard 1.01).

Because of its broad reach, a reasonableness standard must be used in applying this rule. It is meant to address knowingly or recklessly abusive conduct, not the minor insensitivities to which all mortals are subject. It is based on conduct of reasonable people. It does not empower each person to define his or her own standard of sensitivity and require everyone else to meet it. This standard is not meant to restrict or prohibit normal human interaction between individuals who may be physically attracted to each other, and it does not prohibit socialization or even flirtation in the workplace if such interactions are welcome. There are, however, specific prohibitions on such behavior in some situations in which there are significant power differentials such as teacher–student or supervisor–supervisee relationships (see also Standard 1.12).

(b) Psychologists accord sexual-harassment complainants and respondents dignity and respect. Psychologists do not participate in denying a person academic admittance or advancement, employment, tenure, or promotion, based solely upon their having made, or their being the subject of, sexual-harassment charges. This does not preclude taking action based upon the outcome of such proceedings or consideration of other appropriate information.

Standard 1.11b provides special protection for both the individual who alleges sexual harassment and the individual accused of harassment. There should be no penalties for filing such allegations in good faith or for being subject to such allegations if later exonerated. The statement proscribing certain actions based solely on the filing of a charge was designed to avoid inappropriate punitive actions while allowing proper action against a psychologist when rightfully indicated. For example, the chairperson of a psychology department would not be prevented from suspending a faculty member who was involved in a sexual harassment case before that matter was resolved if that individual was abandoning his or her classes or engaging in other behaviors that made the action a reasonable one to take. Likewise, a person who repeatedly files unwarranted sexual harassment charges against disliked colleagues as a means of intimidation or to seek revenge may well be subject to disciplinary action based on this type of unprofessional behavior. If evidence is available of other problematic or unethical behavior on the part of the subject of a complaint, taking action based on those behaviors is not precluded simply because of the pendency of sexual harassment charges.

Sexual harassment complaints should be taken very seriously. Psychologists should listen carefully to complainants, realizing that these are usually difficult issues to discuss, especially for an individual who may be in a subordinate position to the psychologist. If the psychologist is told that his or her conduct is unwelcome, it is incumbent on the psychologist to realistically evaluate and resolve the situation quickly, bring his or her conduct into conformity with the standard, and clarify any misunderstandings that may have precipitated the discussion. Under no circumstances may a psychologist respond in a discriminatory or punitive way to someone who has filed a complaint of sexual harassment. For example, it would be improper to threaten such a person's employment, interfere with their promotion or advancement in the work environment, or otherwise interfere with their personal or professional relationships in the work setting based solely on the filing of a complaint.

1.12 Other Harassment

Psychologists do not knowingly engage in behavior that is harassing or demeaning to persons with whom they interact in their work based on factors such as those persons' age, gender, race, ethnicity, national origin, religion, sexual orientation, disability, language, or socioeconomic status.

The Ethics Code recognizes that sexual harassment is not the only type of harassment to be prohibited. In fact, many times more subtle types of harassment are problematic (e.g., evidence of a consistent pattern of making appointments with a particular student who the faculty member dislikes because of his or her religious preferences and then not showing up at the correct time, when this never occurs with other students; telling offensive ethnic jokes). Standard 1.12 prohibits other types of harassment based on the identified criteria. Harassment may be based on many other factors (e.g., status, mode of dress, epilepsy, facial hair, obesity, acne). The list of factors is not exhaustive.

To be applied, the standard requires that the psychologist was aware (i.e., knew) that the behavior was harassing or demeaning. The use of the word *knowingly* is dictated by the fact that such words as *harassing* and *demeaning* are not objectively self-defining words. Therefore, the words *knowingly engage* were included to overcome the "eye of the beholder" problem that can occur in many situations (e.g., the psychologist will not always know what may be considered harassing by a person who may feel offended). On the other hand, closing one's eyes to the obvious may well be considered as knowing. A psychologist whose behavior would be considered clearly improper to the reasonable person would be hard-pressed to defend such conduct by claiming that he or she was unaware that such behavior is generally considered unacceptable. Finally, if a psychologist has been informed that certain behavior is offensive, then the psychologist certainly knows that the behavior is offensive and continued engaging in the behavior would invite a complaint.

1.13 Personal Problems and Conflicts

(a) Psychologists recognize that their personal problems and conflicts may interfere with their effectiveness. Accordingly, they refrain from undertaking an activity when they know or should know that their personal problems are likely to lead to harm to a patient, client, colleague, student, research participant, or other person to whom they may owe a professional or scientific obligation.

Standard 1.13a states that it is a responsibility of psychologists to be aware of and sensitive to how their personal problems may negatively affect their professional work and effectiveness. The standard recognizes that psychologists, like others, are not always aware of the impact of their personal problems on their work. This, however, does not relieve the psychologist from acting in accordance with the mandate to avoid harm (see also Standard 1.14).

The standard requires that psychologists not engage in activities in which they know or should know that their personal problems are likely to harm someone with whom they work. If a complaint is filed under this standard, the psychologist should keep in mind that the ethics committee will review the complaint against the criteria that the psychologist "knew or should have known" that his or her personal problems were likely to cause harm in the specific situation. Psychologists should be aware of the many situations and symptoms that indicate personal problems that can impair judgment and performance. The psychologist who is unaware of his or her own personal problems may in fact be impaired. Denial or lack of knowledge, however, will not provide a sufficient excuse under this standard. The psychologist is encouraged to listen carefully to the advice of peers who are calling attention to potentially problematic behaviors.

(b) In addition, psychologists have an obligation to be alert to signs of, and to obtain assistance for, their personal problems at an early stage, in order to prevent significantly impaired performance.

Psychologists should be on guard for early signs of impairment (e.g., short temper, family or marital discord, employment problems, depression or anxiety, stress-related illnesses, changes in eating or sleeping patterns, alcohol dependence or use of nonprescribed drugs). In addition, psychologists should be alert to the possible unwanted side affects of certain prescribed medications. If a psychologist is in a personal life crisis, it is incumbent on him or her to be alert to the increased potential for vulnerability and to proceed with heightened caution.

It should also be noted that some state, county, and provincial psychological associations have developed impaired psychologist committees to address this specific issue. Psychologists who think they may have a problem that interferes with the adequacy of their work could contact these programs where available for assistance (see also Standards 1.13c, 8.04, and 8.05).

(c) When psychologists become aware of personal problems that may interfere with their performing work-related duties adequately, they take appropriate measures, such as obtaining professional consultation or assistance, and determine whether they should limit, suspend, or terminate their work-related duties.

Standard 1.13c provides requirements for situations in which psychologists are aware that their personal problems may interfere with their professional responsibilities. Psychologists must take appropriate measures, including consultation, personal therapy, other assistance, impaired professional programs, and so forth, and they must determine whether the problem is serious enough to require that they seek supervision of their professional work or temporarily or permanently limit, suspend, or terminate their professional duties. Seeking proper help is both a service to the psychologists as well as those with whom they work. Psychologists should also keep in mind the importance of early intervention for such difficulties (see also Standard 1.13b).

1.14 Avoiding Harm

Psychologists take reasonable steps to avoid harming their patients or clients, research participants, students, and others

with whom they work, and to minimize harm where it is foreseeable and unavoidable.

The psychologist should always attempt to avoid harm or to minimize harm when it is foreseeable and unavoidable. It may not always be possible to avoid harm (such as in performing forensic evaluations or workplace evaluations), but to take no action to avoid or minimize harm may be grounds for an ethical complaint. In addition, a research participant or patient may be harmed but not be aware of the damage until sometime in the future. Generally, violations of this standard would be charged only if harm is also alleged. Therefore, it would be important for the psychologist to demonstrate that reasonable steps were taken to avoid negative consequences. "Reasonable steps" might include obtaining informed consent, following well-established research and treatment protocols, informing research participants of any possible negative aspects of the research project, establishing a clear agreement with recipients of services to avoid misunderstandings in the future, and discussing the potential uses of test results with those to be evaluated. If a patient, research participant, or student later claimed harm due to an evaluation, referral, participation in a research project, or course of treatment, the reasonable steps, documented in the record, would help demonstrate ethical behavior.

In providing forensic evaluations psychologists should be careful not to make inaccurate, overreaching, or overinclusive statements that are harmful or subject to misinterpretation or that go beyond the purpose of the evaluation (e.g., statements about an individual's sexual orientation or other irrelevant personal factors that may negatively bias a case but are not related to the issue at hand should be avoided).

1.15 Misuse of Psychologists' Influence

Because psychologists' scientific and professional judgments and actions may affect the lives of others, they are alert to and guard against personal, financial, social, organizational, or political factors that might lead to misuse of their influence.

This standard alerts psychologists to the fact that, as highly respected professional members of the community, what psychologists say and do as psychologists have the potential for affecting individuals and groups in important ways and points out that there is a real potential for misuse of that influence. Because of this potential, it is incumbent on psychologists to be sensitive to and guard against misuse on the basis of the psychological factors identified (see also Standard 1.01).

Although not all misuse can always be anticipated, realistically there are many pressures at work that can result in foreseeable misuse of psychologists' influence, and it is incumbent on psychologists to try to prevent this. The range of pressures is great and might include (a) the member of the psychologist's family who asks for a letter of reference to be written on the psychologist's office stationery, which would include some inaccurate statements; (b) the financial crisis that might tempt one to repeat a costly diagnostic test battery unnecessarily or continue to see a patient who pays promptly but might really be ready for termination of therapy; (c) the temptation for a researcher working for a commercial corporation to bias data in the service of making a new test more marketable; (d) the pressure from an attorney who has been a consistent source of referrals to omit contradictory data from a report that would not support the client's position. This standard would require a psychologist, for example, to take reasonable steps to prevent schools or employers from using assessment results to make decisions that cannot fairly be based on the nature of the assessment.

Particularly because it is easy to rationalize engaging in some behaviors, psychologists need to be both introspective and careful. Responsible psychologists should be aware of the power differential that exists in some of their professional relationships and should guard against misusing that differential.

1.16 Misuse of Psychologists' Work

(a) Psychologists do not participate in activities in which it appears likely that their skills or data will be misused by others, unless corrective mechanisms are available. (See also Standard 7.04, Truthfulness and Candor.)

Standard 1.15 addresses situations in which potential misuse of psychology services may be apparent only after the fact. Standard 1.16 deals with situations in which this "appears likely" in advance. Psychologists cannot always be sure that their work products will be used appropriately by others, and there are situations in which inappropriate purposes may be behind the requests for psychologists' services and the resultant work products are obviously likely to be misused. This standard requires that psychologists not participate in professional or scientific activities when misuse seems likely. Psychologists who market and sell products or services need to make a reasonable attempt to restrict access to these products or services if they are likely to be misused or inappropriately applied. For example, selling secure psychological tests or automated testing software to organizations that do not employ persons with appropriate competence and training in the use and interpretation of the test or software are additional situations for psychologists to avoid (see also Standard 2.06).

The attempt to engage a psychologist to present predetermined findings in a case, or to employ a research psychologist whose work will be publicized only when supportive of the industry's vested interests and whose disconfirming data would be suppressed, would be "opportunities" for psychologists to avoid.

Forensic situations, in which mechanisms by which biased or misused findings can readily be challenged by the other side (e.g., cross examinations and depositions), are not subject to this rule (although the psychologist would still be subject to the requirements of other standards, such as Standard 7.04). In such situations, intended or unintended misuse of a psychologist's knowledge or work products can generally be corrected in the course of cross-examinations and depositions, and so, in view of the availability of such corrective mechanisms, the psychologist is free to participate even though *after* the proceeding it may appear that "misuse" of psychology has occurred in some cases. However, in other types of situations that lack corrective mechanisms, it is incumbent on the psychologist to refrain from participation (see also Standards 1.02 and 8.03).

(b) If psychologists learn of misuse or misrepresentation of their work, they take reasonable steps to correct or minimize the misuse or misrepresentation.

It is recognized that psychologists cannot reasonably be held responsible for all misuses or misrepresentations of their work. It is required only that, on becoming aware of such occurrences, psychologists take reasonable steps to correct or minimize the negatives. Reasonable steps might include, for example, a phone call to the individual involved if the error is deemed unintentional, a memo to an attorney or the court, or a letter to the editor of a journal or newspaper with the necessary clarifications or corrections for inclusion in the next possible issue. One may not always achieve the desired result, but, in this standard, as in many standards, it is the *absence* of taking steps that is problematic. Psychologists would be well advised to document the attempts made in their records.

It should also be noted that when it is reasonable to expect that the psychologist would know of the misuse or misrepresentation of his or her work, a claim of unawareness would not appear to be an acceptable excuse for not acting.

1.17 Multiple Relationships

(a) In many communities and situations, it may not be feasible or reasonable for psychologists to avoid social or other non-professional contacts with persons such as patients, clients, students, supervisees, or research participants. Psychologists must always be sensitive to the potential harmful effects of other contacts on their work and on those persons with whom they deal. A psychologist refrains from entering into or promising another personal, scientific, professional, financial, or other relationship with such persons if it appears likely that such a relationship reasonably might impair the psychologist's objectivity or otherwise interfere with the psychologist's effectively performing his or her functions as a psychologist, or might harm or exploit the other party.

In the 1989 Ethics Code, psychologists were instructed to make every effort to avoid dual relationships that *could* impair their professional judgment or increase the risk of exploitation. Although that code did not explicitly prohibit all dual relationships, even the possibility of increased risk of exploitation or loss of objectivity was sufficient to proscribe one. Standard 1.17a addresses situations that begin with the psychologist already in a professional relationship, such as therapist, teacher, or supervisor. Standard 1.17b addresses situations in which there are other relationships already existing prior to the professional relationship being considered. It seems clear that the experiences of a prior or concurrent relationship could have the potential for complicating the scientific or professional work process. (See also Standard 1.19, which addresses exploitative relationships in the context of power differentials with consequent vulnerability.)

The current Ethics Code proscribes entering into multiple relationships based on a threshold defined as appearing *likely* that the relationship *reasonably might* lead to the feared problems. The risks of concern are stipulated as impaired objectivity on the part of the psychologist, other interference with the psychologist's effective performance, harm to the other party, and exploitation of the recipient of the psychological services. It highlights the need for psychologists to be sensitive not only to the dangers of loss of objectivity on their part, but also to the possibility of other potential sources of their decreased effectiveness, as, for example, changes in how the other party may hear and function in the context of the original professional relationship that predated the professional relationship, resulting in less successful outcomes. If a therapist invests with a stockbroker patient, the patient might well become increasingly reluctant to reveal himself or herself in therapy in order to protect his or her financially advantageous broker–client relationship with the psychologist, with consequent harm to himself or herself.

At times a professor may be called on in the same semester to teach a core course in psychology and also supervise a student in a practicum setting. The role of teacher and individual supervisor is a dual role, but not necessarily one that creates conflict; therefore, it would probably be acceptable under the new Ethics Code. However, if the professor were called on to provide psychotherapy to the same student he or she was teaching or supervising, or worse still, if it were a standard part of the curriculum to expose students to therapy experiences with the same individual who also teaches courses, then this would likely present a conflict for both teacher and student. For example, low grades awarded in the classroom could have an impact on the psychotherapy relationship.

The standard recognizes that there are situations in which it may not be feasible or reasonable to avoid social or other nonprofessional contacts with patients, clients, students, supervisees, or research participants, such as in some rural areas, small towns, and close-knit ethnic, religious, or professional or university communities. It might not be feasible for a psychologist in severe health crisis to avoid the emergency care of the one local physician, who happens to be a client. But it might be reasonable for that psychologist to use a physician in the next town for routine care rather than to use his or her own patient as a regular physician.

It is extremely difficult to define with a degree of specificity just when it would appear likely that a relationship reasonably might lead to negative consequences, without describing a particular fact situation. This emphasizes the value of consultation with colleagues as to the reasonable expectation of problems in a given situation.

A psychologist who has a banker as a long-term psychotherapy client would have to consider the cautions stipulated in this standard in deciding whether to use that client as his or her banker. Psychologists who live in metropolitan areas could easily use a bank other than the client's. However, in a very small town, with perhaps only one bank, it might be inconvenient and seem unreasonable not to use that local branch for routine banking matters that would not involve the client personally. However, might the banker-client's being privy to information regarding his or her psychologist's office and personal finances be a possible source of problems? Might the inconvenience of banking by mail with another bank be wise? Consultation might help in making a decision here. On the other hand, if a psychologist needed to apply for a loan that could substantially involve the judgment and goodwill of the banker granting or denying it, he or she might decide without hesitation to use a different bank, despite the inconvenience of traveling to another town. The test is whether "it appears likely" that such an added relationship "reasonably might" lead to one of the listed problems.

A psychologist might, after considerable thought, decide that it was reasonable and therefore appropriate to join the church that one of his or her clients attends, as long as social contacts could be largely avoided and kept superficial. The psychologist might decide, however, not to serve on the same political campaign committee as that client, because loss of objectivity and possibilities for exploitation could easily be envisioned if they had opposing views on an important committee policy. And the psychologist needing some renovation done at home had better proceed with caution in considering whether to engage a contractor-client, because with construction problems and frustrations almost the norm, the psychologist could, by such an involvement in the project, easily put both self and client into a difficult position, potentially exploitative and harmful to the professional relationship or to the new construction see also Standards 1.14 and 1.19).

This standard introduces a new element in the form of the proscription not only against entering into, but also against promising another relationship, because such promises themselves may be sufficient to change the professional relationship by providing impetus for the other party to focus on attaining that new relationship at the cost of the original professional goals. How tempting it might be for the investment counselor patient to report how much better he or she feels if the prospect of a personally pleasurable and lucrative relationship with the therapist is the termination prize, or for the patient who thinks he or she is in love with his or her therapist to deny difficulties in order to seem ready for termination and the hoped-for posttermination fulfillment (see Standard 4.07).

It should be noted that the rule about not promising a future relationship does not preclude the psychologist's explaining the rule to the involved party. But it is important in providing the explanation that the psychologist be very careful to avoid any implications to the effect that a posttermination relationship is a shared goal. Additionally, he or she must be alert to the possibilities for misinterpretation of the explanation given on the part of the client or patient who is seeking such a future relationship. Therapists who subscribe to the practice of brief psychotherapy throughout the lifetime of the client have a built-in explanation to assist them in negating the viability of any relationship other than that of patient and therapist.

> **(b) Likewise, whenever feasible, a psychologist refrains from taking on professional or scientific obligations when preexisting relationships would create a risk of such harm.**

For example, a psychologist who works within an organization's Employee Assistance Program (EAP) providing individual and group counseling for employees may be asked to assist the chief executive officer (CEO) in deciding among employees for a promotion or a reduction in force. Such dual roles within the organization might be unacceptable, because the psychologist, in the course of providing counseling in an EAP, has likely obtained insight into the personal and professional strengths and weaknesses of his or her clients and cannot objectively make such determinations without compromising his or her role with the employee and misusing information that has been obtained in a confidential relationship, even when such information is not shared with others.

It may be tempting to help a close friend in distress who turns to a psychologist-friend in time of crisis, saying, "you're the only one I can trust to talk to." However, by the time the psychologist has questioned how objective he or she could be in working with that friend, and considered the possible harm to that friend and other involved parties, self included, that might well ensue, referral would clearly be indicated. If a psychologist is asked by a corporation to evaluate employee performance, with an eye toward cutting down on staff, the psychologist's prior relationship with some of the top management people who would have to be evaluated would likely make this an offer the psychologist would choose to refuse.

It is certainly safer to avoid taking on relationships with a prior history. But if it is not feasible to avoid doing so, or does not seem necessary, psychologists need to proceed with great care and heightened alertness to the possible emergence of problems. What is important here is that the psychologist consider carefully the circumstances, in the light of the concerns listed previously, and make a decision that reflects this. It may be useful to consider the "worst case scenario" while deciding whether to add a professional role to an existing or prior relationship. Consultation with peers is frequently helpful in making such judgments.

> **(c) If a psychologist finds that, due to unforeseen factors, a potentially harmful multiple relationship has arisen, the psychologist attempts to resolve it with due regard for the best interests of the affected person and maximal compliance with the Ethics Code.**

When, despite the psychologists' alertness and concern, unforeseen factors give rise to potentially harmful multiple relationships, psychologists have the responsibility to try to ameliorate the situation as best they can. Such a circumstance might arise, for example, when a psychotherapist discovers, in the course of working with a patient, that the person whom that patient has begun dating is the therapist's friend and their social interactions would be expected to be frequent and with some degree of intimacy. Such a circumstance could not have been anticipated, but the potential for loss of objectivity, other interference with effective performance, and harm might all emerge as viable concerns. Consultation with knowledgeable, objective colleagues is a course of action that is strongly recommended, because it is most likely to facilitate an optimal outcome for the persons involved. In the deliberations, attention must be addressed to compliance with the stipulations of the Ethics Code (see also Standards 1.14, 1.20, and 4.09).

Although some individuals may be offended by the psychologist's avoidance of or refusal to enter into a nonprofessional or social relationship, it is often possible, by explaining the reasons for refusal and the provisions of this Ethics Code, to help such individuals accept the decision without feeling personally diminished or devalued. If the individual is unable to do so and the professional relationship is undermined, it may be wise to offer a referral to another psychologist but unwise to see a termination under these conditions as license to proceed with a nonprofessional or social relationship.

1.18 Barter (With Patients or Clients)

Psychologists ordinarily refrain from accepting goods, services, or other nonmonetary remuneration from patients or clients in return for psychological services because such arrangements create inherent potential for conflicts, exploitation, and distortion of the professional relationship. A psychologist may participate in bartering <u>only</u> if (1) it is not clinically contraindicated, <u>and</u> (2) the relationship is not exploitative. (See also Standards 1.17, Multiple Relationships, and 1.25, Fees and Financial Arrangements.)

For the first time, the APA Ethics Code has a specific position on barter with assessment and therapy patients or clients. Although barter is not specifically defined in the Ethics Code, it would refer here, in line with dictionary definition, to the provision of goods or services rather than money in exchange for psychological services. The standard emphasizes that psychologists *ordinarily refrain* from barter arrangements. However, it recognizes that there are some circumstances in which barter is the only feasible alternative for a patient or client in need of psychological services, and it provides for protection against most of the actual abuses of barter. It should be noted that in some ethnic groups, the use of valuables other than money may be culturally preferable, and in some communities it may be the only viable option. Pro bono services, although certainly at times an option, may not always be possible, either because of therapeutic issues, the discomfort or unwillingness of the patient or client to accept free service, or financial pressures on the psychologist, particularly in economically depressed areas where many indigent patients may need psychological services.

Bartering may be exercised as an option *only* if the following two conditions are met: (a) Bartering is not clinically contraindicated *and* (b) the relationship is not exploitative. In evaluating the clinical situation, psychologists should consider factors such as the theoretical orientation of the therapist, the patient's diagnosis, the duration of therapy, the dependency needs of the patient, the nature of the problems for which treatment is indicated, and the nature of the barter arrangement. Bartering would clearly be clinically contraindicated, for example, if the patient or client with a borderline personality disorder was offering to provide the therapist with housekeeping or baby-sitting services in exchange for psychotherapy. The exacerbation of boundary problems in an individual with a history of unclear boundaries could be catastrophic. One would not likely barter, either, with a hypomanic individual, or when the resolution of relationship management issues precluded doing so, or, in general because of the obvious problems in setting and maintaining appropriate limits and roles.

The mandate to consider the possibility of exploitation before entering into any bartering arrangement is a recognition of the particular dangers that may occur when, for example, the hourly wage or other value ascribed to the patient-client's work is so low that as therapy hours mount, the degree of indebtedness increases significantly with likely resentment of the arrangement. Although exploitation concerns in this standard are focused on the client or patient, it should be noted that the psychologist's feeling exploited as a result of a patient-client's not performing the arranged-for services satisfactorily could also have a very negative impact on the psychological services rendered (see also Standard 1.19).

In the Ethics Code, the barter standard includes cross-references to Standards 1.17, Multiple Relationships, and 1.25, Fees and Financial Arrangements. The psychologist should be aware that barter may meet the requirements of this standard but be contraindicated by other standards in the Ethics Code. These standards are called to psychologists' attention, because the stipulations and caveats included therein bear on bartering too and need to be considered in making decisions about the use of barter with patients or clients (see also Standards 1.14 and 1.19). All of the stipulations in Standard 1.25, Fees and Financial Arrangements, apply in the context of reaching bartering agreements, and psychologists are cautioned to be very explicit and detailed, perhaps using written contracts to seal agreements, even though these are not required by the standard. Particular attention should be paid to considering and making sure that there is no exploitation of the patient or client.

It is strongly recommended that psychologists who are considering bartering arrangements document in their case records their initial considerations and the rationales underlying their decisions, discussions with clients on the subject, and any ongoing related observations or concerns. Should an ethics complaint ever be filed regarding bartering, such records, showing attention to the requirements of this standard, would likely be most helpful. Consultation with colleagues can also be extremely helpful in making sound judgments about bartering, and psychologists are urged to turn to their knowledgeable peers for help in this type of complex decision-making situation. If, despite the precautions taken, a bartering situation begins to deteriorate, it is suggested that the psychologist take immediate steps to intervene, with the primary consideration in trying to resolve the situation being the patient's or client's best interests. Here again, consultation might be very useful.

It might be noted here that although this standard does not differentiate between the barter of goods and of services, it is generally considered that there is a lower risk in the bartering for goods than for services. Although there are some exceptions, goods usually have an easily verified value and are less "interactive" than are ongoing service relationships. However, even when goods are involved, it is possible to have differing opinions of fair market value; in instances in which products created by clients are involved, there is the added delicate situation possible when, for example, a patient's painting is not one that appeals to the therapist or the price placed on it by the patient seems inappropriate, and so forth. Patients bartering their artistic creations or skills in exchange for assessment or treatment services, and the psychologists who agree to consume their goods or services, are open to a whole new set of experiences involving performance criteria that may or may not be met, possible complications if goods bartered do not stand up well, and so on.

Note that in some areas of the country, local trade associations exist that might be used to help facilitate a type of barter arrangement. Such trade associations are made up of area merchants who agree to conduct business with one another without the use of money, except for an annual membership fee. Points, or credits, are accrued and dispensed, and logged into the company computer. There is no need for the purchaser (therapy patient) and vendor (the psychologist) to ever directly exchange products or services, as long as both belong to the trade association. Although the use of a trade association does distance the parties, it still leaves some of the concerns regarding bartering to be dealt with.

The possibility of the client's being injured while performing work for the psychologist could also be an issue. Therefore, it is very important that the psychologist consider carefully the capacity of the patient to function acceptably in the role designated by the bartering arrangement and the implications of dysfunction for all concerned. Additionally, in this context, it would be wise for psychologists to consider what kinds of insurance coverage might be necessary and to be aware that their professional liability insurance might not cover them in a bartering situation. As a final caution, it should be noted that the value of bartered goods or services must be reported as professional fee income and appropriate taxes must be paid.

1.19 Exploitative Relationships

(a) Psychologists do not exploit persons over whom they have supervisory, evaluative, or other authority such as students, supervisees, employees, research participants, and clients or patients. (See also Standards 4.05–4.07 regarding sexual involvement with clients or patients.)

There are various types of exploitative relationships, and this standard should be interpreted broadly. The exploitation may be sexual, financial, political, or of many other types. In addition to obvious types of exploitation, such as extortion, many more subtle forms of exploitation may occur. Examples could include burdening persons with requests that they feel unable to deny and that go beyond their appropriate responsibilities. The graduate student who is asked by his or her dissertation chairperson to prepare a translation of an article for him or her may not feel free to say he or she really does not have the time to do so. Psychologists who expect employees to house-sit or run personal errands for them, on a regular basis and without fair financial compensation, may well be exploiting them.

Finally, psychologists need to be sensitive to the fact that, although the perception of exploitation may be in the eye of the beholder, it is the ethics committee, licensing board, or equivalent body that judges on the basis of evidence whether exploitation in an objective sense, whether or not subjectively experienced by the complainant, has in fact occurred.

> **(b) Psychologists do not engage in sexual relationships with students or supervisees in training over whom the psychologist has evaluative or direct authority, because such relationships are so likely to impair judgment or be exploitative.**

This is a new standard that applies only to relationships with students or supervisees in training and only when the psychologist has evaluative or direct authority over those students or supervisees in training. It is invoked because of the likelihood of impaired judgment or exploitation in those situations. The standard seems quite clear: No sexual relationships are allowed, even if impaired judgment or exploitation has not occurred or is not proved. The student whose comprehensive examination a psychologist grades, or whom that psychologist evaluates for internship placement, is protected by this standard. So is the supervisee in a predoctoral practicum or the postdoctoral supervisee who may be fulfilling licensing requirements and over whom the psychologist holds legal evaluative authority. Practitioners who are not in training and who are employed in institutions where they are supervised administratively or otherwise by colleagues would not be covered under this standard, but if they were sexually harassed or exploited, they would have recourse under Standard 1.11 or Standard 1.19a.

One of the arguments against maintaining the restrictions delineated in this standard is that behaviors between consenting adults should not be judged unethical and that the psychologist may not be exploiting the student or supervisee. It must be pointed out that, although a particular student or supervisee may not feel exploited, other students or supervisees, who see choice internships and other desirable assignments being given to a faculty member's lover, for example, feel certain that the professor's judgment is biased and therefore that the fairness of evaluating *their* work also has been degraded. Furthermore, the student or supervisee may not "feel exploited" until a later point in time, as, for example, when the professor-supervisor decides to end the relationship. It is then that feelings of exploitation, and an ethics complaint, could materialize.

Questions have been raised about this standard in relation to students whose spouses or partners teach courses they take, or supervisees in training who are married to psychologists who, for example, run the clinics or laboratories in which they are placed. The key issue would appear to be who does the actual grading of examinations or papers or the direct supervision. It might be reasonable to permit one's spouse-partner to register for a course one is teaching if alternative sections are not available. However, in such an instance, it might be important to have someone else do the grading of all but objective tests. And within an organization, direct supervision of a trainee had best not be done by a spouse-partner.

1.20 Consultations and Referrals

(a) Psychologists arrange for appropriate consultations and referrals based principally on the best interests of their patients or clients, with appropriate consent, and subject to other relevant considerations, including applicable law and contractual obligations. (See also Standards 5.01, Discussing the Limits of Confidentiality, and 5.06, Consultations.)

As always, the best interests of the patient or client are a guiding principle in performing psychological functions. The appropriate consent for consultations and referrals required in this section of the standard may be secured from a competent client or from the parent or legal guardian of a minor child. It is recognized that there are times when "other relevant considerations, including applicable law and contractual obligations" direct our actions. In an emergency situation, and if permitted by law, one may consult and refer without consent (see also Standard 5.05). The cross-references are noted to call attention to the need for discussing the limits of confidentiality with recipients of services as early as possible in the relationship so that they understand that there are situations in which their consent may not be required for the psychologist to provide various services or to fulfill various duties such as initiating professional consultations in their behalf, or making needed referrals. In order to give some guidance on the content of consultations, Standard 5.06 is cited here as well, and psychologists are reminded that it is wise to document in their records the significant actions taken.

(b) When indicated and professionally appropriate, psychologists cooperate with other professionals in order to serve their patients or clients effectively and appropriately.

Psychologists frequently collaborate with a physician to manage the medical aspects of the case as appropriate, and they commonly consult with the individual therapists of couples they are seeing for marital therapy. Of course, consent must be secured as stipulated earlier. It is the patients or clients of the psychologist, not those of the other professional, who are the focus of concern in this standard. The standard also recognizes that such cooperation may not always be indicated or professionally appropriate, alluding, for example, to situations in which other professionals may make requests that are inappropriate, such as asking for data that a research psychologist is not free to provide, trying to obtain agreement to a course of treatment that the referring psychologist views negatively, or just trying to get privileged information from the psychologist.

(c) Psychologists' referral practices are consistent with law.

This standard appears to be self-explanatory. It alludes, for example, to federal (and some state) statutes that bar payments in exchange for or as inducement to referrals of patients. In addition to federal statutes, psychologists are cautioned that there may be state-by-state differences in legal requirements, as, for example, regarding confidentiality, and it is important for them to be familiar with the statutes and rules and regulations in those states in which they work.

1.21 Third-Party Requests for Services

(a) When a psychologist agrees to provide services to a person or entity at the request of a third party, the psychologist clarifies to the extent feasible, at the outside of the service, the nature of the relationship with each party. This clarification includes the role of the psychologist (such as therapist, organizational consultant, diagnostician, or expert witness), the probable uses of the services provided or the information obtained, and the fact that there may be limits to confidentiality.

The third parties requesting services might be parents concerned about a child's behavior, the court ordering a child custody or presentencing evaluation, a legal guardian, an employer seeking help in hiring, an organization contracting for services on behalf of its employees, and so on. In addition to explaining the kinds of roles the psychologist may play as, for example, a therapist, an expert witness, evaluator or consultant, the psychologist is expected to let each party know how the services rendered or the information garnered would probably be used, and to warn about possible limits to confidentiality. Unlike most situations, in which what transpires between patient or client and psychologist remains confidential unless the privilege is waived by the patient or client, the third party may also be a corporate client and may have rights to receive information as outlined in the employment contract. Likewise, the individual who is to be the subject of a presentencing evaluation for the court must be told before the service is rendered that the results and recommendations, which might or might not be favorable, from that person's viewpoint, will be provided to the court. And the psychologist hired by an organization to evaluate a corporate officer at the request of the CEO needs to tell that person beforehand that he or she is serving as an organizational consultant, as well as a psychologist doing assessments, and that a report will be sent to the CEO for use in evaluating his or her suitability for promotion. If the psychologist is paid by a corporation to provide psychotherapy to employees, the psychologist may secure agreement from the corporate representative that the content of the therapy will not be shared, and the employee would need to be so advised (see Standard 5.01).

> **(b) If there is a foreseeable risk of the psychologist's being called upon to perform conflicting roles because of the involvement of a third party, the psychologist clarifies the nature and direction of his or her responsibilities, keeps all parties appropriately informed as matters develop, and resolves the situation in accordance with the Ethics Code.**

There are times when the involvement of a third party in the relationship between a psychologist and the recipient of his or her services results in identifiable potential problems, and these problems may become particularly difficult when forensic issues are involved.

Suppose that a psychologist has been treating a divorced woman in therapy for about a year. She comes in, distressed, and states that her ex-husband is seeking custody of their children and that a custody battle is anticipated. As her therapist, the psychologist might, of course, be called, voluntarily or under subpoena, to testify during the custody hearing concerning the services rendered. But suppose that the patient's lawyer calls requesting that the therapist do a custody evaluation of the family and testify as to the results. To the role of therapist, the psychologist is now being asked to add the role of expert witness on custody matters. The role of therapist includes the responsibility of making the client's welfare a first consideration, and keeping confidentiality, within the limits of the law. However, in the role of an expert witness providing a forensic custody workup, the responsibilities would include doing a competent assessment of the whole family and rendering honest, professionally sound, and appropriate findings based on the data, in light of the welfare of the children, even though these findings might not be in the therapy client's best interests. If the psychologist does not simply reject the request, it is important for him or her to explain to both clients and lawyers the potential conflict in assuming both roles, the fact that a therapist's objectivity might well be questioned, and that the therapeutic alliance would likely be endangered if not destroyed if the findings were not as hoped for by the therapy client.

Although this standard does not *require* that the psychologist reject the added role in all circumstances, great caution is recommended here. Many psychologists feel strongly that the assumption of additional roles by the therapist in such a situation should be avoided completely because they consider it impossible for a therapist to maintain the objectivity necessary for doing a custody evaluation. And even if such objectivity could be maintained, it is not unlikely that the credibility of the evaluation would be questioned because of the dual roles. Even psychologists who believe themselves capable of complete objectivity in the added role would have to acknowledge the possibility that the role addition could be problematic, for example, because of the potential

for harm to the therapeutic relationship and consequent feelings of abandonment on the part of the patient. It certainly would appear wise to consider
suggesting that another forensic psychologist conduct the evaluation. (Many
standards are relevant here, including Standards 1.14–1.15, 1.17, 4.01a, and
7.02–7.05.)

Another example might involve a school psychologist in a juvenile deten-
tion facility who is instructed by the administration to facilitate a therapy
group for troubled teenage boys, some of whom the psychologist has evaluated
in the past when employed in the regular school system. After clarifying the
ground rules and roles with all parties, so that, for example, the limits of
confidentiality are clear and acceptable to the administrator as well as the
group members, the psychologist begins the group sessions. However, a few
months later, a new administrator is appointed who wants to change the rules
regarding confidentiality in a direction of concern to the psychologist. These
changes would have to be addressed and dealt with by all parties. After an
unsuccessful attempt to modify the new requirements, the psychologist would
need to let the group members know of the changes being imposed so that they
understand what they can expect. The responsibility of psychologists to keep
all parties informed "as the situation develops" refers to the possibility that,
in the course of carrying out the services as explained initially, and illustrated
earlier, the best laid plans may change, the cast of characters may be altered,
third parties may try to change the ground rules, and these changes must be
dealt with the parties involved. Ultimately, of course, it is the psychologist's
responsibility to make the often complicated decisions that must be faced, with
due regard for the requirements of this Ethics Code.

1.22 Delegation to and Supervision of Subordinates

**(a) Psychologists delegate to their employees, supervisees, and
research assistants only those responsibilities that such persons can reasonably be expected to perform competently, on
the basis of their education, training, or experience, either
independently or with the level of supervision being provided.**

Psychologists need to be aware of the levels of education, training, and
experience of those they employ, supervise, or use as research assistants, so
that they themselves can assign and supervise or delegate supervision appropriately. Research assistants are not assigned to do surgical procedures on
experimental animals without supervision until their competency to perform
the required procedures has been ascertained. The supervisee well trained in
the administration of the Wechsler Adult Intelligence Scale–Revised (WAIS-
R) may be assigned to test clients with that examination and do the scoring
independently. But that same supervisee may not be assigned to do neuropsychological test battery interpretations if that individual's level of competence is insufficient to make it appropriate, given the available level of supervision (see also Standard 2.06).

(b) Psychologists provide proper training and supervision to their employees or supervisees and take reasonable steps to see that such persons perform services responsibly, competently, and ethically.

Here, the focus is on the psychologist's responsibility both to provide proper training and to take "reasonable steps" to see that those they employ and supervise perform appropriately. Failure to provide appropriate training or supervision is an ethical violation. Planning such services, but not actually following through by doing the supervision or seeing that the training actually occurs, is not enough.

In the course of stipulating the pertinent ethical responsibilities of psychologists, this standard touches on risk management issues as well. It is important to note that the supervisor-employer can be and often is held legally responsible for the performance of those he or she hires, trains, or supervises. Independent practitioners who supervise service providers, licensed or not and psychologists or not, are particularly cautioned about the significant professional as well as legal responsibility that arises from such roles, even if signing of their insurance forms is not part of the arrangement.

(c) If institutional policies, procedures, or practices prevent fulfillment of this obligation, psychologists attempt to modify their role or to correct the situation to the extent feasible.

A key word here is *attempt*. The standard acknowledges that psychologists may not have the power to change institutional policies, procedures, or practices so that they can conform fully to the requirements of Standards 1.22a and Standard 1.22b. What is required by Standard 1.22c is only that psychologists try to effect appropriate change. This might take the form of trying to modify their role or adjust their workload in such a way as to allow for more observation of supervisees and advising the powers that be of the requirements of this Ethics Code, perhaps suggesting some changes that might be negotiated, perhaps pointing out the vulnerability of the institution if appropriate work assignments are not made, sufficient supervision time is not provided, and so on. It is always wise to document the attempts made to correct the problematic situation (see also Standard 8.03).

1.23 Documentation of Professional and Scientific Work

(a) Psychologists appropriately document their professional and scientific work in order to facilitate provision of services later by them or by other professionals, to ensure accountability, and to meet other requirements of institutions or the law.

All scientific or professional work must be documented appropriately. This facilitates replication of research and allows for not only peer review of results, but also for general accountability. For therapy services, proper documentation enhances continuity of care whether by the original therapist over time or by a subsequent therapist whom a patient might consult. Documentation is required, too, so that psychologists can demonstrate accountability and institutional and legal requirements are met. Psychologists need to be familiar with the documentation requirements of the institutions where they work and with the provisions of their state laws and federal law. Psychologists may find themselves and their clients ineligible for reimbursement from an insurance company or government agency if they cannot provide the required information or are unable to demonstrate, via their records, for example, the frequency and type of services they rendered, consultations secured, major treatment issues of concern, and so forth. Such documentation is also important in the event that an ethical or legal violation is charged.

> **(b) When psychologists have reason to believe that records of their professional services will be used in legal proceedings involving recipients of or participants in their work, they have a responsibility to create and maintain documentation in the kind of detail and quality that would be consistent with reasonable scrutiny in an adjudicative forum. (See also Standard 7.01, Professionalism, under Forensic Activities.)**

In a sense, this standard is simply a specific corollary to the general requirement that psychologists appropriately document their work (see Standard 1.23a). It is recognized that in the ordinary course of therapy, psychologists' customary record-keeping practices vary widely. However, Standard 1.23b requires that when psychologists have reason to expect that their records will be involved in the resolution of important rights of patients or others in court or other legal proceedings, they have an obligation to create records in the quality and detail that can be used in such proceedings. This does not require that psychologists know every rule of evidence or procedure as to admissibility and use of evidence in court. Rather, they simply must create records in a manner generally acceptable for use in legal proceedings. This would, of course, usually be more than intermittent, scanty, and illegible process or progress notes (see Standard 1.23a, Standard 1.24, and Appendix B for additional information on record keeping).

1.24 Records and Data

> **Psychologists create, maintain, disseminate, store, retain, and dispose of records and data relating to their research, practice, or other work in accordance with law and in a manner that permits compliance with the requirements of this Ethics Code. (See also Standard 5.04, Maintenance of Records.)**

Psychologists should be aware of their individual state and federal record-keeping requirements and, as stipulated in this standard, follow the law while complying with this code's requirements. This would suggest, for example, that records be kept under lock and key to protect confidentiality; that they be disposed of by burning or shredding in order to preserve that confidentiality; and that the contents of records reflect such important matters as identifying data, dates and type of service, the obtaining of consent, treatment plans, and significant interventions, for example. It is helpful if records are legible, so that they can be useful to other professionals when patients or clients are referred and their records follow them.

There are a number of APA documents that, although not enforceable by the APA Ethics Committee, provide additional guidance on these issues. These include the 1993 Record Keeping Guidelines (APA, 1993c) developed by the Board of Professional Affairs and adopted by the APA Council of Representatives (see Appendix B). The APA General Guidelines for Providers of Psychological Services (1987a) include some minimal record-keeping suggestions. Also, the *Standards for Educational and Psychological Testing* (APA, 1985) stipulate some provisions for the retention and deletion of testing and assessment records. These materials may be secured through the Order Department of the APA.

1.25 Fees and Financial Arrangements

(a) As early as is feasible in a professional or scientific relationship, the psychologist and the patient, client, or other appropriate recipient of psychological services reach an agreement specifying the compensation and the billing arrangements.

The clause "as early as feasible" recognizes that, although it is desirable to discuss compensation arrangements in the first meeting between the parties, there may be legitimate reasons why it is impossible to do so. For example, it might be inappropriate even to attempt such a discussion with extremely agitated individuals or those in great psychological pain who need to be heard and cannot focus on anything but their problems. Clinical judgment would have to enter into the decision about the timing of the discussion, but it is necessary that the psychologist keep in mind the serious consequences of not having a clear understanding of finances and talk about finances as early as possible. When the discussion is held, an agreement needs to be reached about fees, billing arrangements, and payment policies. If the psychologist charges for telephone calls, writing letters, or reading patient diaries, for example, or levies interest on unpaid balances, these policies should be included in that discussion. Although the standard does not require that the agreements be put in writing, many psychologists now find it prudent to establish such agreements in writing and to document in progress notes other discussions and agreements that occur regarding finances. It would certainly appear wise to at least document in the record that a verbal agreement was reached and stipulate its provisions. Note that the standard requires only that an agreement be reached, not for the psychologist to be the person to discuss each element of the agreement (see Standard 1.25f).

(b) Psychologists do not exploit recipients of services or payors with respect to fees.

Psychologists are free to set their fees as they see fit, as long as those fees are nonexploitative and other requirements of the Ethics Code and applicable statutes are met. Exploitation in this standard might refer, for example, to taking advantage of emotionally distraught patients by inflating fees because the clients are so upset that they are incapable of contracting in their own best interests (see also Standards 1.14 and 1.19a).

In this Ethics Code, psychologists are not required to establish "fee floors," "fee ceilings," "standard fees," or any such designations, nor does this standard preclude the use of sliding fee scales based on economic ability to pay. Quite the contrary. Its sole concern is the avoidance of exploitation in regard to fees, and any fees may be charged, at the discretion of the psychologist, as long as they are not exploitative and are agreed to in advance by patients and are truthfully disclosed to payors.

(c) Psychologists' fee practices are consistent with law.

Psychologists need to know their state laws regarding professional practice and fees. Many of the problems regarding fee practices arise in connection with insurance billing. For example, psychologists need to know that double billing, back billing, billing for telephone sessions without differentiating these from office or house sessions, and consistently billing insurance companies higher fees than those for clients not covered by insurance or billing services provided to one family member as though provided to another family member who has insurance coverage all may raise concerns about insurance fraud. The motivation of helping the patient secure reimbursement for needed and even provided services does not make these practices acceptable or legitimate. Likewise, some types of division of fees may violate state fee-splitting laws (see also Standards 1.26–1.27).

(d) Psychologists do not misrepresent their fees.

Whether in public statements, advertisements, or in discussion with patients or clients within the consultation room, psychologists are expected to present an accurate picture of their fees. This means not only providing accurate information, but also not withholding pertinent information. If the psychologist charges patients for phone calls and letter writing, for example, patients need to be told this because they may expect to be billed only for the hourly fees discussed if other charge policies are not mentioned (see also Standards 3.03a and 4.08–4.09).

(e) If limitations to services can be anticipated because of limitations in financing, this is discussed with the patient, client, or other appropriate recipient of services as early as is feasible. (See also Standard 4.08, Interruption of Services.)

The industrial/organizational psychologist who, in the course of his or her work uncovers problems that need to be addressed and anticipates running out of allocated funds for needed services, would be required to discuss this problem with the individual with whom the psychologist contracted in order to resolve the problem most constructively. In some situations, as when a preferred provider psychologist knows that the managed care plan benefits on which the patient may depend will run out before therapy goals can be reached, it is important to discuss this with the patient early, so there is not an abrupt and unexpected "bombshell" dropped later on. It should be noted that, although psychologists may occasionally choose to provide some services on a pro bono basis, this Ethics Code does not require them to do so. The psychologist is not required to "fix" the problem, just to inform the patient or client and discuss it. However, psychologists who have the option of appealing what they consider to be inappropriate denials of authorization to continue treatment should consider doing so. This is true because of client welfare concerns and because recent case law suggests that filing of such appeals may be considered a duty of the psychologist (see also Standards 1.14 and 4.08–4.09).

> **(f) If the patient, client, or other recipient of services does not pay for services as agreed, and if the psychologist wishes to use collection agencies or legal measures to collect the fees, the psychologist first informs the person that such measures will be taken and provides that person an opportunity to make prompt payment. (See also Standard 5.11, Withholding Records for Nonpayment.)**

This is a new standard that acknowledges that it is not unethical per se to use collection agencies or legal services in order to secure payment for their services and that provides guidance when psychologists choose to do so. It directs both that psychologists inform the patients or clients of their intent to do so and that an opportunity for prompt payment be offered (see also Standard 5.02). Although it is required only that psychologists discuss their collection actions with patients or clients prior to invoking them, they might find it helpful to consider whether their policies regarding the use of collection agencies or legal measures should be discussed early in the professional or scientific relationship, and the confidentiality exceptions noted (see also Standard 5.01).

Psychologists are advised to check state law regarding both collections and confidentiality. Although the use of collection agencies or legal measures automatically involves a loss of some confidentiality, it is appropriate that only the minimum amount of information essential for pursuing collection be revealed, in accordance with the fourth stipulation in Standard 5.05a, and that the substantive content of services rendered not be shared.

Before engaging a collection agent, it might be wise to discuss the tactics and procedures that will be used, because psychologists are the ones ultimately responsible for whatever actions are taken.

1.26 Accuracy in Reports to Payors and Funding Sources

In their reports to payors for services or sources of research funding, psychologists accurately state the nature of the re-

search or service provided, the fees or charges, and where applicable, the identity of the provider, the findings, and the diagnosis. (See also Standard 5.05, Disclosures.)

This standard appears to be quite clear in its focus on the requirement of accuracy in reports to funding sources, whether these be related to research or practice funding sources and involve, for example, reports to foundations providing research monies, or to insurance companies providing coverage for therapeutic services. Altering of diagnoses and other falsifications of billing are clearly unacceptable and illegal. This means that, for example, submitting claims for individual psychotherapy when couples therapy is the factual description of services in order to ensure insurance coverage is not acceptable practice. The treatment reports rendered must be honest and factual, preserving the confidentiality of the relationship to the extent that is possible while providing enough information to meet the aims of the report, consistent with the fourth stipulation in Standard 5.05a. Psychologists are also cautioned about signing or cosigning insurance forms for services provided by supervisees and are reminded that even when doing so is legally and ethically acceptable, it involves the assumption of legal and professional responsibility, with potentially significant risk to the signer (see also Standards 1.22 and 4.01b).

1.27 Referrals and Fees

When a psychologist pays, receives payment from, or divides fees with another professional other than in an employer–employee relationship, the payment to each is based on the services (clinical, consultative, administrative, or other) provided and is not based on the referral itself.

Provisions in prior APA Ethics Codes prohibited giving or receiving remuneration for referring clients for professional services. The FTC challenged this prohibition as anticompetitive on the theory that it could restrict psychologists' participation in referral services and similar institutions.

The current standard does not prohibit payment of referral fees to a referral service or similar institution, including but not limited to state, county, or provincial psychological association referral services that charge psychologists for the administrative services of listing on the referral rosters, nor does it prohibit payments to referral services by psychologists that may be based on the referrals received. The rule does not prohibit referral fees between institutions and individual professionals, or participation by psychologists in preferred provider organizations, health maintenance organizations, and other managed care organizations. Also, the standard specifically allows payments between individual professionals provided that the fee is based on *actual* services, not just obtaining or referring a patient. The standard is implicated when a professional refers a patient he or she is seeing professionally to another professional in exchange for a fee. A point of concern would be the temptation to make referrals on the basis of the payments anticipated rather than on the basis of the best interests of the client.

If Dr. A. refers a patient to Dr. B., Dr. A. may not accept payment solely for doing so. But if Dr. A. refers a patient to Dr. B., who sees that patient in office space provided by Dr. A., and if Dr. A.'s secretary answers the phone for Dr. B. and does his or her billing, then Dr. A. may indeed expect payment from Dr. B. based on the overhead costs and services rendered. This standard does not stipulate how payment is to be made. Therefore, this payment may be determined to be a percentage of Dr. B.'s collections or a flat monthly fee, for example. But however constituted, the fee must be based on costs and services rather than on the referrals themselves. The standard certainly does not explicitly prohibit psychologists from making a profit in the normal course of a business arrangement. By contrast, if Dr. B.'s office space and office operations were completely separate from Dr. A.'s and no services were provided by Dr. A. to Dr. B., referrals received from Dr. A. would warrant no payment to Dr. A. from Dr. B. It should be noted that employer–employee relationships are exempted from this standard.

State laws may be relevant to this standard, and psychologists should be familiar with their requirements, including the possibility that behavior determined to be ethical under this standard may nevertheless constitute an illegal remuneration under the "antikickback" law. Also, the APA has no control over licensure laws or board rules that continue enforcing earlier prohibitions against all referral fees. Furthermore, psychologists should take note of provisions in their managed care contracts that relate to fees, consider how these fit with the provisions of this Ethics Code, and deal with any issues that may emerge in accordance with Standard 8.03.

Chapter 4 _____

Evaluation, Assessment, or Intervention

This section relates to the use of evaluation, assessment, and intervention techniques and procedures in educational, employment, health care, and other settings. It evolved largely from Principle 8, Assessment Techniques, of the 1981 version and is of particular significance to industrial/organizational psychologists and those who use such procedures in conducting research as well as psychologists who deliver clinical, counseling, neuropsychological, or other health care services. These standards, drafted to provide specific mandates and prohibitions, have broad applicability to various practice and research areas.

This section, in conjunction with Standards 1.04, 1.07, and 1.24, covers the construction and use of psychological tests, informing patients and other consumers of the procedures or instruments to be used, providing them with feedback, testing special populations, and the uses and abuses of raw data.

The Ethics Code specifically limits any statements by psychologists about individuals whom they have not formally assessed. It also restricts the release of raw data to those who are qualified to interpret it, reflecting the overall concern about competence and the importance of responsible use of tests. There is a standard exclusively devoted to automated test scoring and interpretation services, and how vendors should promote, and buyers should select, such services.

It should be noted that the Ethics Code does not provide an explicit standard that requires informed consent for assessment if it is not part of treatment and therefore not subject to Standard 4.02. However, one might view such a requirement as inherent in Standard 2.01 (Evaluation, Diagnosis, and Interventions in Professional Context), Standard 1.14 (Avoiding Harm), or other standards. Also, in most cases psychology board or institutional rules, case law, or the prevailing standard of practice will require similar informed consent in many types of assessment or intervention activities.

2. Evaluation, Assessment, or Intervention

2.01 Evaluation, Diagnosis, and Interventions in Professional Context

(a) Psychologists perform evaluations, diagnostic services, or interventions only within the context of a defined professional relationship. (See also Standard 1.03, Professional and Scientific Relationship.)

Standard 2.01a, repeats the mandate found in Standard 1.03: that professional services be provided only in the context of a professional relationship. A defined professional relationship exists within a specific context that is acknowledged by both parties (i.e., when the client has sought services of the psychologist and the psychologist has agreed to provide the help). Such relationships generally, but not always, involve the exchange of money or some other form of monetary value for the services rendered by the psychologist. Psychological services offered in agencies without charge or on a pro bono basis would also fall within the context of a professional relationship. Depending on the circumstances, a professional relationship may or may not involve a written contract. Consulting with other professionals about a case, however, would not appear to violate this standard.

Psychologists should always avoid discussing cases or appearing to express a professional view about a person's personality type or diagnosis in casual or social situations. Likewise, psychologists should not give professional advice in such causal circumstances because such advice would be out of context and based on inadequate information. Using psychological judgments in a casual way will ultimately undermine the credibility of the psychologist as well as the profession (see also Standard 5.03b).

> **(b) Psychologists' assessments, recommendations, reports, and psychological diagnostic or evaluative statements are based on information and techniques (including personal interviews of the individual when appropriate) sufficient to provide appropriate substantiation for their findings. (See also Standard 7.02, Forensic Assessments.)**

Standard 2.01b requires that psychologists use information and techniques that will substantiate their findings. The standard recognizes that there are situations in which a personal interview may not be appropriate, may not be possible, may be inadvisable, may not be required by the accepted standard of care (e.g., when a psychologist uses an assistant to collect standard data through testing or interviewing), or may be precluded by the nature of the services (e.g., a consultation restricted to a review of the record). Under such circumstances, a personal interview of the individual is not mandated. In all cases, however, the findings must be based on information and techniques that clearly support the findings. It is important to note the cross-reference to Standard 7.02, Forensic Assessments, which addresses the same issue. In general, a clinical interview is prudent as an assessment procedure, but when none is done the psychologist should note that fact (see also Standards 1.06 and 2.05).

2.02 Competence and Appropriate Use of Assessments and Interventions

(a) Psychologists who develop, administer, score, interpret, or use psychological assessment techniques, interviews, tests, or instruments do so in a manner and for purposes that are ap-

propriate in light of the research on or evidence of the usefulness and proper application of the techniques.

The standard requires that psychologists be familiar with and adhere to basic principles related to proper use of assessment techniques, interviews, tests, and other instruments. Assessment techniques should not be used to address questions beyond the scope of their purpose or design. Psychologists should always read the test manual. They should be formally trained in the use of sophisticated projective techniques such as the Rorschach Psychodiagnostic Test or the Thematic Apperception Test if they use them. "Pop psychology" books must not contain tests or what appear to be psychological instruments that are not properly validated without the appropriate disclaimer. Likewise, for other than classroom purposes, in the absence of validation and reliability studies, a psychologist should not "make up" tests or "reinterpret" test results based on formulas known only to the psychologist. Psychologists should not make diagnostic statements, recommendations, or similar judgements unless they have obtained adequate information on which to base their judgements.

Psychologists who perform custody evaluations or special education determinations should use instruments that have evidence of relevance to the specific issues at hand. Psychologists who evaluate individuals for employment selection, promotion, or placement use instruments that demonstrate evidence of validity and reliability for such uses and are relevant for the chosen jobs. For example, a verbal intelligence test standardized on a hearing population may have little predictive validity for job placement when used with those who are hearing impaired. An intelligence test or clinical personality test having usefulness in educational or clinical applications, respectively, should not be used for employment selection unless there is evidence of their usefulness in that specific application. In addition, psychologists involved in personnel assessment should be familiar with the numerous state and federal laws and regulations governing these practices, including the Americans with Disabilities Act, which addresses the use of psychological tests with individuals with disabilities, and the Uniform Guidelines for Employee Selection.

(b) Psychologists refrain from misuse of assessment techniques, interventions, results, and interpretations and take reasonable steps to prevent others from misusing the information these techniques provide. This includes refraining from releasing raw test results or raw data to persons, other than to patients or clients as appropriate, who are not qualified to use such information. (See also Standards 1.02, Relationship of Ethics and Law, and 1.04, Boundaries of Competence.)

Standard 2.02b recognizes that under some laws and regulations, patients or clients may be entitled to raw test results or raw data. In the normal course of practice, however, only another professional competent to evaluate the data is considered qualified to use such information. When psychologists are required to provide raw data or test results to a patient or client, they attempt to assist the patient or client to understand the data and interpretations based on the data.

Raw test data is frequently requested by subpoena or by other health care providers. Before releasing raw data or other confidential information, psychologists should determine that the recipient of the information has a legal right to obtain it and has the proper experience and skill to use it appropriately. When a subpoena has been issued, the psychologist may need to seek a protective order from the court to avoid improper disclosure and will want to consider consulting with his or her legal counsel to determine legal rights and responsibilities.

In any case, psychologists must respond to a subpoena issued by proper authority and to an order issued by the court. A subpoena signed by a clerk, service bureau, or attorney requires a response, but the proper response often is *not* simply turning over the records. The psychologist is advised to consult with legal counsel in these situations.

Even if a subpoena is issued by the court, it does not necessarily mean that all raw data or test protocols must be turned over to any source requesting the information, especially if the request comes from a source not qualified to use the information. On the other hand, it is recognized that in forensic situations, opposing counsel may have the right to determine whether data were collected accurately, the tests scored properly, the interpretations of the data are valid, and that significant issues were not overlooked or excluded from the evaluation. Opposing counsel also has the right to question the psychologist on each of these issues as appropriate. The psychologist may wish to request that the information be turned over to another psychologist for review. The request for the release of information may be modified or limited by the judge in order to protect the material that is not relevant to the particular situation or to protect the welfare and confidentiality of the recipient. In many situations the court will permit an "in camera" review of the record or data (i.e., the judge reviews the material alone) to determine what, if any, data or information are probative, are nonprejudicial, relevant to the case at hand, and do not represent an unnecessary breach of the client's confidentiality (see also Standards 1.02 and 7.06).

If, despite the psychologist's efforts to the contrary, the court still demands that raw data or proprietary test information be turned over to an unqualified individual, attempts to protect the security of test material should be made (e.g., the psychologist might request special restriction on the use of the data or test material by the recipient). The psychologist might also advise the other party of the importance of having the data interpreted by a qualified mental health professional to ensure valid interpretations of the data and to avoid improper use or distribution of the test material.

2.03 Test Construction

Psychologists who develop and conduct research with tests and other assessment techniques use scientific procedures and current professional knowledge for test design, standardiza-

tion, validation, reduction or elimination of bias, and recommendations for use.

This standard covers the use of a variety of assessment techniques including personal interviews, paper-and-pencil tests, computerized tests, and other forms of assessment procedures. In developing tests or other measurement instruments for specific purposes, psychologists must be sure to use appropriate target populations and to provide appropriate cautions regarding any limitations that may apply to the particular instrument. Familiarity with the population being studied is important to the development of valid tests. In order to eliminate bias in test construction and use, it may be necessary to consult with professionals knowledgeable about the population in question (see Standard 1.08). Exaggerated claims of the usefulness of a test technique or instrument would clearly be in violation of this standard.

2.04 Use of Assessment in General and With Special Populations

(a) Psychologists who perform interventions or administer, score, interpret, or use assessment techniques are familiar with the reliability, validation, and related standardization or outcome studies of, and proper applications and uses of, the techniques they use.

Psychologists must be familiar with and understand the statistical concepts related to reliability, validity, and standardization, as well as the appropriateness of test norms. They should be familiar with the procedures for administering, scoring, and interpreting specific tests. In addition, psychologists should review the test manual to be sure that the test may be properly used with the population under consideration. Psychologists should not attempt to interpret results from assessment measures for which they have not had adequate training.

It is also essential that psychologists use tests that are appropriate for the purpose at hand, based on normative and validation studies. It would be improper, for example, to attempt to derive an IQ score from a Minnesota Multiphasic Personality Inventory profile unless solid research existed that supported such an extrapolation.

(b) Psychologists recognize limits to the certainty with which diagnoses, judgments, or predictions can be made about individuals.

Psychologists recognize that their diagnostic work, predictions, or judgments about individuals are limited by the extent and nature of the data that these judgments are based on. In other words, psychologists should never go beyond the data in making statements. This is especially important when working in the schools with diverse ethnic and cultural populations and in forensic settings, such as performing custody evaluations or in personnel work (see Standard 7.02).

Psychologists should also be aware of the extent that available research and the standardization sample might limit the certainty of interpretations made when using a specific assessment instrument. For example, a test that has no available norms, or norms based only on college freshmen, may have very limited utility with most groups and this limitation should be acknowledged in any reports or recommendations.

> **(c) Psychologists attempt to identify situations in which particular interventions or assessments techniques or norms may not be applicable or may require adjustment in administration or interpretation because of factors such as individuals' gender, age, race, ethnicity, national origin, religion, sexual orientation, disability, language, or socioeconomic status.**

Psychologists should be aware of and attempt to identify those situations that mandate the use of special procedures or that, because of other factors, require adjustments in the administration of psychological procedures or interpretations of results. This standard clearly applies to situations in which there are language or cultural barriers that interfere with the proper use of psychological techniques. In such circumstances, the psychologist may need to use more appropriate instruments, seek consultation, use interpreters, or make proper referrals. If adjustments are made in the use of specific techniques, the psychologist must be cautious regarding any conclusions drawn from the procedures. Conclusions drawn or generalizations offered in such situations must be stated tentatively and with relevant limitations described. Special attention should be paid to the use of language-based tests with individuals with hearing impairments or performance tests with persons having physical disabilities. Psychologists should be familiar with the Americans with Disabilities Act.

2.05 Interpreting Assessment Results

> **When interpreting assessment results, including automated interpretations, psychologists take into account the various test factors and characteristics of the person being assessed that might affect psychologists' judgments or reduce the accuracy of their interpretations. They indicate any significant reservations they have about the accuracy or limitations of their interpretations.**

In their reports or other statements concerning the recipient of assessment services, psychologists clearly acknowledge any significant reservations they may have about the accuracy or other limitations of their results (e.g., if the patient was fatigued during the testing or if under stress due to some unrelated incidence, or if the patient is bilingual with English as a second language).

The psychologist should consider issues such as age, ethnic background, educational opportunities, family values, and so on when drawing conclusions about the test results. This standard is also applicable to judgments and interpretations based on information obtained in personal interviews.

2.06 Unqualified Persons

Psychologists do not promote the use of psychological assessment techniques by unqualified persons. (See also Standard 1.22, Delegation to and Supervision of Subordinates.)

Those who use objective and projective tests, behavioral observation, clinical interviews, or any other diagnostic or assessment procedure with patients or clients must be competently trained and supervised when appropriate. It is potentially damaging to consumers for a psychologist to invite or condone such a diagnostic procedure by a layperson or an inadequately trained mental health care provider. Such practices could result in the erroneous documenting or reporting of a diagnosis, resulting in recommendations or interventions that are unnecessary or even detrimental to the individual. In order to avoid such an outcome, and to help ensure the integrity of the evaluation process, it is important to delegate responsibility only to those individuals who are qualified to carry it out competently.

It should be remembered that the psychologist may bear ultimate responsibility for the professional performance of persons whom he or she trains and currently supervises in assessment skills. This obligation also extends in part to psychologists who teach workshops on assessment. It is their obligation to ensure that appropriate screening for workshop attendees occurs. This could be done by establishing minimal requirements for participation, such as licensure or other credentialing or training (see also Standard 6.04).

2.07 Obsolete Tests and Outdated Test Results

(a) Psychologists do not base their assessment or intervention decisions or recommendations on data or test results that are outdated for the current purpose.

In making diagnostic or other decisions about an individual, it is essential to use tests or other data that accurately and currently reflect the construct being measured. Some test results, such as those from aptitude or intelligence tests, may be expected to vary less significantly over time than others, such as measures of depression or state anxiety. It is important to determine in each situation whether data are accurate for the immediate purpose. This requires a good working knowledge of the instrument being used, the concepts being assessed, and the current purpose for the use of the data. For example, IQ or aptitude test scores used for class placement of a student may be considered obsolete if as old as 5 years, whereas scores of that vintage or older may be very useful as an estimate of premorbid intelligence or aptitude in a patient with a head injury. It is important to note that criteria for test obsolescence may be established by some school systems and states; it is the psychologist's obligation to know whether such standards exist and to take them into account.

(b) Similarly, psychologists do not base such decisions or recommendations on tests and measures that are obsolete and not useful for the current purpose.

In general, psychologists use the most recently published form of a test in formulating professional judgments and decisions unless there is some justifiable reason to use an earlier version. This does not necessarily require the use of a particular version of a test just because it has been revised, however. This standard defines obsolescence of a particular test in terms of the purpose for which it is being used. A test would likely be considered obsolete if it had lost its efficacy or was surpassed by a newer version or better instrument for the current purpose. If an earlier version of a test produced more accurate discriminations than a later version, with certain populations, then it might well be the test of choice with those populations. For example, in assessing certain special populations, such as the very gifted or severely developmentally retarded, the instruments used must have appropriate floors and ceilings to measure accurately those who are outliers in the distribution, and the most recent editions of these tests may not always prove to be the most useful. Or, for research purposes, one may appropriately choose an older version of a test, because of the relationship of older scores to the research in the field. Some longitudinal studies may introduce less extraneous variability by using the same instrument instead of a newer one introduced after earlier testings have already been carried out.

2.08 Test Scoring and Interpretation Services

(a) Psychologists who offer assessment or scoring procedures to other professionals accurately describe the purpose, norms, validity, reliability, and applications of the procedures and any special qualifications applicable to their use.

This standard focuses on assessment or scoring procedures and requires psychologist vendors, psychologists who provide assessment and scoring procedures, to make accurate statements in manuals and advertisements. Specifically, it requires them to accurately describe information about the test's norms, validity, and reliability, as well as the intended applications of the procedures. Special qualifications of users might include the training necessary for adequate administration. Any limitations to the use of the test itself or scoring procedures must also be made clear, such as the lack of generalizability to certain age groups, ethnic groups, and so on. Obviously, this standard does not require vendors to reprint information from the test manual, but they must not make promotional or other statements that are deceptive or misleading concerning the applicability or usefulness of the test (see Standard 2.06).

(b) Psychologists select scoring and interpretation services (including automated services) on the basis of evidence of the validity of the program and procedures as well as on other appropriate considerations.

Some appropriate considerations on which psychologists base their choices of scoring and interpretation services are information about the software's capability, flexibility, appropriateness for a particular population, availability of special scales, a technical support "hotline," and other factors. Additional considerations are the availability of fax scoring services and the "turnaround time" required for scoring tests. In the absence of information important in making an informed choice about services for scoring, the psychologist should make an effort to acquire that information or select another service instead. No assumptions about the validity or efficacy of the scoring service should be made by psychologists unless they are substantiated by the vendor; psychologists should request appropriate documentation as needed.

(c) Psychologists retain appropriate responsibility for the appropriate application, interpretation, and use of assessment instruments, whether they score and interpret such tests themselves or use automated or other services.

Psychologists are ultimately accountable for psychological assessment services regardless of their use of automated scoring services. It is their responsibility to implement proper test administration procedures and to be familiar with the instruments so that they can make competent decisions about their application with each client or population being served. Although psychologists would not be held accountable for errors by the vendor, they should be aware of updates and errors that have been detected by the vendor. In short, the burden is on the psychologist to demonstrate that steps have been taken to evaluate the automated scoring service prior to using it, and it is recommended that such an evaluation be done periodically over the time it is used.

When there is a significant disparity between the automated report and the psychologist's clinical impression of the patient, the psychologist should explore the possibility of an erroneous report and take appropriate action.

Psychologists should note that the narrative reports of some automated services are copyrighted and require specific acknowledgment whenever an automated report is being used. Some vendors consider an automated report to be a colleague-to-colleague consultation that does not need citation or referencing. They should bear in mind that they retain ultimate responsibility for the contents of the psychological report even when the vendor supplied the narrative. It is the psychologist's responsibility to observe the copyright law at all times and act accordingly (see Standards 6.22 and 1.04).

2.09 Explaining Assessment Results

Unless the nature of the relationship is clearly explained to the person being assessed in advance and precludes provision

of an explanation of results (such as in some organizational consulting, preemployment or security screenings, and forensic evaluations), psychologists ensure that an explanation of the results is provided using language that is reasonably understandable to the person assessed or to another legally authorized person on behalf of the client. Regardless of whether the scoring and interpretation are done by the psychologist, by assistants, or by automated or other outside services, psychologists take reasonable steps to ensure that appropriate explanations of results are given.

In this standard the obligations between psychologists and those being assessed are delineated. It is essential for psychologists to provide an explanation of assessment results to those being assessed, unless another arrangement has been explained and agreed to *in advance*, in situations such as those mentioned in the first part of the standard. If results are not to be provided, as in the case of many personnel or forensic situations, the psychologist must explain this to the individual at the outset. At all times the psychologist should use easily understood language, or, if necessary, an interpreter should be used.

This rule does not require that the psychologist personally will provide the interpretation. Rather, the rule requires that he or she ensures that an interpretation will be given to the individual, in some form, unless it is precluded by the setting. In an academic setting, for example, it might be necessary for the supervisor to provide the interpretation of a WAIS that had been administered by an intern who is no longer on the site.

2.10 Maintaining Test Security

Psychologists make reasonable efforts to maintain the integrity and security of tests and other assessment techniques consistent with law, contractual obligations, and in a manner that permits compliance with the requirements of this Ethics Code. (See also Standard 1.02, Relationship of Ethics and Law.)

Psychologists bear the legal and ethical responsibility of trying to protect the test materials (e.g., Rorschach cards, WAIS-R Vocabulary items, etc.). It is important that psychologists make reasonable efforts to protect assessment instruments from being released to unauthorized individuals or agencies.

Psychologists who work in school systems should be aware that under certain federal or state laws, disclosure of psychological records is mandated when the proper request is made by the client or legally authorized representative of a minor client. In determining whether to release test protocols psychologists should determine not only the source of the request but the intended audience of the materials as well.

Even when the right, generally, to examine records on request is clear, copies of *test protocols* should not be released unless required by law. Psychologists complying with a subpoena for production of the test protocol may seek the court's help in resolving such an ethical and legal dilemma. The court may narrow the scope of the subpoena, issue a protective order limiting further disclosure or use, or permit a psychologist to submit the raw data to another psychologist for review (see also Standards 2.02b and 7.06).

Chapter 5 _____

Advertising and Other Public Statements

These standards apply to all psychologists. The current provisions are quite permissive in allowing a wide range of communications but emphasizing primarily the avoidance of "false, fraudulent, and deceptive" statements and clarifying the psychologist's responsibilities for statements made by others. This section also includes provisions regarding media presentations and solicitation of testimonials from, and in-person solicitation of, vulnerable persons. Due to the importance of this area, chapter 2 of this book includes a historical comparison of changes in the advertising and promotional area, as well as a description of the process and content of the FTC investigation and subsequent changes.

3. Advertising and Other Public Statements

3.01 Definition of Public Statements

Psychologists comply with this Ethics Code in public statements relating to their professional services, products, or publications or to the field of psychology. Public statements include but are not limited to paid or unpaid advertising, brochures, printed matter, directory listings, personal resumes or curriculum vitae, interviews or comments for use in media, statements in legal proceedings, lectures and public oral presentations, and published materials.

This standard states the scope of Section 3, which includes public statements and advertising broadly defined. Note that the list given is not exhaustive and applies regardless of whether payment is made to disseminate the statement. Public statements also subject to these rules could include, for example, yellow pages listings, newspapers articles, and radio and TV interviews. "Gray areas" might include statements regarding psychological matters made at social gatherings or association meetings or, for example, a statement of a psychological nature made by a psychologist in his or her role as a school board member when it is known that he or she is a psychologist (see also Standard 1.01).

3.02 Statements by Others

(a) Psychologists who engage others to create or place public statements that promote their professional practice, products,

or activities retain professional responsibility for such statements.

3.02a addresses situations in which the psychologist can control the public statement, whereas 3.02b and 3.02c address situations in which the psychologist cannot do so.

The phrase "engage others" would include activities such as hiring a practice management firm or advertising agency to promote a psychologist's practice and hiring a consultant to write a resume. Professional responsibility is reflected in activities such as prior review of materials and requiring the delegated person to consult with the psychologist on professionally significant decisions about the statements, such as how to designate credentials. This standard does not mean that the psychologist is automatically responsible for every error made by the person or group engaged for the statements. For example, if the psychologist approved proof copies of a brochure, and the printer used an earlier version, the psychologist would not be responsible for the printer's error. However, the psychologist would be responsible for ensuring that the printer corrected the error once it was discovered and for discontinuing the use of the document containing the error.

The important action for compliance is to determine appropriate professional responsibility in each advertising activity and to ensure that the required actions are taken.

(b) In addition, psychologists make reasonable efforts to prevent others whom they do not control (such as employers, publishers, sponsors, organizational clients, and representatives of the print or broadcast media) from making deceptive statements concerning psychologists' practice or professional or scientific activities.

This standard addresses the responsibility of the psychologist for attempting to prevent deception when statements about the psychologist's work are made by persons whom the psychologist does not control. The list of such persons provided in the standard is not exhaustive. Deception does not require that there was the intent to mislead, but may be unintentional. It may involve dissemination of inaccurate information or omissions of important information.

Problems here include the occasional efforts of media or marketing personnel (e.g., of hospitals where the psychologist works) to sensationalize or exaggerate information to deceptive effect. This standard requires that the psychologist be alert to attempts to get him or her to make unsupported claims beyond the data or to *misleadingly* sensationalize professional information.

The standard addresses action taken ahead of time to prevent problems, but recognizes that the psychologist does not control such persons and requires only that "reasonable efforts" be made. Reasonable efforts might be, for example, asking a reporter to read back quotations to be asked in an interview, asking editors to review galleys, or sending an employer a note clarifying the proper interpretation of data.

(c) If psychologists learn of deceptive statements about their work made by others, psychologists make reasonable efforts to correct such statements.

This part addresses correction of deception after the fact in situations in which the statement is made by someone other than the psychologist. The standard recognizes that the psychologist will not always be able to make such a correction and requires only that "reasonable efforts" be made.

Examples of efforts to correct such problems would be printed corrections or retractions or writing or calling the person who provided the incorrect information to ask that it be corrected (see also Standard 3.02b). For example, if a psychologist's credentials are not stated correctly in a news article, the psychologist could contact the reporter and ask that a correction be printed.

(d) Psychologists do not compensate employees of press, radio, television, or other communication media in return for publicity in a news item.

The focus is on a *news* item and on *compensation*. The obvious concern is about a blatant action such as paying a newspaper reporter money for the express purpose of the reporter including a quote from the psychologist in a news article.

This standard does not restrict any paid advertising, however, and does not necessarily prohibit such practices as buying lunch for a media person as long as this is not "in return for publicity in a news item." A gray area is buying gifts that may cost no more than lunch but that might be perceived as a "payoff" for publicity.

(e) A paid advertisement relating to the psychologist's activities must be identified as such, unless it is already apparent from the context.

This section requires careful consideration of the context. If not apparent from the context, a paid advertisement would ordinarily carry a "paid advertisement" notice. If the context is clear, such a notice would not be needed, as, for example, when the advertisement is a business-card-type ad in a publication's advertising section.

Context can produce many gray areas that may be difficult to address without specifying the full details. The issue in such matters is the balance between whether this is a paid ad versus whether it is a news item or educational piece for which no compensation is paid.

Special concerns are raised by "canned columns," wherein the psychologist buys a column and runs it in a newspaper. If the psychologist pays a fee to the newspaper to run the column, this might be a paid advertisement and should so state. In fact, the APA Ethics Committee adopted a formal statement on such columns April 18, 1993, without regard to payment:

> Identifying oneself as the author of canned columns or pre-authored news-
> letters (using the term "by") is unethical because it violates Standards 3.02
> (a & b) Statements by Others, 3.03a Avoidance of False or Deceptive State-
> ments, and 6.23 (a & b) Publication Credit. Such columns must clearly
> identify the source of the material. ("Ethics Committee," 1993)

Consider a situation in which a psychologist, Dr. H., has contracted for
newsletters written by Write For You Enterprises and that the service provides a quantity of newsletters every month. The newsletters carry Dr. H.'s
practice name and logo, and all of the articles are written by the staff of the
service. The previous comments and the Ethics Committee statement suggest
that Dr. H. must not say "by John H., PhD" on any articles and that credit
should be indicated somewhere in the newsletter indicating that the articles
are provided by Write For You Enterprises. If Dr. H. actually wrote one of
articles, Dr. H. could then indicate "by John H., PhD" on the article that he
wrote.

3.03 Avoidance of False or Deceptive Statements

**(a) Psychologists do not make public statements that are false,
deceptive, misleading, or fraudulent, either because of what
they state, convey, or suggest or because of what they omit,
concerning their research, practice, or other work activities
or those of persons or organizations with which they are affiliated. As examples (and not in limitation) of this standard,
psychologists do not make false or deceptive statements concerning (1) their training, experience, or competence; (2) their
academic degrees; (3) their credentials; (4) their institutional
or association affiliations; (5) their services; (6) the scientific
or clinical basis for, or results or degree of success of, their
services; (7) their fees; or (8) their publications or research
findings. (See also Standards 6.15, Deception in Research, and
6.18, Providing Participants With Information About the Study.)**

This section is stated in terms of public statements that are prohibited
and requires careful consideration of context. Note that the list of areas (1–
8) is not exhaustive, but is stated as examples. The focus is on "public statements that are false, deceptive, misleading, or fraudulent." This rule covers
problems of commission ("what [statements] state, convey, or suggest") and
omission ("what they omit"), so it requires that the psychologist actively consider the accuracy of his or her public statements. Under the law, "deceptive"
and "misleading" statements are ones that, given their commonsense meaning,
would be likely to be misunderstood in some material way by an appreciable
percentage of readers or hearers. Thus, the fact that some readers could tease
out a "correct" meaning is not a defense, and careless misunderstanding by
one reader does not prove an offense.

Examples of problems of commission would be a psychologist's listing a
degree that the psychologist does not have, listing under "publications" on a

resume papers that the psychologist did not write, or claiming in an advertisement "lasting results" when the psychologist has data only to support short-term results. Problems of omission are very dependent on context. If a psychologist runs an ad stating "initial consultation $20" but does not state that the consultation is provided only if the client also pays for a psychological inventory, the ad would be misleading.

There are a variety of practices that are considered clearly improper by most psychologists but that are asked about with some frequency. For example, listing "ABD" after one's name is misleading, because "All But Dissertation" or "All But Doctorate" is not a degree, and the public would assume that it is a legitimate degree. Similarly, listing a designation for "Doctoral Candidate" (e.g., PhD(c)) as if it were a degree is misleading.

It is acceptable to list such information as APA, division, or other membership as long as the context is appropriate, as in a description of credentials in a brochure for a continuing education workshop. However, listing such memberships or one's APA membership number after one's signature on a report or insurance form would be misleading. It suggests that APA membership is a credential, which it is not. Similarly, descriptions such as "Board Eligible" may be misleading, because it implies that a recognized group has designated that the psychologist meets certain standards.

Also note that this rule covers psychologists' own activities as well as their "representations of activities of persons or organizations with which they are affiliated." For example, a psychologist *making* a public statement that the hospital with which he or she is affiliated has a 90% success rate with adolescent clients when the psychologist knows that the hospital's data shows 60% would violate this standard. Similarly, stating that an associate in a private practice is licensed when the individual is not is prohibited.

As noted in chapter 2 and in the introduction to chapter 5, the current provisions reflect the APA's continuing evolution and modernization of its advertising standards. The standard does not include language from earlier Ethics Codes stating that advertising may include any information that is not prohibited, because the context now makes that point clear.

(b) Psychologists claim as credentials for their psychological work, only degrees that (1) were earned from a regionally accredited educational institution or (2) were the basis for psychology licensure by the state in which they practice.

This standard separately and specifically allows the claiming as credentials for psychological work only two types of degrees. The first, the provision found in previous APA Ethics Codes, is any degree that is earned from a regionally accredited educational institution (e.g., accredited by the North Central Association of Schools and Colleges) or another regional accreditation body approved by the U.S. secretary of education. For doctoral degrees, as long as the degree is otherwise qualified, the degrees PhD, PsyD, and EdD would be equivalent in this rule. Note that a psychologist listing such a degree implies that the degree is in psychology, so that this provision notwithstanding, listing a degree that is not received in psychology (e.g., in English or business) could be a violation of 3.03a as "misleading" if used in connection with offering psychology services. Context would be important in determining the accuracy of use of nonpsychology degrees from related fields (e.g., social work or occupational therapy).

The second type of degree, a new provision in this Ethics Code, is a degree that, although it may not have been earned from a regionally accredited educational institution, was nonetheless used as the basis for the granting of licensure in a state in which the individual is practicing. The phrase "the basis for psychology licensure by the state in which they practice" addresses the dilemma faced by APA members (frequently associate members) who have been licensed as psychologists in their state on the basis of doctoral degrees from institutions that are not regionally accredited. This may be the case when the state licensure board recognizes doctoral degrees from schools that are not regionally accredited but are state licensed. The "regionally accredited" standard still appears to be the most meaningful one to use generally, but providing the "basis of licensure" alternative helps to ensure that unreasonable restrictions are not applied. 3.03b does not require that the degree be in psychology, so a nonpsychology mental health degree that meets the criteria in 3.03b (e.g., a PhD in social work that was accepted by a state licensure board as the basis on which psychology licensure was granted) would be appropriate.

The following scenario is illustrative. An APA associate member is licensed based on a master's degree from a school that is not regionally accredited. Later the member receives a doctoral degree from a school that is also not regionally accredited. The degree that was "the basis for psychology licensure" was the master's degree, so this member could sign "MA" but could risk ethical violation if he or she signs "PhD" after his or her name on reports or uses "PhD" on professional business cards. This would be true regardless of whether the psychologist believed that the licensure board would grant licensure based on the later degree. However, if this member received a PhD from a school that is regionally accredited, the PhD could be claimed as a credential.

The behavior at issue in this section is claiming an educational degree "as a credential." Application of this standard should include consideration of the special contextual meaning of degrees listed after an individual's name on letterhead and business cards and on signatures on letters, professional reports, and official forms such as insurance claims. Listing a variety of degrees in a resume in the usual manner may not be prohibited, because the ordinary person would not see it as a credential and the school would be listed, along with other information about the person's background, allowing further independent review of the significance of the degree. Consider the difference in signing "PhD" after one's name on an evaluation report; the usual consumer will see this as a "credential," qualifying the member to do psychological work.

3.04 Media Presentations

When psychologists provide advice or comment by means of public lectures, demonstrations, radio or television programs,

prerecorded tapes, printed articles, mailed material, or other media, they take reasonable precautions to ensure that (1) the statements are based on appropriate psychological literature and practice, (2) the statements are otherwise consistent with this Ethics Code, and (3) the recipients of the information are not encouraged to infer that a relationship has been established with them personally.

Media is defined broadly in this rule, providing a nonexhaustive list, including prerecorded tapes and "other media" (e.g., public computer bulletin boards). The rule requires taking "reasonable precautions to ensure" that three requirements are met, recognizing that the psychologist may not be able to control some of the conditions.

The first requirement is that "the statements are based on appropriate psychological literature and practice." This addresses, for example, the importance of resisting the temptation (and the efforts by many media personnel) to go beyond the data and create a misleading impression through sensationalism or exaggeration. It can be difficult in an interview format to provide appropriate qualifications or disclaimers, but preliminary discussion with the interviewer can help achieve compliance with this standard. (Standards 3.02b and 3.02c, which address psychologists' responsibilities for preventing and correcting deceptive statements about their work, is also relevant to these situations.)

The second requirement, "the statements are otherwise consistent with this Ethics Code," would include many standards with which the psychologist must comply in giving advice in the media. Examples are compliance with Standard 3.03, which requires not making false or deceptive public statements; Standard 1.04, which indicates that a psychologist must not give advice in an area in which he or she is not competent; and Standard 2.01b, which indicates that a psychologist must not render a diagnosis of an individual without sufficient information to make the diagnosis.

The last requirement, "the recipients of the information are not encouraged to infer that a relationship has been established with them personally," addresses the problem of individuals incorrectly believing that they are in a therapy relationship. Although this can be a subjective judgment, the psychologist should consider the differences in the passive listener, the radio call-in participant, and the active interviewee in a therapylike TV talk show interchange. The psychologist could periodically use some statement to emphasize the difference in roles, such as "you might talk to a therapist about . . . ."

Media psychology is a traditionally difficult area in ethics that is still evolving. It is important in the light of established procedures such as suicide hotlines and evolving developments such as "1-900 telephone therapy" to differentiate between "therapy" and "media psychology." When therapy services as such are offered, whether by telephone or on a TV program, many other rules in the Ethics Code may apply. For purposes of this section, the principal issue is the provision of educational information or advice through the media or mass distribution materials. Some applications, such as a psychologist's being involved in a discussion among participants on a TV talk show, can present a fine line between conducting group therapy and playing a media psychology role.

There is no explicit provision that addresses appearing on media programs with current or former clients, but this can involve elements of coercion and prohibited multiple relationships depending on the circumstances. Also, note that testimonials should not be solicited from current psychotherapy clients (see the following standard).

3.05 Testimonials

Psychologists do not solicit testimonials from current psychotherapy clients or patients or other persons who because of their particular circumstances are vulnerable to undue influence.

This provision applies to solicitation of testimonials from "persons who because of their particular circumstances are vulnerable to undue influence." It prohibits solicitation of testimonials from all current psychotherapy clients. Note that this standard applies only to the *solicitation* of a testimonial, not to the use of an unsolicited testimonial. Other standards might be relevant to such use, such as regarding confidentiality, but this standard prohibits only certain solicitation.

For example, the standard would apply if a psychologist took advantage of a custody evaluation client who ordinarily would not agree to publicly state his or her receiving psychological services, but who did agree because she feared that the psychologist would provide a negative report if the solicitation was refused. Similarly, it would apply if a psychologist took advantage of a current psychotherapy client who ordinarily would not agree to publicly state his or her involvement in therapy, but who does agree due to feeling unrealistic gratitude for the psychologist's treatment.

The consent agreement between the APA and the FTC defines some terms for purposes of that agreement. These definitions do not apply to the APA Ethics Code generally, but are relevant to consider when applying those portions of the Ethics Code covered by the FTC agreement. The definitions include "psychotherapy" and "current psychotherapy patient."[1] The FTC does not have a specific definition of "vulnerable to undue influence."

---

[1] "Psychotherapy" means the therapeutic treatment of mental, emotional, or behavioral disorders by psychological means, and excludes programs, seminars, workshops, or consultations that address specific limited goals, such as career planning; improving employment skills or performance; increasing assertiveness; losing weight; giving up smoking; or obtaining non-individualized information about methods of coping with concerns common in everyday life. ("FTC Consent Order," 1993)

"Current psychotherapy patient" means a patient who has commenced an evaluation for or a planned course of individual, family, or group psychotherapy, wherein the patient and the therapist have not agreed to terminate the treatment. However, a person who has not participated in psychotherapy with the psychologist for one year shall not be deemed a current psychotherapy patient. ("FTC Consent Order," 1993)

3.06 In-Person Solicitation

Psychologists do not engage, directly or through agents, in uninvited in-person solicitation of business from actual or potential psychotherapy patients or clients or other persons who because of their particular circumstances are vulnerable to undue influence. However, this does not preclude attempting to implement appropriate collateral contacts with significant others for the purpose of benefiting an already engaged therapy patient.

The current provision limits the prohibition to persons "who because of their particular circumstances are vulnerable to undue influence," including vulnerable psychotherapy clients (see Standard 3.05 regarding definitions of psychotherapy). It should be apparent from the context that this provision is not relevant to psychologists soliciting business from companies.

It is important to note that this prohibition applies only to contacts that are *uninvited* and *occur in person* whether by the psychologist or through an agent of the psychologist, as opposed to contacts invited by the individual or conducted through the mail or other methods, such as placing flyers on windshields. Case law in this area includes telephone contacts as being "in person."

An example of the behavior prohibited by this standard is "ambulance chasing"; for psychologists, perhaps this would be soliciting mourners at a funeral home or going by the residences of survivors located through names listed in obituaries. Generally, however, this rule makes it clear that it is *acceptable* to engage in direct solicitation as long as the "vulnerability" problem is not present. Because of concerns over both the First Amendment and permitting free competition, the FTC sought to ensure that this standard does not, for example, prohibit passing out professional cards to individuals at a shopping mall.

The second sentence of the standard—"However, this does not preclude attempting to implement appropriate collateral contacts with significant others for the purpose of benefiting an already engaged therapy patient"—makes it clear that this rule does not prohibit the psychologist suggesting, for example, that the spouse or partner of a client be treated by the same psychologist.

Chapter 6 _____

Therapy

This section applies only to therapy patients and clients, not to persons involved only in nontherapy assessment, to nontherapy organizational consulting, or to other nontherapy clients. The purpose of this section is to address standards specific to therapy relationships, for example, the need to explain therapy to clients and to provide guarantees of special protection of therapy client's welfare.

A major continuing standard is the prohibition against sexual involvement with clients. Important new standards are provisions regarding sexual involvement with former clients, therapy with former sexual partners, an explicit requirement for informed consent to therapy, and more guidance regarding discontinuing and terminating treatment, including implications for psychologists' employment and partnership contracts. New standards also include clarifying relationships when treating couples and families and informing clients of supervision and the therapist's intern status. Although most of the other provisions in this section are continuations of previous Ethics Code requirements, the format has been changed, and all provisions should be carefully reviewed.

4. Therapy

4.01 Structuring the Relationship

(a) Psychologists discuss with clients or patients as early as is feasible in the therapeutic relationship appropriate issues, such as the nature and anticipated course of therapy, fees, and confidentiality. (See also Standards 1.25, Fees and Financial Arrangements, and 5.01, Discussing the Limits of Confidentiality.)

This standard requires that several issues be discussed, and this discussion would ordinarily occur at the beginning of therapy. Note that the list of areas to be discussed is not exhaustive, but includes any "appropriate issues." Other standards provide guidance as to some of the other appropriate issues, and this standard refers to two of them: 5.01, Discussing the Limits of Confidentiality, and 1.25, Fees and Financial Arrangements.

In addition to issues that are always appropriate to discuss, some may vary depending on the situation. For example, when seeing a child client, the discussion, with the child and with the parent or guardian, should include the role of the psychologist with both individuals (see Standard 4.03, which requires that discussion).

(b) When the psychologist's work with clients or patients will be supervised, the above discussion includes that fact, and the name of the supervisor, when the supervisor has legal responsibility for the case.

The issue involved in this standard is that clients have the right to know whether their therapist is qualified to treat them independently or whether the work must be supervised. In addition, when the supervisor has ultimate legal responsibility for their treatment, as, for example, in an internship setting or for a nonlicensed therapist in a private practice, the client should know the name of the supervisor. Legal responsibility must be determined based on applicable state and federal laws but is generally the case if (a) the supervisee is an employee and not qualified to practice independently, (b) the supervision is required for the supervisee to practice lawfully, or (c) the supervisee is in training or is being supervised in order to obtain a license (e.g., the postdoctoral year of required supervised experience). Signing an insurance form as supervisor for a supervisee's services requires special considerations, but it is generally considered to reflect legal responsibility by the supervisor for the services. (See Standard 1.26 for a discussion of cosigning insurance forms.)

In most cases, "supervision" (as opposed to "consultation") implies greater levels of legal responsibility. (Also see Standard 1.22 for a discussion of the responsibilities of supervisors.) Note that state law, or other regulations, may require special notifications or procedures when the therapist's work is supervised, and it is the psychologist's responsibility to be aware of such requirements.

(c) When the therapist is a student intern, the client or patient is informed of that fact.

The issue involved in this standard is that patients have the right to know if the therapist is still in training. The term *student intern* would cover any formal student status, such as internship, practicum, or residency. Explanations about student, intern, or resident status (rather than just the "fact" of being an intern, as required by this rule) are provided in most settings. When the supervisee is a student intern (or other trainee status), it is assumed that the work is always supervised and that indicating the name of the supervisor is required as provided in 4.01b.

Note that state law, or other regulations, may require special notification of student status. Also, if the student is called "Dr." by the patient and has not already earned that degree, an explanation should be provided so the patient is not misled. (Also see Standard 3.03a regarding omissions in statements regarding one's credentials.)

(d) Psychologists make reasonable efforts to answer patients' questions and to avoid apparent misunderstandings about therapy. Whenever possible, psychologists provide oral and/

or written information, using language that is reasonably understandable to the patient or client.

The standard requires that the psychologist provide an opportunity for the client to ask questions and allows giving oral and written information, as long as the information uses language that is understandable to the person. (See the commentary on Standard 1.07a for additional discussion of "understandable language.") Many psychologists are now using lengthier consent forms or educational brochures on treatment, given either before treatment begins or in response to specific questions. The standard does not require endless or provably "successful" clarification of explanations, only that "reasonable efforts" be made.

For example, clients often ask how long therapy will last. This standard does not require giving a specific amount of time but that the psychologist address the client's concern and provide appropriate information, by either talking with the client or providing written educational information.

The psychologist's efforts notwithstanding, the standard acknowledges that the psychologist will not always be aware of and may not be responsible for "private" misconceptions that the client or patient may hold. For example, a psychologist may explain that the client may experience uncomfortable emotions associated with therapy, but the client may secretly hold onto the belief that therapy will immediately lead to feelings of relief and happiness. If the misunderstanding is expressed, the therapist would then address it.

4.02 Informed Consent to Therapy

(a) Psychologists obtain appropriate informed consent to therapy or related procedures, using language that is reasonably understandable to participants. The content of informed consent will vary depending on many circumstances; however, informed consent generally implies that the person (1) has the capacity to consent, (2) has been informed of significant information concerning the procedure, (3) has freely and without undue influence expressed consent, and (4) consent has been appropriately documented.

The method of obtaining the informed consent required in this standard is subject to a variety of considerations and may vary depending on the circumstances, including possible state-by-state variations in law. The process should include using language that is understandable to the person. (See the commentary on Standard 1.07a for additional discussion of "understandable language.") "Related procedures" might include assessment, consultation, and supervision.

The specific provisions (1–4) are stated as *generally* implied by the concept of "informed consent" but are not requirements imposed by the rule; the requirement is that there be "appropriate informed consent." However, these conditions would almost always have to be met for the consent to be valid as understood legally in most jurisdictions. Accordingly, consent that does not meet the four conditions is likely to be found as not being "appropriate informed consent" and is therefore inadequate under this Ethics Code. Each provision deserves specific discussion.

The client's capacity to consent must be based on the psychologist's understanding at the time at which the consent is given and does not require that the psychologist have formal documentation of the capacity. This provision will be most difficult to comply with when the person's capacity has been called into question, such as during an assessment for dementia in a formal competency hearing process. Under those conditions, the psychologist should document how the person's welfare and rights have been considered and protected. For example, the psychologist's progress note might document which of the following types of steps the psychologist has taken. The psychologist can engage in as appropriate a discussion as possible with the client, can obtain the client's regular health professional's feedback regarding the client's understanding of the nature of the assessment, and can determine whether the client's attorney believes he or she has capacity to consent. Furthermore, the psychologist can contact the family or guardian, and hospital administrator or hospital attorney as necessary, to apprise such persons of the situation and to elicit their input, so as to add to the protection of the patient's rights. If the psychologist has good reason to believe that the person's ability to consent or refuse is significantly impaired, the psychologist may urge that the processes for court intervention or substituted consent be activated in order to comply with this standard.

The second provision of this standard involves information such as the type of services to be provided and confidentiality information (see the commentary on Standard 5.01) and might include a discussion of the risks and alternatives to the service. This provision does not, however, require that any specific set of information be provided, only that the person be informed of "significant information." The third requirement is that consent must not be obtained through coercion or unreasonable reliance on the person's vulnerable situation.

The documentation required by the fourth requirement could be, for example, in the form of a signed consent for treatment or a progress note entry; the standard does not specify the method of documentation and does not require a signed consent form. Legal requirements may be more specific regarding the methods of obtaining and documenting informed consent, and psychologists should know laws to which they are subject.

> **(b) When persons are legally incapable of giving informed consent, psychologists obtain informed permission from a legally authorized person, if such substitute consent is permitted by law.**

Persons legally incapable of giving informed consent would include children and adults who have been found legally incompetent to give consent. In such situations, the psychologist must obtain consent as provided in this section and must comply with section 4.02c.

(c) In addition, psychologists (1) inform those persons who are legally incapable of giving informed consent about the proposed interventions in a manner commensurate with the persons' psychological capacities, (2) seek their assent to those interventions, and (3) consider such persons' preferences and best interests.

Even though a child may not be able to provide the legal consent, the child must be told about the nature of the intervention (testing, observation, therapy) and asked if he or she will agree (assent) to the procedure. The therapist proceeds with therapy only after having considered the child's preference (e.g., "no") and the child's best interest. "*Seeking* assent" does not mean that the child must agree. For example, a therapist might say to a child client, "we're going to talk together and see if we can help you be happier. Is that okay? Will you be willing to talk to me?" If the child says yes, the decision is easy, assuming that the psychologist believes that the child needs to be treated. (Even in these circumstances, however, consent from a legally authorized person must be obtained.) If the child says no, the psychologist considers the child's preference not to be seen, but might decide to see the child anyway, if it would still be in the child's best interest. This decision is made only after obtaining the *consent* from a legally authorized person required in 4.02b.

4.03 Couple and Family Relationships

(a) When a psychologist agrees to provide services to several persons who have a relationship (such as husband and wife or parents and children), the psychologist attempts to clarify at the outset (1) which of the individuals are patients or clients and (2) the relationship the psychologist will have with each person. This clarification includes the role of the psychologist and the probable uses of the services provided or the information obtained. (See also Standard 5.01, Discussing the Limits of Confidentiality.)

This standard applies only when more than one individual is being treated and when the individuals have a continuing relationship with each other. It applies to formal family or marital therapy as well as "collateral" contacts: limited contacts with family members in support of the treatment of an individual. Confidentiality is an important issue in this discussion, and state and federal law may be important considerations in determining what clarification is needed regarding confidentiality.

The standard requires that the psychologist make an effort to clarify several areas and that the discussion occur at the outset of the joint meetings. The orientation of the therapist, nature of the treatment, and the nature of the problems and diagnosis are factors that affect the clarifications required by this standard.

The first area of clarification, "which of the individuals are patients or clients," can be particularly complicated. This does not mean that the psychologist must designate an "identified patient." This rule does not require that each individual's status as patient or client be absolutely determined, only clarified. However, Standard 1.26 becomes relevant regarding accuracy in insurance reports.

The second area would be handled differently for the therapist who will see a couple separately in individual sessions as well as conjointly, but requires that the psychologist help each participant understand what their relationship with the psychologist is to be. It may also entail keeping separate records.

> **(b) As soon as it becomes apparent that the psychologist may be called on to perform potentially conflicting roles (such as marital counselor to husband and wife, and then witness for one party in a divorce proceeding), the psychologist attempts to clarify and adjust, or withdraw from, roles appropriately. (See also Standard 7.03, Clarification of Role, under Forensic Activities.)**

This standard addresses a difficult area in which an ethical dilemma can arise easily. It requires that the psychologist not ignore the need to address potentially conflicting roles *as soon as* it becomes apparent that the psychologist *may* be called on to perform them. The emphasis is on *attempting* to take one of several actions. "Clarifying" the potentially conflicting roles might consist of explaining what the roles are, in what ways they might conflict, and what effects such a conflict might have on the therapy. "Adjusting" roles might involve changing from being a couple's therapist to being the individual therapist for one member of the couple if it is clinically indicated. (Obviously, adjusting roles may itself be problematic.) "Withdrawing" from an existing role must be considered in light of the possibility of abandonment, but because the role is a "potentially conflicting" one, the psychologist might also decline to play the role.

The classic version of this problem is the psychologist who treats a couple in marital therapy and later finds that he or she is to be called as an expert witness for one party or the other in a divorce or custody action. "As soon as" the psychologist realizes that this may occur, the standard requires clarifying the potential problem and adjusting or withdrawing (or refusing) roles. The underlying issues are the potential for problems with objectivity and with feelings of betrayal in the therapy relationship. In fact, many psychologists establish, and communicate to clients, a policy that when treating couples, they will not become involved in giving opinions in later divorce or custody actions. Unfortunately, they cannot always contrive this, and they may later be compelled by a court to testify. Note the reference to Standard 7.03, which provides additional rules regarding clarification of role in forensic activities.

4.04 Providing Mental Health Services to Those Served by Others

> **In deciding whether to offer or provide services to those already receiving mental health services elsewhere, psycholo-**

gists carefully consider the treatment issues and the potential patient's or client's welfare. The psychologist discusses these issues with the patient or client, or another legally authorized person on behalf of the client, in order to minimize the risk of confusion and conflict, consults with the other service providers when appropriate, and proceeds with caution and sensitivity to the therapeutic issues.

This standard must be understood in the context of its appearing in the Therapy section of the Ethics Code and of provisions in the Advertising section. A similar provision in the 1981 Ethics Code, rescinded in 1989, prohibited *offering* services to "someone receiving similar services from another professional." That appeared in a section that applied to all psychologists and all psychology services. Standard 3.06 provides that psychologists do not engage in uninvited, in-person solicitation of psychotherapy clients or other persons who because of their particular circumstances are vulnerable to undue influence. Both the previous and the current Ethics Code (Standard 4.04) allow *providing* services requested in the first instance by the client as long as this is done with sensitivity. The FTC action is discussed in chapter 2 and in the introduction to chapter 5.

Compliance with this standard requires that certain steps be taken. The psychologist first considers the treatment issues in terms of the client's welfare and discusses them with the potential client. For example, a client might be therapist shopping because he or she is angry with a therapist who provided needed confrontation. The therapist should recognize the special problems this would pose in a new therapy relationship and should discuss this with the client.

Ordinarily, the psychologist would consult with the other service providers in order to obtain background information and possibly coordinate treatment, but on rare occasions this may not be possible or appropriate. For example, the patient may refuse permission and the psychologist would then not be free to communicate with the other provider. It would be wise to document such refusal in the record. Standards 5.03 and 5.05–5.06 are relevant to contacts with other providers.

The required discussion should occur with the client's legally authorized representative if the client is not able to provide competent consent to treatment.

4.05 Sexual Intimacies With Current Patients or Clients

Psychologists do not engage in sexual intimacies with current patients or clients.

This standard specifically prohibits sexual intimacies with current patients or clients, a provision that has been explicit in the APA Ethics Code since 1977. Note that this provision in the 1992 Ethics Code appears in the Therapy section and applies only to patients or clients receiving therapy and related services. Relationships involving nontherapy clients may be covered by Standards 1.14, 1.17, and 1.19.

The term *sexual intimacies* is far broader than sexual intercourse. It would be difficult to define or to catalogue the large range of physical, verbal, and nonverbal behaviors that are sexual intimacies, but in addition to sexual intercourse, they include kissing, any erotic or romantic hugging, touching, or other physical contact. Actions that do not involve touch may also be sexually intimate, for example, explicit, verbal sexual invitations or masturbating in front of a client or therapist. The Ethics Committee has generally addressed this on a case-by-case basis. Although the term used is *sexual intimacies*, most sexual interactions between therapists and clients contain issues of abuse of power and exploitation and do not deserve the usual emotionally relevant definition of *intimacy*. *Sexual intimacies*, however, is a term that is readily understood.

This standard does not prohibit nonsexual touching between therapist and client, but the ease with which touch is misunderstood strongly suggests caution in how and when touch is used. For example, a therapist's supportive hug may well be interpreted as a sexual overture by some patients, particularly those with a history of incest or other similar problems or those whose relationship issues have not been worked through. Strong caution is indicated when the psychologist considers initiating or responding to touch.

It should be noted that "sex therapy" does not involve romantic or erotic interaction between the therapist and client, even though it may involve dealing with explicitly sexual information, instructions, or readings. Psychologists must be cautious, however, because clients may perceive activities or comments as erotic, without regard to the psychologist's intent. The use of sexual surrogates is often considered controversial, but this rule makes it clear that even if the psychologist endorses the use of surrogates, the surrogate is *never* the psychologist.

4.06 Therapy With Former Sexual Partners

Psychologists do not accept as therapy patients or clients persons with whom they have engaged in sexual intimacies.

This standard is a new provision in the 1992 Ethics Code that recognizes that treating former lovers in therapy is problematic. Concerns include loss of objectivity, role confusion (by both psychologist and client), and risk for further sexual involvement. Nontherapy professional relationships involving former lovers are covered by Standards 1.14 and 1.19. (See also the discussion under Standard 4.05 regarding sexual intimacies.)

4.07 Sexual Intimacies With Former Therapy Patients

(a) Psychologists do not engage in sexual intimacies with a former therapy patient or client for at least two years after cessation or termination of professional services.

This is the first time that the APA Ethics Code has explicitly addressed sexual involvement with former therapy clients or patients. The APA Ethics Committee did establish a policy statement in 1987 that addressed such behavior when there was an improper termination, but a change in the Ethics Code provides an explicit rule. Note that this provision applies only to therapy patients or clients. Relationships involving nontherapy clients may be covered by Standards 1.14 and 1.19 (see also Standard 4.05, which discusses sexual intimacies generally).

Standard 4.07a establishes an absolute prohibition on such conduct for 2 years after cessation or termination of therapy. The rule means that such behavior is *always* wrong in less than 2 years. It does not mean that such behavior is automatically acceptable after 2 years; Standard 4.07b addresses behavior after the 2 years.

Note that the last clause, "cessation or termination of services," indicates that if the psychologist sees the patient on an intermittent basis, then the 2-year period does not begin until the last date of service and that if the psychologist is still available as the client's therapist, then the 2-year period does not begin until the formal termination of therapy. In fact, some approaches, including those that provide brief periods of psychotherapy throughout the individual's lifetime, would argue against ever being involved. Any professional contact or service would reflect that services have not been terminated and would restart the 2-year time period, for example, telephone follow-up contacts, brief consults, and providing psychological reports about the person. An absence of any *personal* contact during the 2 years was not made part of the rule, but is addressed under Standard 4.07b regarding "promises" of a future relationship (see the commentary on Factor 7 in Standard 4.07b).

> **(b) Because sexual intimacies with a former therapy patient or client are so frequently harmful to the patient or client, and because such intimacies undermine public confidence in the psychology profession and thereby deter the public's use of needed services, psychologists do not engage in sexual intimacies with former therapy patients and clients even after a two-year interval except in the most unusual circumstances. The psychologist who engages in such activity after the two years following cessation or termination of treatment bears the burden of demonstrating that there has been no exploitation, in light of all relevant factors, including (1) the amount of time that has passed since therapy terminated, (2) the nature and duration of the therapy, (3) the circumstances of termination, (4) the patient's or client's personal history, (5) the patient's or client's current mental status, (6) the likelihood of adverse impact on the patient or client and others, and (7) any statements or actions made by the therapist during the course of therapy suggesting or inviting the possibility of a posttermination sexual or romantic relationship with the patient or client. (See also Standard 1.17, Multiple Relationships.)**

Standard 4.07b of the rule, which applies *after* a 2-year period, is best understood as an "almost never" rule. Standard 4.07b emphasizes that sexual involvement after 2 years would occur only "in the most unusual circumstances." It places the burden on the psychologist who engages in such activity to demonstrate that "there has been no exploitation, in light of all relevant factors." Standard 4.07b does not give an exhaustive list but states that relevant factors would include at least seven considerations.

The first factor recognizes that shorter time periods after termination argue against involvement, but in all cases must exceed 2 years.

The second factor points out that there is a difference between the intensity and depth of different therapies, such as intensive psychoanalytic or psychodynamic therapy on the one hand and biofeedback for headaches on the other, and that there is a great deal of difference between a one- to two-session therapy as opposed to several years' duration. (Also see the commentary on 4.07a regarding "termination" and "brief intermittent treatment.")

The third factor recognizes in part that a termination that occurs *due to* problems in managing the therapeutic relationship, for example, substantial transference–countertransference issues, may permanently prevent a relationship ever occurring without a very high likelihood of exploitation and harm. In fact, some therapies may result in unresolved transference over very long periods of time. Other signs of problems may include abrupt or explosive terminations.

The fourth factor recognizes that events in the patient's history such as boundary violations like child sexual or other abuse may result in special meaning to involvement with a person with whom there is a power differential, such as a former therapist. Factor 4 recognizes that such variables may increase the risk of exploitation and harm. This may occur in part due to the client's tendency to reenact past events in a current relationship, but the psychologist bears the responsibility of not exploiting this tendency.

The fifth factor recognizes that an individual who is distraught and vulnerable is more susceptible to exploitation than a person whose mental status is stable. Also, disorders such as dependent or borderline personality disorders involve factors that are relevant to mental status at any point in time. *Current* refers to "at the time of the new relationship," but mental status "at the time of termination" would be relevant under Factor 3.

The sixth factor requires consideration of the adverse effects of the involvement, including factors such as impaired ability to trust, identity confusion, and increased suicidal risk. The consideration is not only with regard to the former client, but also to other persons such as their family members, ex-spouses, children, and other clients in the psychologist's practice, including clients referred by the former client.

The seventh factor deals with indications that the psychologist suggested that at the end of 2 years he or she could have a romantic or sexual relationship with the client or patient. This factor does not make the psychologist responsible for a client's misperception of a "promise," but this rule becomes an issue only if the psychologist did in fact become involved with the client. (See also the commentary on Standard 1.17, which addresses promising of a multiple relationship.)

It should be stressed that this listing of factors is illustrative and not exhaustive. The rule requires proof that there has been no exploitation "in light of *all* relevant factors."

This standard is written in a form that addresses enforcement: "the psychologist . . . bears the burden of demonstrating." The psychologist who is considering entering a romantic or sexual relationship with a former client needs to consider this action prior to entering the relationship. One option is to obtain consultation, using the seven variables as minimal considerations. The consultation should be with a psychologist with expertise in ethics and professional and personal boundary issues, and not, for example, with a friend or colleague. Bad or misguided advice from a consultant, whether an expert or not, may not protect the patient or client adequately and is not likely to be considered an adequate defense to an ethics complaint. The role of the consultant is to help the psychologist become more aware of considerations and consequences, and perhaps to look at options, not to give or withhold "permission."

It should be noted that some psychologists strongly believe in a "perpetuity rule," a prohibition against a psychologist ever becoming sexually involved with a person who has once been the psychologist's client. As noted, the current standard is a very restrictive rule, and a perpetuity rule might be more difficult to defend constitutionally and socially than the current rule.

4.08 Interruption of Services

(a) Psychologists make reasonable efforts to plan for facilitating care in the event that psychological services are interrupted by factors such as the psychologist's illness, death, unavailability, or relocation or by the client's relocation or financial limitations. (See also Standard 5.09, Preserving Records and Data.)

This standard is new and essentially requires a *prior plan* for addressing several potential interruptions to services. The rule does not state how the plan is to be made, but several steps are apparent. The therapist's death or relocation can be addressed in documents such as contracts and organizational rules. Illness and unavailability can be addressed through agreements with other psychologists to provide coverage in such circumstances and for the psychologist's answering service, secretary, and so on, to be aware of the arrangement. The client's relocation is routinely addressed by making referrals. Financial limitations can be addressed by clear financial agreements and an early understanding of insurance or other third-party payment limits. Psychologists should be aware that several courts have ruled in effect that when a physician makes a decision to discharge a patient because an insurance company refuses to pay benefits, *both* the physician *and* the insurer can be held liable if their conduct was a "substantial factor in bringing about the harm" (*Wickline v. California*, 1986; *Wilson v. Blue Cross*, 1990).

Note that the list of potential interruptions is not exhaustive, and if additional problems can be anticipated, they should be planned for. There is no requirement that the plan be written, and the various interruptions to services may require different methods for executing the plan. The most adequate plan for the therapist's death would be written, whereas a verbal plan for relocation would be workable.

The rule only requires "reasonable efforts," so if the psychologist is prevented from making an adequate plan, it is the psychologist's efforts that would be examined, not just the absence of a plan.

It should also be noted that psychologists who work as part of treatment teams in institutional settings may, on the one hand, easily have a documented plan for continuity of care, but have limited control over various interruptions in services, on the other hand. Standard 8.03, Conflicts Between Ethics and Organizational Demands, should be consulted.

> **(b) When entering into employment or contractual relationships, psychologists provide for orderly and appropriate resolution of responsibility for patient or client care in the event that the employment or contractual relationship ends, with paramount consideration given to the welfare of the patient or client.**

Problems most often arise at the point at which an agreement ends, and therefore this provision, new in the 1992 Ethics Code, relates to the point at which a psychologist enters into an agreement and can take steps to avoid problems down the road. The rule applies to all psychologist parties to agreements: employer and employee, partners in partnership agreements, and contractor and contract employee. Note that "employment or contractual relationships" includes not only employment, but group practices and managed care agreements. Also note that other standards should also be considered in the agreements, such as 5.04 and 5.09, which deal with patient records.

The "paramount consideration" is a high standard and suggests that financial considerations in agreements will be held to be secondary to the client welfare concerns. There is no specific mention of noncompete agreements and no suggestion that they are prohibited per se. However, the provisions of such agreements could be reviewed under this rule.

An example may help to clarify one way in which this standard may be interpreted. An employment contract (completed after the effective date of this Ethics Code: December 1, 1992) contains a noncompete agreement that requires that if Dr. Green leaves the practice, he or she cannot continue seeing any current clients; there are no provisions for exceptions. If (a) Dr. Green has a client who would be harmed by discontinuing at this time and (b) Dr. Green could in fact continue seeing the client (in another or the same office) were it not for the agreement, then Dr. Green (and the employers if psychologists) would have failed to meet the standard. However, if the agreement allowed for Dr. Green to continue to see clients—whether within or outside the practice—until the clients can be referred or terminated appropriately, the standard would probably be met. Fee issues are addressed by other standards, so contract requirements such as that Dr. Green may "buy out the noncompete" or pay compensation to the practice as provided by their agreement, if reasonable and not a ruse to prevent all continued therapy, would likely not violate this standard (see also the discussion of Standard 1.27, Referrals and Fees).

Although this standard does not mention client "freedom of choice" as such, agreements should be clear regarding whether clients will be free to exercise choice or whether client "welfare" is being defined on the basis of the psychologists' perceptions.

Note that this section covers termination of the agreement for whatever reason and therefore requires that contracts address the other relevant factors in 4.08a: the therapist's illness, death, and unavailability.

4.09 Terminating the Professional Relationship

(a) Psychologists do not abandon patients or clients. (See also Standard 1.25e, under Fees and Financial Arrangements.)

Legal standards are very important in this area, because there may be definitions of "abandonment" and appropriate termination in statute and case law. This is a new standard that was previously addressed more generally as part of client welfare. No definition of abandonment is provided. However, on the basis of the professional practice and literature, this concept is commonly understood to mean that a client is (a) left without an appropriate resource to turn to when the therapist is unavailable and (b) is discontinued as a client without formal termination and referral as needed. Standard 4.09c provides guidance regarding proper termination; compliance with that section would argue against having "abandoned" the client.

It should be noted that some clients may feel abandoned no matter how much the termination is in the client's best interest and no matter what steps the psychologist has taken. This standard does not require a psychologist to continue to see a client who is unwilling to accept an appropriate termination.

(b) Psychologists terminate a professional relationship when it becomes reasonably clear that the patient or client no longer needs the service, is not benefiting, or is being harmed by continued service.

This standard identifies three conditions under which therapy *must* be terminated, but does not say that termination may not be appropriate for other reasons (e.g., due to financial limitations of the client). The standard implies that psychologists regularly consider whether these conditions are present in therapy. Compliance with this rule might be reviewed by considering whether the progress notes include information that indicates that the psychologist should have discontinued or considered discontinuation of the treatment. Clinical judgment is a critical element in making the decision, as is sensitivity to the actual circumstances.

The first two conditions, addressing the client no longer needing or not benefiting from therapy, involve substantial clinical judgment. The standard does not state a specific time frame and does not require, for example, terminating a client who is working through a "plateau" in therapy or who is being seen in supportive therapy. It may be important for the psychologist to discuss these concerns with the client as appropriate. Consultation can be an important adjunct in making these decisions (see Standard 1.20).

The third condition addresses harm from continued service, and consultation is frequently indicated in such situations. For example, if a psychologist is treating a client and discovers that the client's problems are beyond the psychologist's competence, it may be difficult for the psychologist to tell whether their treatment is simply not benefiting or is harming the client. This requires the knowledge and competence to determine what may be accomplished by alternative treatments. Continued service may "harm" by preventing or delaying the provision of effective treatment. The standard allows for the addition of other services, when needed to enhance effectiveness, rather than simply discontinuing.

> **(c) Prior to termination for whatever reason, except where precluded by the patient's or client's conduct, the psychologist discusses the patient's or client's views and needs, provides appropriate pretermination counseling, suggests alternative service providers as appropriate, and takes other reasonable steps to facilitate transfer of responsibility to another provider if the patient or client needs one immediately.**

This standard addresses a wide range of circumstances, not only those in which the client wants or agrees to termination, but those in which the client may not want termination or transfer or abruptly leaves therapy. Examples of being precluded from discussing termination are clients who abruptly discontinue treatment and do not return, who refuse to respond to calls or letters, who do not want to terminate and refuse cooperation, or who are so disturbed that further discussion or contact is contraindicated.

Except in these situations, the discussion required by the rule may vary depending on therapist orientation and the nature of services, but it typically would involve a review of problems and progress and of planning for future services as needed. The discussion and steps required generally do not require lengthy interventions. This standard does not require that psychologists continue to see clients when termination is indicated.

When further treatment is needed, the psychologist should make necessary referrals. The psychologist cannot assure that the client will accept a referral, but referrals should be made and noted in the client's file. The requirement of facilitating transfer of the client applies only when the client needs another provider "immediately." This is most often the case when there is an emergency situation and only requires that "reasonable steps" be taken. Such steps might be calling for an appointment before the client leaves the office or calling a client to see if he or she has scheduled an appointment with one of the referrals provided. Even when the need is not "immediate," the goal is always for there to be continuing care with as little interruption a possible.

As noted under Standard 4.08, psychologists who work as part of treatment teams in institutional settings may have limited control over the processes used in some terminations of services (see also Standard 8.03, Conflicts Between Ethics and Organizational Demands).

Chapter 7 ———————————

Privacy and Confidentiality

The importance of respecting people's rights to privacy and of maintaining the confidentiality of the information imparted in the course of their work with psychologists has long been recognized and has been reflected in prior APA ethical codes.

This section of this Ethics Code reflects the increasing complexity of the legal requirements for psychologists regarding reporting of information, the issues generated by new techniques and approaches to treatment, the development of electronic and other technologies with their accompanying responsibilities, and, in general, the thrust of a culture that deemphasizes professional power, focuses more and more on the rights of service recipients, and emphasizes formal dispute resolution.

What has emerged in this context is a need for more guidance in dealing with issues of privacy and confidentiality. Privacy generally refers to the right of individuals not to have their physical person or mental or emotional process invaded or shared without their consent. It entails the ideas that the results of testing or other evaluations will be used only for appropriate purposes and that they can trust that information shared with the psychologist will not in any way, other than mandated by law, be used against them. Confidentiality means that nonpublic information about a person will not be disclosed without consent or special legal authorization. Except in special circumstances (e.g., mandatory reporting laws), psychologists are required by the Ethics Code and by law to maintain the confidentiality of communications shared with them. The recipients of psychological services retain the right to release the confidential information in most situations.

This section of the Ethics Code details matters such as creating and handling of records, communication regarding the limits of confidentiality, sharing data, the use of confidential information for didactic or other purposes, preparing for the eventuality of death or incapacity of a therapist, and so on. A high value is placed on respecting each person's right to information about the limits of confidentiality, information without which truly informed consent cannot be given.

5. <u>Privacy and Confidentiality</u>

These Standards are potentially applicable to the professional and scientific activities of all psychologists.

Psychologists should note that the provisions of Section 5: Privacy and Confidentiality have potential broad applicability to psychologists' work in a wide variety of situations and circumstances, ranging from teaching and research to the applied areas of practice, including school, clinical, and counseling, as well as industrial/organizational work.

5.01 Discussing the Limits of Confidentiality

(a) Psychologists discuss with persons and organizations with whom they establish a scientific or professional relationship (including, to the extent feasible, minors and their legal representatives) (1) the relevant limitations on confidentiality, including limitations where applicable in group, marital, and family therapy or in organizational consulting, and (2) the foreseeable uses of the information generated through their services.

Confidentiality is a central aspect of psychological services and the standard requires that psychologists discuss issues related to confidentiality with individuals or organizations with whom they work or provide services. Such information includes relevant limitations on confidentiality, to the extent they are predictable, and how the information may be used in the future. This is especially important when psychologists are providing services to individuals who may become involved in forensic issues (e.g., marital separation, custody, visitation, relocation disputes, personal injury cases, or other legal matters). When working with minors, or, although not explicitly stated, with other persons under legal guardianship, psychologists discuss these limitations when feasible. The psychologist should document the fact that information was released under these circumstances (see also Standard 4.03).

Psychologists working in or consulting with organizations may encounter some unique conflicts surrounding issues of confidentiality. A psychologist assisting an organization (the client) in the development of employee effectiveness gains access to personal information about an employee that is not directly relevant to development but could affect performance on the job. Such instances suggest that psychologists should be certain to define the limits of confidentiality with clients in advance or at the onset of specific circumstances.

Psychologists should note that there may be a number of statutory exclusions to confidentiality, such as child abuse reporting acts, situations involving duty to warn or protect others from potentially dangerous patients, responsibilities under commitment procedures, or the delivery of group therapy services (see Standard 5.05).

(b) Unless it is not feasible or is contraindicated, the discussion of confidentiality occurs at the onset of the relationship and thereafter as new circumstances may warrant.

The qualifier "unless it is not feasible or is contraindicated" acknowledges that there are times, particularly in an initial session, when a recipient of services may be so upset or dysfunctional that it would be inappropriate to enter into any discussion of confidentiality issues. The psychologist must share the relevant information as early as practical and as new circumstances may warrant. Following the initial discussion, psychologists will further discuss issues related to confidentiality as are required by the nature of the services delivered. There are times when a psychologist may choose to allude to a confidentiality limit on recognizing that the client may be on the verge of sharing information unaware that such information could not be kept confidential.

(c) Permission for electronic recording of interviews is secured from clients and patients.

Standard 501c is a new standard that acknowledges the growing importance of new technologies for recording and maintaining information in psychological practice. This standard requires that psychologists obtain formal consent from clients and patients in order to use such technology, including such activities as tape recording, videotaping, and filming. Logically, the permission is obtained prior to the recording, although this is not explicitly stated in the standard. Psychologists should also see standards related to informed consent: 4.01b, 4.02, 4.04, 5.03–5.06, and 6.13.

5.02 Maintaining Confidentiality

Psychologists have a primary obligation and take reasonable precautions to respect the confidentiality rights of those with whom they work or consult, recognizing that confidentiality may be established by law, institutional rules, or professional or scientific relationships. (See also Standard 6.26, Professional Reviewers.)

This standard establishes that confidentiality is a primary professional obligation and recognizes that there are limits to what psychologists can do to protect such rights. The standard also recognizes that confidentiality is established by a number of diverse mechanisms, including law, institutional rules, and professional and scientific relationships. The psychologist must be aware of or obtain advice about the basic requirements and constraints and relevant current laws and regulations regarding confidentiality. It is clear that there are no hard and fast rules that apply to all situations. The psychologist must be cognizant of these issues and be able to provide a priori evidence that such precautions were taken into consideration in a timely fashion. Reasonable precautions might include having knowledge of state and federal laws, as well as institutional rules (e.g., psychologists reviewing grant applications should keep proprietary information confidential; see also Standard 6.26).

5.03 Minimizing Intrusions on Privacy

(a) In order to minimize intrusions on privacy, psychologists include in written and oral reports, consultations, and the like,

only information germane to the purpose for which the communication is made.

Psychologists receive vast amounts of personal and private information from recipients of services. This standard requires that psychologists limit the information they provide in reports and consultations to material that is relevant to the purpose of the report. This standard is of great importance when providing information required for third-party payment for services or in forensic cases, or when collaborating with other therapists. A psychologist who inappropriately discloses confidential information not pertinent to the presenting problem (e.g., the sexual orientation of an individual who has sought help for smoking cessation) would be at risk for violating this standard. It is important to remember that reports and consultations may be subpoenaed in the future for purposes not related to the specific issue currently under consideration (see Standard 5.05a related to requirements of insurance carriers). In addition, psychologists should note that these requirements may be modified when working in a forensic setting (see Standards 7.02 and 1.23b).

(b) Psychologists discuss confidential information obtained in clinical or consulting relationships, or evaluative data concerning patients, individual or organizational clients, students, research participants, supervisees, and employees, only for appropriate scientific or professional purposes and only with persons clearly concerned with such matters.

The standard permits discussion only for appropriate purposes and only with appropriate persons. Presenting case information in a classroom lecture would be permitted if identifying information is not revealed (see Standard 5.08). Psychologists should be especially aware of this prohibition as it relates to social situations and discussions held in public places. A signed release of information for clinical or other proper purposes is not a license to speak without limit—in other words, do not gossip.

The standard also applies to industrial/organization work and research conducted by psychologists, and it extends to supervisees and employees of psychologists. It also extends to relatives of a patient. For example, a psychologist would not discuss the Minnesota Multiphasic Personality Inventory profile of one spouse with the other without consent and a justification for sharing such information.

It is well-known that psychologists are constantly subjected to subtle social pressures to discuss "their most interesting cases" or to discuss "how tests really work." It is important that psychologists refrain from such interaction in order to protect the confidentiality of recipients and testing material as well as to maintain the integrity of the profession. Social gossip or casual chatter is clearly inappropriate and should be avoided. Although the audience may be fascinated by the psychologist's "cases," the real message is that psychologists talk about their patients in social gatherings and that the listener may be the next subject of some future conversation.

5.04 Maintenance of Records

Psychologists maintain appropriate confidentiality in creating, storing, accessing, transferring, and disposing of records under their control, whether these are written, automated, or in any other medium. Psychologists maintain and dispose of records in accordance with law and in a manner that permits compliance with the requirements of this Ethics Code.

Psychologists have the ultimate responsibility for maintaining the appropriate confidentiality of any information in their possession, whether it be written or electronic information. The psychologist maintains responsibility for office staff access to such records and must assure that proper staff training procedures are used to maintain confidentiality. Records should be kept in secure places (e.g., locked offices or file cabinets), with access limited to appropriate individuals. Special procedures should be followed to completely destroy records when applicable (e.g., completely shredding or burning all confidential documents would be ideal).

Psychologists should keep in mind that letters, billing statements, and other materials that contain confidential identifying information are protected under Standard 5.04 and also may implicate other standards (see Standards 1.24, 4.08, and 5.09). The Record Keeping Guidelines adopted by the APA Council of Representative in 1993 should also be consulted for guidance, although they are not enforceable by the APA Ethics Committee. (See Appendix B.)

5.05 Disclosures

(a) Psychologists disclose confidential information without the consent of the individual only as mandated by law, or where permitted by law for a valid purpose, such as (1) to provide needed professional services to the patient or the individual or organizational client, (2) to obtain appropriate professional consultations, (3) to protect the patient or client or others from harm, or (4) to obtain payment for services, in which instance disclosure is limited to the minimum that is necessary to achieve the purpose.

Standard 5.05a addresses situations in which a psychologist may disclose confidential information without consent. The standard restricts such disclosure to situations that (a) are mandated or required by law or (b) permitted by law and for a valid purpose. Such provisions may vary significantly from state to state, and psychologists should be familiar with all statutes that mandate reporting (e.g., mandatory child or elder abuse reporting acts, or some duty-to-protect statutes).

The standard provides several examples of valid purposes for release where permitted by law. The list is only illustrative and should not to be considered exhaustive. It should not be assumed that being on the list means that your state law allows the disclosure, or even if permitted, generally, that it applies to every specific instance.

Psychologists should note that the fourth example (to obtain payment for services) provides that disclosure should be limited to the information necessary to achieve the stated purpose of the disclosure. Other examples may include providing clinical details to insurance companies when only a diagnosis is required for payment, or collection action, in which case the necessary information must be limited to the recipients identifying information. In this latter case, clinical information should not be included. Under no circumstances should psychologists intimidate a recipient by threats to disclose any confidential information in order to collect a debt (also see Standards 1.25f and 8.03).

> **(b) Psychologists also may disclose confidential information with the appropriate consent of the patient or the individual or organizational client (or of another legally authorized person on behalf of the patient or client), unless prohibited by law.**

Standard 5.05b extends the disclosure provisions to include disclosure with proper consent of the recipient, including organizational clients, unless prohibited by law. Psychologists should make sure that the consent provided is in conformity with the statutory requirements in their jurisdiction or the requirements that apply to the instant situation. This standard states that psychologists "may disclose" information; it does not mandate disclosure even if the psychologist has the required consent. If the psychologist refuses to disclose information, even with consent, this does not necessarily constitute an ethical violation. For example, a psychologist might be able to ethically refuse to disclose information if the psychologist believes that such disclosure, even with proper consent, would be harmful to the patient or client. The psychologist is reminded of pertinent state and federal laws related to disclosure of confidential information that may not allow this discretion and may absolutely require the release.

5.06 Consultations

> **When consulting with colleagues, (1) psychologists do not share confidential information that reasonably could lead to the identification of a patient, client, research participant, or other person or organization with whom they have a confidential relationship unless they have obtained the prior consent of the person or organization or the disclosure cannot be avoided, and (2) they share information only to the extent necessary to achieve the purposes of the consultation. (See also Standard 5.02, Maintaining Confidentiality.)**

Under this standard, psychologists do not need to obtain consent to consult as long as identifying information is not revealed or if the disclosure cannot be avoided. In addition, psychologists limit the information disclosed to that necessary for the purposes of the consultation. There may be certain circumstances in which confidential information may be shared without consent (e.g., when mandated by law) or when permitted by law (e.g., the patient is in a coma), or a request is received by a legal guardian in an emergency, or to protect the individual or others from harm (see also Standards 1.14, 5.03, and 5.05).

5.07 Confidential Information in Databases

(a) If confidential information concerning recipients of psychological services is to be entered into databases or systems of records available to persons whose access has not been consented to by the recipient, then psychologists use coding or other techniques to avoid the inclusion of personal identifiers.

Psychologists must protect the identity of recipients by using coding systems or other techniques to protect confidential information in databases when access to the database is available to individuals who do not have permission to view such information. This standard would prohibit using the recipient's name for purposes of identification in such databases, necessitating development of a coding system (see also Standard 6.16).

(b) If a research protocol approved by an institutional review board or similar body requires the inclusion of personal identifiers, such identifiers are deleted before the information is made accessible to persons other than those of whom the subject was advised.

Standard 5.07b addresses the problem that could occur if a research protocol required the inclusion of information that is personally identifiable. In such circumstances, psychologists must make sure that such identifiers are deleted prior to the release of any information to persons other than those to whom the subject has consented.

(c) If such deletion is not feasible, then before psychologists transfer such data to others or review such data collected by others, they take reasonable steps to determine that appropriate consent of personally identifiable individuals has been obtained.

Standard 5.07c addresses the situation in which psychologists are not able, for some appropriate reason, to delete personal identifiers (e.g., it may not be possible to delete personal identifiers due to the manner in which the data are stored). The standard requires that psychologists "take reasonable steps" to determine that appropriate consent of identifiable individuals was obtained. This requirement may be satisfied by, for example, contacting the original researcher or institution as appropriate to determine whether consent was obtained. It is not a requirement that psychologists assure that the consent was obtained but that they take reasonable steps in that direction. If it is not possible to make this determination, the psychologist should assume that such consent was not obtained. To do nothing—or something that was less than reasonable—would be a clear ethical violation (see also Standard 6.16).

5.08 Use of Confidential Information for Didactic or Other Purposes

(a) Psychologists do not disclose in their writings, lectures, or other public media, confidential, personally identifiable information concerning their patients, individual or organizational clients, students, research participants, or other recipients of their services that they obtained during the course of their work, unless the person or organization has consented in writing or unless there is other ethical or legal authorization for doing so.

The standard prohibits psychologists from disclosing the identity or personally identifiable confidential information obtained from individuals in public presentations, including lectures and writings. The standard lists two exemptions to this prohibition: (a) when there is written consent from the individual or organization involved or (b) when such disclosure is ethically permitted or there is legal authorization to reveal such information. An example of legal authorization might include a situation in which the data or information are part of the public record, such as records of court proceedings or public hearings.

Psychologists working for organizations frequently collect data (e.g., test scores on job applicants, turnover data) that are generally considered to be the property of the organization. The psychologist will often require approval from an organization to publish or present findings from research or interventions in organizations.

(b) Ordinarily, in such scientific and professional presentations, psychologists disguise confidential information concerning such persons or organizations so that they are not individually identifiable to others and so that discussions do not cause harm to subjects who might identify themselves.

The purpose of this standard is to protect the identity of the person or organization and to assure that such presentations do not in any way harm a person who might be able to be identified by others or to identify himself or herself due the nature of the presentation. This may be accomplished by changing the references to the sex, the age, or the ethnic background or other demographic characteristic of the subject. In addition, the time frames may be changed (e.g., discussing a case that "occurred 15 years ago"). Finally, the psychologist may wish to consider melding different aspects of various cases together in such a manner as to present the case without divulging personally identifiable information. In all cases, the psychologist should remain sensitive to the fact that some students, clients, or others may identify themselves, though erroneously, and be prepared to deal with them. When discussing specific situations, it is always advisable to inform audiences that details have been changed.

5.09 Preserving Records and Data

A psychologist makes plans in advance so that confidentiality of records and data is protected in the event of the psychologist's death, incapacity, or withdrawal from the position or practice.

This new and important standard requires psychologists to plan in advance for the protection of their confidential records and data in the event of their death, incapacity, or withdrawal from their position or practice.

The reason for the standard is clear when considering the problems that may occur upon a psychologist's unexpected death. This standard, however, also applies to psychologists who terminate employment with an agency or organization, relocate their practice, retire, or become disabled and are unable to continue work. In addition to possible harm that might come to patients without such plans, there is the possibility of legal suit against the psychologist's estate should the confidentiality of records and data not be protected.

Because the future is not predictable, psychologists should develop plans for such eventualities and review their plans on a regular schedule. The standard does not specify the nature or type of plan that must be available, but it does mean that if some type of plan has not been made, the psychologist must do so now (see also Standard 4.08).

5.10 Ownership of Records and Data

Recognizing that ownership of records and data is governed by legal principles, psychologists take reasonable and lawful steps so that records and data remain available to the extent needed to serve the best interests of patients, individual or organizational clients, research participants, or appropriate others.

The standard recognizes that in certain circumstances, such as agency or organizational practice, data and records may be outside the direct control of psychologists. Therefore, the standard mandates only that psychologists act to reasonably assure that such information is available. The psychologist should be sure that records and data are stored in an organized manner, in a safe and secure place, and that there is an acceptable filing system used to identify the records. A loss of records through personal carelessness or shoddy practices would not be acceptable under this standard. To have knowledge that the record-keeping system is inadequate and do nothing to attempt to improve the situation or to bring the concerns to the attention of the proper authority would be an ethics violation. Stealing records from an agency or institution to assure their availability would also violate this standard (see also Standards 4.08 and 5.09).

The psychologist must also seek to implement ethical and legal mechanisms to release records when appropriate, becoming familiar with the legal, regulatory, and institutional requirements that affect the availability of records. For example, patients and clients may request a copy of their record (see also Standard 2.02b). The statutes regulating the release of recipients' records vary from jurisdiction to jurisdiction. Some states require that records or copies of the records be turned over to the patient; other states may require that the psychologist sit down with the patient to help interpret and discuss the record. The psychologist should also be willing to advise organizational clients about the appropriate use of records, potential misuses of records, ethical and legal regulations, and ways to minimize access to records containing confidential information.

5.11 Withholding Records for Nonpayment

Psychologists may not withhold records under their control that are requested and imminently needed for a patient's or client's treatment solely because payment has not been received, except as otherwise provided by law.

Psychologists may not refuse to release—or hold hostage—certain records of a patient or client unless legally authorized to do so. The standard applies only to records requested for treatment and requires that the records were requested and are imminently needed for the continuity of the recipient's care (e.g., the request comes from a hospital emergency room where the patient has been admitted or a subsequent provider requests the records in order to provide for coordination of treatment services). The only exception would be one provided by law. This standard generally would not apply to custody evaluations, personal injury evaluations, or other forensic evaluation except when they are being requested and imminently needed for treatment. Note that the Record Keeping Guidelines read somewhat differently from Standard 5.11. The guidelines state that "psychologists do not withhold records that are needed for valid healthcare purposes solely because the client has not paid for prior service." The concept of a "valid health care purpose" would appear to be broader than "imminently needed" for the continuity of care. Regardless of the nature of the request, the psychologist must always follow the "imminently needed" for treatment criteria.

Chapter 8 _____

Teaching, Training Supervision, Research, and Publishing

The standards addressing teaching activities limit what may be taught to whom, with critical variables being the qualification of the teacher, the expertise or legal scope of practice of the student or trainee, and the possible effect on the public. Also, there are new standards that address in detail the process of evaluation of students and actions affecting affect academic promotions.

Changes in the research area address the process of undertaking research and carrying out appropriate consultations, providing adequate informed consent to research participants, and a stronger cautionary statement about the use of deception in research than was in the 1989 code.

The new publication standards address in a specific way the claiming of publication credit, duplicate publication, reporting and correcting errors in research, sharing of data with those wishing to replicate the study, and the obligations of professional reviewers. These topics are addressed in more detail than in any previous code.

6. Teaching, Training Supervision, Research, and Publishing

6.01 Design of Education and Training Programs

Psychologists who are responsible for education and training programs seek to ensure that the programs are competently designed, provide the proper experiences, and meet the requirements for licensure, certification, or other goals for which claims are made by the program.

This standard would apply to psychologists teaching in the program as well as psychologists who serve in various administrative roles (e.g., director of training, department chairperson, dean of the graduate school, or head of the curriculum committee). If an educational program purports to lead to licensure or other stated goals, the program must be competently designed and provide experiences that will meet the requirements for such goals. In essence, this standard is a "truth in advertising" provision that will assist current and prospective students in evaluating educational and training programs.

It should be noted that psychologists cannot guarantee the results for the students, but they have a responsibility related to the design of the programs under their direction (i.e., they "seek to ensure" that the programs are competently designed). This requirement might be met by assuring that the psychologist can demonstrate direct involvement in the development of program content, program requirements, program goals, and the purposes of the training programs (see also Standards 3.02–3.03).

6.02 Descriptions of Education and Training Programs

(a) Psychologists responsible for education and training programs seek to ensure that there is a current and accurate description of the program content, training goals and objectives, and requirements that must be met for satisfactory completion of the program. This information must be made readily available to all interested parties.

This standard requires that those psychologists responsible for these programs "seek to ensure" that the descriptions of the content, requirements, and goals are accurate, current, and readily available. Once again, the requirement is not to ensure, only to seek to ensure. This might involve calling to the attention of those responsible the need for changing descriptions or reprinting the program brochure as appropriate.

(b) Psychologists seek to ensure that statements concerning their course outlines are accurate and not misleading, particularly regarding the subject matter to be covered, bases for evaluating progress, and the nature of course experiences. (See also Standard 3.03, Avoidance of False or Deceptive Statements.)

Psychologists who are responsible for courses "seek to ensure" that statements about their own course outlines, subject matter, evaluation procedures, and any required experiences are accurate and reflect the true nature of the course offered. Psychologists are expected to exercise their power, however substantial or limited it may be, to seek compliance with these stipulations. Psychologists must avoid misrepresentation of important issues such as subject matter, the time involved in the course, or procedures for evaluation. Students should not enroll for a course only later to find out that it is not what they were led to expect.

(c) To the degree to which they exercise control, psychologists responsible for announcements, catalogs, brochures, or advertisements describing workshops, seminars, or other non-degree-granting educational programs ensure that they accurately describe the audience for which the program is intended, the educational objectives, the presenters, and the fees involved.

Standard 6.02c relates to non-degree-granting educational programs such as continuing education workshops. The standard recognizes that psychologists may not always have ultimate control over how the program is presented or marketed. The standard requires that psychologists responsible for such programs must, to the degree to which they exercise control, ensure that participants have been given information related to the target population to whom the program is directed (for undergraduates, licensed psychologists, laypersons, etc.), the goals of the program, who will be the presenters, and the fees that are involved. If relevant brochures and announcements do not contain this information, it may well represent an ethical violation (see also Standard 3.02).

6.03 Accuracy and Objectivity in Teaching

(a) When engaged in teaching or training, psychologists present psychological information accurately and with a reasonable degree of objectivity.

Psychologists engaged in teaching or training do not present unreasonably biased, inaccurate, or distorted information about the subject matter. This does not mean that psychologists may not advance a particular theoretical orientation, but when doing so they must be sure to be accurate and appropriately objective in the presentation. The reference to a "reasonable degree of objectivity" acknowledges that no one is wholly objective. This standard does not give everyone the right to challenge as "unethical" everyone of a different orientation. It seeks to sanction only those who abandon normally recognized standards of professionalism and accuracy in teaching. For example, an instructor who is primarily Jungian in orientation, who teaches a survey course in psychotherapy theories, must also be conversant with and able to teach a range of theories objectively, as would normally be part of a survey course. To promote Jungian theories as superior to others, without fairly presenting them and in the absence of supporting data, might constitute a violation of this standard.

(b) When engaged in teaching or training, psychologists recognize the power they hold over students or supervisees and therefore make reasonable efforts to avoid engaging in conduct that is personally demeaning to students or supervisees. (See also Standards 1.09, Respecting Others, and 1.12, Other Harassment.)

Psychologists must not minimize the importance of power differentials that exist between students and professors and between supervisors and supervisees. When such relationships exist, the student or supervisee is vulnerable to both subtle and blatant demeaning treatment by the person in the powerful position. The "make reasonable efforts" portion of the standard recognizes that the standard contains an "eye of the beholder" problem (e.g., a student may feel demeaned by a professor's comments that were not intended to offend and that would not offend most people). Blatant or repeated examples of demeaning conduct that most reasonable people would regard as demeaning (e.g., recurrent derogatory or disrespectful comments against homosexuals, Mormons, people who smoke, behaviorists, or members of certain ethnic or cultural groups) place the psychologist at risk for an ethical complaint (see also Standard 1.08).

6.04 Limitation on Teaching

Psychologists do not teach the use of techniques or procedures that require specialized training, licensure, or expertise, including but not limited to hypnosis, biofeedback, and projective techniques, to individuals who lack the prerequisite training, legal scope of practice, or expertise.

Psychologists who teach these types of techniques to others must first ascertain that the person has the prerequisite training, legal scope of practice, or expertise to learn the skill or technique. When offering special training or workshops in specialized areas of practice (e.g., in neuropsychological testing or use of analytic interpretations in therapy), the psychologist takes steps to ensure that the target market for the workshop are individuals who can competently and ethically use the techniques. Graduate-level training, proper licensure, or documented expertise would meet the requirements of this standard. It should be noted that psychologists may teach about such techniques (e.g., hypnosis) without teaching how to do it (see also Standard 2.06).

6.05 Assessing Student and Supervisee Performance

(a) In academic and supervisory relationships, psychologists establish an appropriate process for providing feedback to students and supervisees.

Procedures for providing feedback should be clear and should be available to the students and supervisees. Ordinarily, these procedures are developed by programs with the input of individual psychologists. When specification of program requirements are inadequate and not under the total control of the psychologist, the psychologist should encourage and document attempts to develop new ones (see also Standards 6.01–6.02).

(b) Psychologists evaluate students and supervisees on the basis of their actual performance on relevant and established program requirements.

Psychologists do not base evaluations on extraneous variables such as monetary contributions to a school, referrals received from a student, help the student offers in a research project, physical characteristics, gender, ethnic background, and so forth. This standard requires the establishment of program requirements that identify the criteria for evaluation. In the absence of objective and identifiable criteria, proper evaluation cannot occur (see also Standards 1.17a, 1.19, and 6.01–6.02).

6.06 Planning Research

(a) Psychologists design, conduct, and report research in accordance with recognized standards of scientific competence and ethical research.

This standard refers both to the need for *competence* in research (e.g., not exposing research subjects to unpleasant experiences under a study design so obviously flawed that no useful data could ever be yielded) and the need for *ethical* conduct (e.g., not forgetting to obtain informed consent). It should be noted that compliance with this standard requires special attention to various provisions of the Ethics Code, including but not limited to all provisions of Section 6. Psychologists should be familiar with relevant state and federal regulations and institutional review board criteria governing their research activities. Psychologists should also be familiar with the codes of ethics of other specialists, especially when conducting interdisciplinary research (e.g., the psychologist who conducts research with a multidisciplinary team or with a neurologist must have at least basic knowledge of standards promulgated by the respective professional groups; see also Standard 1.03).

(b) Psychologists plan their research so as to minimize the possibility that results will be misleading.

Standard 6.06b requires that psychologists plan their research in such a way that the results will not be likely to be misconstrued or presented in a misleading manner. Improper selection of research subjects, too few subjects, improper statistical methodology, inadequate control groups, biased questionnaires, or instruments of questionable validity may negatively affect the conclusions drawn from the research. A psychologist is not responsible for every misinterpretation of his or her research. However, a design in which results are almost unavoidably misunderstood, in a way that can harm social groups, would be improper.

(c) In planning research, psychologists consider its ethical acceptability under the Ethics Code. If an ethical issue is unclear, psychologists seek to resolve the issue through consultation with institutional review boards, animal care and use committees, peer consultations, or other proper mechanisms.

Psychologists must consider the various provisions of the Ethics Code in planning their research. In the event of uncertainty, psychologists must take some type of action to resolve the issues (e.g., by consulting with proper authorities). If a complaint is filed it will be important for the psychologist to demonstrate that he or she gave serious consideration to the various provisions of the Ethics Code and consulted with other knowledgeable people regarding any unclear issues.

(d) Psychologists take reasonable steps to implement appropriate protections for the rights and welfare of human participants, other persons affected by the research, and the welfare of animal subjects.

The Ethics Code identifies many methods that may help meet this standard, such as informed consent to participate in a research project, which is a major protection for human participants, and debriefing following completion of the research. Adherence to Standard 6.20, which provides the guidelines for use of animal subjects, would satisfy the requirement for this population. In addition, the standard asserts that psychologists have a responsibility to protect the rights and welfare of others that are affected by the research, such as friends, relatives, spouses, roommates, and clients of supervisees (see also Standards 6.07–6.20).

6.07 Responsibility

(a) Psychologists conduct research competently and with due concern for the dignity and welfare of the participants

This standard does not apply to differences of opinion on a specific research design or methodology or to various resulting interpretations. It refers to incompetent research (i.e., to not having the training or expertise to do the type of research undertaken). In addition, the standard requires psychologists to be concerned with the dignity and welfare of research participants. For example, consulting someone with expertise about Native American culture could help avoid problems such as using explanatory materials for research participants that are demeaning to them.

(b) Psychologists are responsible for the ethical conduct of research conducted by them or by others under their supervision or control.

Psychologists have ultimate responsibility for research conducted by them or under their supervision, such as other psychologists, assistants, and non-credentialed helpers. The net effect is that the senior psychologist could be sanctioned for unethical conduct of a subordinate researcher. It is important that psychologists maintain ongoing review of research projects and pay special attention to the hiring and supervision of research assistants or colleagues working under the direction of the senior researcher.

(c) Researchers and assistants are permitted to perform only those tasks for which they are appropriately trained and prepared.

Psychologists limit the activities of researchers and assistants under their direction to tasks that they are trained and prepared to perform. Psychologists must train assistants in relevant tasks such as the proper methods of conducting structured interviews, administering and scoring standardized tests, or handling animal subjects. Psychologists do not assign tasks to individuals absent proper training, preparation, and supervision (see also Standards 1.04 and 6.20).

> **(d) As part of the process of development and implementation of research projects, psychologists consult those with expertise concerning any special population under investigation or most likely to be affected.**

Psychologists seek consultation with experts as necessary concerning research that involves any special population or that may affect any special population. This standard applies only when there is a special population involved or affected by the research and the psychologist does not have expertise with the population under consideration. Such populations may include people with disabilities, ethnic and racial minorities, and so on.

6.08 Compliance With Law and Standards

> **Psychologists plan and conduct research in a manner consistent with federal and state law and regulations, as well as professional standards governing the conduct of research, and particularly those standards governing research with human participants and animal subjects.**

Although Standard 6.08 requires that psychologists engaged in research be familiar with and follow all relevant federal and state laws and regulations and professional standards, it does not imply that the psychologist will be held accountable to follow a rule that is not widely known and accepted. Federal laws and regulations such as those of the U.S. Department of Health and Human Services and its National Institutes of Health, when relevant, appear to be enforceable under this standard. Professional standards appear to be addressed by widely known and accepted documents such as the Nuremberg Code, the World Medical Association's *Declaration of Helsinki*, and the Belmont Report. Many federal agency committees and professional associations have regulations or standards with which the psychologist may wish to be familiar.[1]

6.09 Institutional Approval

> **Psychologists obtain from host institutions or organizations appropriate approval prior to conducting research, and they provide accurate information about their research proposals. They conduct the research in accordance with the approved research protocol.**

---

[1] Copies of these and other regulations and codes may be obtained from the National Institutes of Health, Office for Protection from Research Risks, Building 31, Room 5B63, 31 Center Dr., MSC 2180, Bethesda, Maryland 20892-2180.

This principle addresses the relationship between the psychologist and those institutions or organizations that provide a setting in which research activities will occur. It asserts the obligation to inform those entities about the nature of the research and obtain approval before proceeding. It would be wise, in general, to carry this out in writing, whereby the proposal and all intended activities are clearly described.

Specifically, psychologists must give accurate information about their research proposal. This information generally includes (a) the fundamental purpose and goals of the research, (b) methodology, (c) any intrusion or disturbance to participants in the research milieu as a result of data gathering, (d) possible risks to human participants or animal subjects, (e) debriefing procedures for human participants, (f) confidentiality issues, and (g) any other aspect of the research project that might affect the institution's willingness to cooperate.

Having received formal approval, psychologists then must carry out the research in accordance with their protocol. This implies that any significant changes that are made subsequent to approval must again be formally submitted for approval to the host institution or organization.

6.10 Research Responsibilities

Prior to conducting research (except research involving only anonymous surveys, naturalistic observations, or similar research), psychologists enter into an agreement with participants that clarifies the nature of the research and the responsibilities of each party.

This standard discusses the contract that principal investigators or their associates clearly establish with each research participant before actually beginning to carry out the research. The general obligations are to explain what the research is about and the responsibilities of researchers and participants, insofar as possible.

Although agreements with participants are normally required, the standard states that it may not be necessary in situations such as naturalistic observations, surveys of anonymous subjects, or other similar research or settings that place no demand on the individual or expose his or her identity to the researcher or to others. It generally addresses the requirements as to the content of the discussions that are spelled out more explicitly in other standards. In general, there should always be strong concern for the welfare and confidentiality of those who contributed to the data (see also Standards 1.03 and 6.11–6.12).

6.11 Informed Consent to Research

(a) Psychologists use language that is reasonably understandable to research participants in obtaining their appropriate informed consent (except as provided in Standard 6.12, Dispensing With Informed Consent). Such informed consent is appropriately documented.

It is important to use language that is commensurate with a research participant's comprehension and level of education, because informed choices must be predicated on information that is meaningful to the participant (see 6.11b for a description of what information should be part of an informed consent agreement). This may include strategies such as using very simple language (for children), using an interpreter (for someone who speaks English as a second language, or not at all, or who is hearing impaired), using diagrams or drawings, inviting questions, or some other creative approach (see also Standard 1.07).

It also is essential to document that informed consent has been properly obtained. Although not required, a printed consent form is commonly read and signed by participants, or their legal representative (parent, custodian, etc.). The documentation should comply with the standards outlined in this section, as well as any additional legal or institutional requirements.

> **(b) Using language that is reasonably understandable to participants, psychologists inform participants of the nature of the research; they inform participants that they are free to participate or to decline to participate or to withdraw from the research; they explain the foreseeable consequences of declining or withdrawing; they inform participants of significant factors that may be expected to influence their willingness to participate (such as risks, discomfort, adverse effects, or limitations on confidentiality, except as provided in Standard 6.15, Deception in Research); and they explain other aspects about which the prospective participants inquire.**

This standard reviews five essential concepts that must be included in any discussion with research participants. Investigators must also clarify any institutional, state, or federal regulations that may apply.

1. *Discussion of the nature of the research.* This would include a broad statement about the purpose and goals of the research. Relevant information might include the range or description of specific activities that could be expected of the participants; the amount of time required; the extent of monetary or other compensation, if any, for their role in the research effort; possible ultimate applications or use of the research results; possible adverse implications for populations that might be affected by the research results; and any other information that the investigator deems relevant and important for a prospective participant to know. Although the investigator bears the obligation of informing prospective participants about the research, he or she is not required to prejudice the study by destroying naivete of the participants that might be essential to the investigation. Nor is he or she required to conduct a literature review and seminar for each subject. Here, as throughout the standards governing consent, the key issue

is communicating the kind of information that could be significant to a reasonable person in deciding whether to participate.

2. *Statement about participants' freedom to decline or withdraw.* The investigator does not coerce, prod, threaten, or intimidate research participants when discussing the optional nature of their involvement in the research. This is particularly important when there might be an ascribed or real power differential between investigator and participant, such as teacher and student or supervisor and supervisee. In any case, the investigator clearly instructs prospective participants that they may either choose to become involved in the research or decline, without prejudice or penalty of any sort. Once an individual has already begun the work of participating as a research subject, he or she always has the option of withdrawing, at any time, for any reason, again without prejudice or penalty; research participants should be clearly informed of these facts in advance.

   Particular care should be taken in working with children and adolescents, older people, or those with diminished capacity, so that they fully understand the continuously voluntary nature of their participation, and the range of options that might apply.

3. *Statement about foreseeable consequences of declining or withdrawing.* Any foreseeable consequences should be fully explained to prospective research participants concerning their decision to abstain from participating or to withdraw after they have already become involved. If there is normally a debriefing session for participants who complete the study, then this should be offered to participants who withdraw as well, if it is warranted, regardless of the extent of their involvement or commitment.

   If monetary or other compensation is contingent on completion of the participation, then this must be clearly stated at the outset.

4. *Factors that may influence willingness to participate.* Full disclosure of known or suspected factors that obviously might significantly affect one's decision to participate in the research is an essential aspect of informed consent. This would include a full exposition of possible risks, unpleasant experiences, the use of chemical substances introduced into the body, distress due to exposure to experiences or activities that might conflict with one's values or normal range of experience, fear or anxiety in connection with the research activities, sensory deprivation, unpleasant sensory stimulus, unpleasant psychosocial stimulus, autonomic arousal, sexual arousal, physical exertion, or any other aspect of the research that might affect the individual's willingness to participate. Certainly, there are individuals who may be particularly vulnerable to experiences that would be considered relatively innocuous to others. For example, those with a history of traumatic experiences of the type that might be reexperienced during the course of the experiment would likely run a higher risk of dysphoric reactions than those who had no such life experience.

   Any risks to the participants' anonymity should also be communicated; this is especially important when behavior will be videotaped or data might be made available to future researchers or become a part of a database to be shared with an indeterminate number of researchers for an indefinite period of time.

Debriefing procedures must also be described in advance if they are a part of the research design, so that prospective participants understand the opportunities and resources available to process any adverse experiences.

It is crucial that descriptions of the research experiences be sufficiently explicit so as to permit appropriate informed decisions by prospective participants. Clear and unambiguous language is important with everyone, but, again, it is crucial in communicating with children, older people, and those who might have difficulty comprehending for any reason. As mentioned previously, the naivete of a prospective participant may be maintained as needed for the purposes of the design, within the aforementioned limits. Certainly, full disclosure may be provided at the conclusion of the participant's involvement or at the conclusion of the study, although it may be withheld at the outset as necessary.

5. *Answers to inquiries.*   Within these limits, and reasonable limits of time, researchers are to answer all questions by prospective participants about any aspect of their involvement in the research without misrepresentation, distortion, or omission of important factual information in responding to such inquiries. The participant should be informed about how to seek additional information or answers to questions during or after participation; specifically, it should be made clear who the responsible party is and how to contact him or her (see Standard 6.15, Deception in Research).

(c) When psychologists conduct research with individuals such as students or subordinates, psychologists take special care to protect the prospective participants from adverse consequences of declining or withdrawing from participation.

This standard, which is new, recognizes that it is necessary to protect those prospective research participants who decline to participate or withdraw from a project already underway, when a real or ascribed power or authority differential exists. This is particularly true with students, supervisees, patients or clients, and employees, or in any situation in which participants may be selected from a closed, hierarchical system (e.g., a prison population or an introductory psychology course in which grades are partially based on participation on research). The psychologist must make an effort to protect such individuals from any adverse consequences of declining or withdrawing, such as a lowering of a grade or evaluation, loss of privileges, or any other negative consequence over which the researcher has some degree of control (see Standard 1.14, Avoiding Harm).

(d) When research participation is a course requirement or opportunity for extra credit, the prospective participant is given the choice of equitable alternative activities.

This new standard asserts that students must be given a free choice about volunteering to be a research participant, without social pressure or other aversive consequences. Furthermore, students not wishing to participate must be offered a choice of reasonable alternative activities in lieu of the research. Instructors providing such alternatives should take into account factors such as the amount of time and energy that might be expected of a student in carrying out the alternative project. They might also attempt to provide an alternative experience that carries an equivalent educational value. For example, an experiential opportunity, such as participating in assisting or performing research with a senior graduate student, might serve such a purpose.

(e) For persons who are legally incapable of giving informed consent, psychologists nevertheless (1) provide an appropriate explanation, (2) obtain the participant's assent, and (3) obtain appropriate permission from a legally authorized person, if such substitute consent is permitted by law.

Psychologists are required to inform prospective research participants about the investigation even if the latter are legally incapable of giving informed consent, such as children, people with mental retardation, impaired older people, or those who are cognitively impaired. In these cases, an "appropriate explanation" might consist of a description of the basic concepts involved in the research. Investigators must obtain participants' clear assent or agreement to participate. In these cases, prospective participants are less knowledgeable about the research but are still able to accept or decline personal involvement. In the absence of assent investigators may not proceed with enlisting the participant's cooperation in the research. If substitute consent is permitted by law, they must then obtain formal consent from a legally authorized individual, such as the parent, custodian, or other responsible party, before proceeding with the research (see also Standards 1.07, 1.14, 5.07, 5.09, 6.14, and 6.18).

6.12 Dispensing With Informed Consent

Before determining that planned research (such as research involving only anonymous questionnaires, naturalistic observations, or certain kinds of archival research) does not require the informed consent of research participants, psychologists consider applicable regulations and institutional review board requirements, and they consult with colleagues as appropriate.

Certain types of research may not require informed consent. The standard cites, as examples, naturalistic observations, obtaining information from an existing database (with all identifying information being deleted), or requesting participants to fill out an anonymous questionnaire. These are situations, presumably, either in which the research participants are unaware of their involvement in the study and hence unaffected by it, or in which they may choose to be anonymous participants. However, even in these situations, psychologists are still obliged to consider the policies and requirements of their institutional review board as well as any applicable federal or local regulations (see Standard 6.08).

A good resource for determining whether to dispense with informed consent is the Department of Health and Human Services' guidelines on minimal risk research. Although Standard 6.12 does not specifically address the concept of minimal risk, it substantially describes situations in which it may apply. Minimal risk is defined as follows: "A risk is minimal where the probability and magnitude of harm or discomfort anticipated in the proposed research are not greater, in and of themselves, than those ordinarily encountered in daily life or during the performance of routine physical or psychological examinations or tests" (National Institutes of Health [NIH], 1993, p. 3-1). A relatively simple example in the area of educational research that might be considered "minimal risk," and therefore not requiring informed consent, might be a project that evaluates various aspects of an elementary school curriculum, requiring only unobtrusive observation.

As with all matters that may be not be entirely clear, it would be important to seek the consultation of knowledgeable colleagues when there is doubt about the need for obtaining consent. It would be wise to seek the advice of colleagues who are experienced researchers, preferably in a similar area of investigation.

6.13 Informed Consent in Research Filming or Recording

Psychologists obtain informed consent from research participants prior to filming or recording them in any form, unless the research involves simply naturalistic observations in public places and it is not anticipated that the recording will be used in a manner that could cause personal identification or harm.

Formal consent must always be obtained when psychologists plan to videotape, film, or audiotape research participants if those who are being recorded may be personally identified by viewers or listeners. Of special concern is the future use to which any permanent records might be put or who might have access to them at some time as yet unspecified or unknown (see also Standard 6.15).

There is no need to obtain informed consent for such recording if it involves naturalistic observations in public places and it will not be used in a way that could identify the research participant or cause harm. By way of example, consider a study contrasting the facial expressions or driving behavior of male with female automobile drivers confronted with certain frustrating traffic information displayed on an electronic sign. A hidden camera could record all the necessary information. However, because drivers and some passengers could be identified by close-up facial shots, and it is conceivable that some might not wish to be involved or be part of a permanent record, and for various reasons, it might be necessary to at least obtain their consent after the fact before proceeding with the analysis of the data. If this could not be done, then the investigators should be prepared to destroy the photographic record immediately rather than plan to release them to other researchers or store them permanently in an archive.

6.14 Offering Inducements for Research Participants

(a) In offering professional services as an inducement to obtain research participants, psychologists make clear the nature of the services, as well as the risks, obligations, and limitations. (See also Standard 1.18, Barter [With Patients or Clients].)

Inducements to participate in research, such as offering a limited number of biofeedback sessions, counseling sessions, interpretation of psychological tests used in the research, lectures, or other psychological service can be a useful means of obtaining cooperation. However, the researcher is obliged to describe clearly what is being offered, including risks, obligations, and limitations.

In short, if a psychological service is offered as an inducement, such as assessment or therapy sessions, the terms must be clearly elaborated and, whenever possible, quantified (e.g., type of test, number of interventions). Enough information must be given so that the prospective participant can freely decide about the risk:benefit ratio and whether it would be a potentially positive experience. Other standards in this Ethics Code should be observed as they may apply to various forms of inducement.

(b) Psychologists do not offer excessive or inappropriate financial or other inducements to obtain research participants, particularly when it might tend to coerce participation.

An example of an excessive inducement would be a large sum of money for a relatively small amount of time expended. This is essentially "an offer that one could not refuse." The investigator must consider the relative worth accorded the money by the recipient, not necessarily its actual value. Fifteen dollars to a homeless person or a young teenager may seem like a large sum, whereas the same amount constitutes "pocket change" to a successful business man or woman. Inappropriate inducements that are not financial would include things such as supplying participants with substances or opportunities that could be potentially be harmful or illegal. This would include giving a bottle of Scotch to someone who is alcohol dependent or child pornographic material to a pedophile.

Another consideration is the situation in which an inducement would create a dual role relationship, have the appearance of a conflict of interest, or could be confusing or destructive to the individual, or any inducement that would violate any other section of this code would be specifically prohibited. Examples of these inducements would be offering a raise to an employee or a good letter of reference to a graduate student if he or she would agree to be a research participant (see also Standards 1.15 and 1.17–1.18).

6.15 Deception in Research

(a) Psychologists do not conduct a study involving deception unless they have determined that the use of deception techniques is justified by the study's prospective scientific, educational, or applied value and that equally effective alternative procedures that do not use deception are not feasible.

This is a prohibition against the use of deception, such as exposing participants to confederates, false premises, false assumptions, spurious data or feedback, or other forms of disinformation unless several conditions are met. The use of deception in research has the potential for harming individuals, depending on the type and extent of the deception; hence, it should be used only as a last resort.

The investigator always bears the responsibility of specifically demonstrating that the prospective scientific, educational, or applied value of the study would warrant the use of deceptive techniques. This involves carefully considering the potential risks to participants who will be exposed to deceptive practices and weighing those risks against the potential benefit in a scientific, educational, or applied context.

The researcher always has a clear obligation to attempt to develop procedures that do not use deception, which, it is hoped, at the same time would not compromise hypothesis testing. With deception research, there may be perceived harm to participants that could result in ethical or legal action taken against the psychologist; it behooves investigators to be extremely cautious in this area (see also Standard 1.14).

(b) Psychologists never deceive research participants about significant aspects that would affect their willingness to participate, such as physical risks, discomfort, or unpleasant emotional experiences.

After a thorough review of alternatives, if the investigator opts to use deception, he or she should be careful not to deceive prospective participants about aspects of the experiment that would have a bearing on their decision to become involved. This would include specifically informing them about any possible physically dangerous aspects of the research, such as the use of or exposure to certain equipment, instruments, or drugs that might have a potential for causing physical harm. It would also include informing them about the likelihood of unpleasant emotional experiences during the research, which might generate strong affect states such as fear or panic, humiliation, rage, dejection, or other dysphoria.

An investigator should be knowledgeable about empirically based psychological vulnerabilities of the population being researched and not be deceptive about significant aspects of the research relevant to these identified vulnerabilities. However, an investigator is not expected to be aware of the totality of a research participant's past and the resulting potential vulnerabilities to the current research.

> **(c) Any other deception that is an integral feature of the design and conduct of an experiment must be explained to participants as early as is feasible, preferably at the conclusion of their participation, but no later than at the conclusion of the research. (See also Standard 6.18, Providing Participants With Information About the Study.)**

It is the investigator's responsibility to offer the opportunity to debrief participants thoroughly about deceptive aspects of the research as soon as is feasible. Usually, this would be at the end of their involvement in the study. However, debriefing may be delayed to the end of the data-gathering phase, when there is concern that the integrity of the study might be threatened if facts about the deception might be "leaked" to future research participants, thereby contaminating the research project. Certainly, in research projects that have an extended data-gathering phase, there might be a concern about maintaining an appropriate amount of participant naivete.

In debriefing children or those with diminished mental capacity, researchers would be well advised to exercise great care in using comprehensible language and concepts commensurate with their level of understanding (see Standard 6.18, Providing Participants With Information About the Study).

At the time of debriefing, investigators must also be prepared to discuss and review any negative psychological reactions that might have been experienced by the participant and even offer the opportunity for counseling or some other intervention if it is needed. Obviously, if a strong reaction has occurred, such as a panic attack or a flashback memory, this must be addressed. The investigator is responsible for selecting an appropriate intervention for the participant, as might be needed. The researcher may not be obligated to arrange for lifetime therapy, but brief intervention or referral may well be called for. Also, the risk of negative reactions may significantly escalate when the participants are children or those with diminished mental capacity. Certainly, an ounce of prevention is worth a pound of cure. The rationale is clear for disclosing any and all information *at the outset* about the research protocol that could be a factor in an individual's willingness to participate (see Standard 1.14).

6.16 Sharing and Utilizing Data

> **Psychologists inform research participants of their anticipated sharing or further use of personally identifiable research data and of the possibility of unanticipated future uses.**

It is essential to tell prospective participants about their known future plans for using personally identifiable data, if any. Although not required by the standard, it is prudent to inform participants at the outset, because it may affect their willingness to continue (see also Standards 5.01–5.02, 5.07, and 5.10). "Personally identifiable" means that either accompanying information reveals the identity of the research participants or the nature of data storage itself reveals their identity (e.g., videotape or audiotape recordings). Prospective participants also should be informed about plans for sharing research data with others, reanalyzing the data for a new study, or any other intentions of the investigator that could possibly expose the identity of the participants to others. For example, an investigator who has placed code numbers on answer sheets, and intends to release the coding key to another researcher so that participants could be recontacted or any other reason, would have to so inform the participants in advance. Although the standard does not specifically address disclosing the anticipated use of data that are not personally identifiable, it may be wise for the researcher to consider this in advance. In the interest of more comprehensive informed consent it may be important to discuss with participants all of the anticipated uses of such data.

It is also required that prospective participants be told about the possibility of unanticipated future uses to which the personally identifiable research data might be put. Such uses might include addition to a database, didactic purposes in an academic or training setting, or any other foreseeable application in which the participants' identity could be revealed. Again, any potential compromise to the confidentiality of participants should be discussed in advance (see Standard 5.01). Participants are then free to decline, without prejudice, if they do not wish to risk being identified in future research (see Standards 5.03 and 6.11).

6.17 Minimizing Invasiveness

In conducting research, psychologists interfere with the participants or milieu from which data are collected only in a manner that is warranted by an appropriate research design and that is consistent with psychologists' roles as scientific investigators.

Investigators do not gratuitously seek information about participants or pry into irrelevant aspects of their lives for the psychologists' own gratification, power, or any other reason. In a variety of situations this may require special consideration, such as topics that are socially sensitive. This might include research such as investigations with individuals who are chemically dependent or HIV-positive, studies about sexual behavior, or other topics requiring self-disclosure about potentially emotionally loaded information. It is in keeping with the standard to avoid interference with the normal habit patterns and life routines of the participants that is unwarranted by the research design, including participating in the lifestyle or activity. As scientific investigators, psychologists must conform to the research design and gather information in a pragmatic and prudent fashion, always being sensitive to the privacy and welfare of the participants.

An example might be an analysis of classroom behavior in which the researcher has several equally useful options for gathering data: videotape, human raters, or teacher evaluations. All other things being equal, the investigator is well advised to use the procedure that interferes least with the activities of the students and teacher, but not to the extent of compromising data gathering.

6.18 Providing Participants With Information About the Study

(a)   Psychologists provide a prompt opportunity for participants to obtain appropriate information about the nature, results, and conclusions of the research, and psychologists attempt to correct any misconceptions that participants may have.

The investigator bears a responsibility to make the nature, results, and conclusions of the research available to all participants who may be interested. This might include having an individual or group discussion with participants. It could also include making a copy of the dissertation, research paper, or summary available at a central location for participants to view or offering to send a copy of an abstract or explanation of the study to interested parties. The psychologist is not expected to incur a prohibitive cost in time or money in honoring this standard; rather, a reasonable means should be selected for instructing former participants about the nature of the research. There should also be a focus on correcting any lingering false ideas or misimpressions about the research, so that participants have a reasonably good understanding about the research, regardless of whether deception was used (see Standard 6.15).

(b) If scientific or humane values justify delaying or withholding this information, psychologists take reasonable measures to reduce the risk of harm.

There may be situations in which it would be humane or necessary to delay or withhold providing this information to former participants. This would include research with those near death or those who would not comprehend because of their age or their diminished mental capacity. Individuals in extreme distress, or others who would have little or no interest and capability in learning the results, would probably not be candidates for receiving such information, and the researcher most likely would have no obligation to inform them about the outcome of the research. In order to reduce the risk of harm in these situations, psychologists should attempt to give such information to the participants' parents or legal guardians at the conclusion of the study, as appropriate. In any case, if it is necessary to delay or withhold information, investigators take whatever steps are necessary to reduce the risk of harm from misconceptions after the research is over (see Standard 6.11).

6.19 Honoring Commitments

Psychologists take reasonable measures to honor all commitments they have made to research participants.

In this standard psychologists are exhorted to abide by agreements made with participants to fulfill certain roles or responsibilities either during or after the conclusion of the research effort. Investigators do what they say they are going to do. If there is a promise to have a debriefing session with a participant who decides to withdraw from the research, then the session must occur. If compensation in the form of money, goods, psychological services, or some other form is promised in return for research participation, then it must be delivered as stated in compliance with the terms of the agreement. If there is a need to renegotiate the agreement, this should be done promptly, openly, and fairly with the participants, with regard for their needs and welfare concerning the project (see Standard 6.07).

6.20 Care and Use of Animals in Research

(a) Psychologists who conduct research involving animals treat them humanely.

This standard reflects clearly the concerns of psychologists who work with animals, urging a humane spirit and high standard of care. It is quite general in nature and leaves the operational definition of humane treatment to existing legal and professional standards. Research involving animals should reflect this awareness by the investigator. Unnecessary or gratuitous cruelty to animals as well as carelessness would be counter to the dictates of this standard (see Standards 1.04–1.05, and 1.14).

(b) Psychologists acquire, care for, use, and dispose of animals in compliance with current federal, state, and local laws and regulations, and with professional standards.

In this standard investigators are reminded of their requirement to know and abide by rules and regulations set forth by any legal, organizational, or institutional body that might exercise control over their conduct as scientists, as well as professional standards. This applies to every aspect of involvement with animal subjects, including the acquisition, care at every phase of the research, and their ultimate disposition.

At the federal level, there are a number of regulations promulgated by the National Institutes of Health (NIH), the U.S. Department of Health and Human Services (DHHS), the National Academy of Sciences (NAS), and the Animal Welfare Information Center (AWIC) of the Department of Agriculture. The publications that are particularly relevant are (a) the (U.S.) *Public Health Service Policy on Humane Care*: *The Use of Laboratory Animals* (NIH, 1986), (b) the (U.S.) *Guide for the Care and Use of Laboratory Animals* (NIH, 1985; developed by DHHS in conjunction with the Institute of Laboratory Animal

Resources [NAS] and NIH), (c) *The Institutional Administrator's Manual for Laboratory Animal Care and Use* (NIH, 1988) and (d) Title 9 C.F.R. (1992). Although the guidelines in these publications are not necessarily specifically enforceable under the rules of this Ethics Code, they should routinely be perused by animal researchers as often as necessary in order to remain current. Furthermore, states may have their own statutes and regulations that pertain to animal research; it is the investigator's duty to be aware of these as well (see Standard 6.08).

Professional associations also provide guidelines and standards for investigators and should be consulted as needed. This would include the *Guidelines for Ethical Conduct in the Care and Use of Animals* (APA, 1993a) and relevant publications of the American Association for Accreditation of Laboratory Animal Care, the American Association of Laboratory Animal Science, the American College of Laboratory Animal Medicine, the American Society of Laboratory Animal Practitioners, and the American Veterinary Medicine Association. The researcher should try to obtain the most current versions of policies, standards, and guidelines in making decisions about research design and risk to animal subjects.

(c) Psychologists trained in research methods and experienced in the care of laboratory animals supervise all procedures involving animals and are responsible for ensuring appropriate consideration of their comfort, health, and humane treatment.

This principle affirms that psychologists must supervise all procedures in animal experimentation and must be well trained in research methods and experienced with animals. This would include ensuring appropriate qualifications of fellow investigators, as well as attention to the custodial responsibilities that have been delegated to assistants, who may have minimal training at the outset. It is their obligation to see to it that animals have proper housing or caging (temperature, humidity, illumination, noise, bedding, sanitation, preventive medical care, etc.). They must also ensure that there are appropriate technical and husbandry resources, that there is proper personal hygiene of those in contact with animals, and that there is humane treatment of the animals involved in research.

(d) Psychologists ensure that all individuals using animals under their supervision have received instruction in research methods and in the care, maintenance, and handling of the species being used, to the extent appropriate to their role.

Animal researchers are responsible for ensuring that their research assistants or others working under their supervision who have direct contact with the animals are qualified and have adequate training and supervision. This is for the protection of both the animals and humans, in order to maintain safety for each in avoiding injury or illness. Proper instruction would include imparting a knowledge of and familiarity with the particular species being used by any suitable means, such as direct training and supervised experience handling the animals, reading materials, training films or tapes, or any other didactic means that are appropriate. The level and type of instruction is commensurate with the assistants' needed level of expertise within the research effort. This standard also requires appropriate instruction in relevant research methods.

(e) Responsibilities and activities of individuals assisting in a research project are consistent with their respective competencies.

Assistants in animal research are expected to perform duties only within their level of skill, competence, and training. Exceeding these expectancies could place both animals and humans at risk of accident, illness, or injury. If new levels of competence should be demanded as the research continues, the researcher bears the responsibility of ensuring the teaching or training of assistants to meet this new demand and continuing to provide adequate supervision as needed.

(f) Psychologists make reasonable efforts to minimize the discomfort, infection, illness, and pain of animal subjects.

This is consistent with all preceding standards on the care and maintenance of animals and highlights the areas of concern that are articulated in 6.20b. It specifically addresses the requirement to be attentive to and minimize any infection, illness, discomfort, or pain of the animal for the duration of the research. This would include (a) attending to the housing and care of animals (e.g., suitable cages, feeding schedules, overall conditions); (b) maintaining sanitary and antiseptic procedures, as appropriate; (c) providing appropriate medical care when needed; and (d) taking steps to avoid unnecessary physical pain (e.g., using anesthetics when warranted and avoiding gratuitously inflicting pain and suffering).

(g) A procedure subjecting animals to pain, stress, or privation is used only when an alternative procedure is unavailable and the goal is justified by its prospective scientific, educational, or applied value.

This is a strong prohibition against using an experimental design that would subject animals to pain, stress, or privation unless it can amply be demonstrated that there is a justifiable prospective value to humanity for using such a procedure. Alternate methods must always be thoroughly explored before an investigator decides to implement a research design that would subject animals to pain, stress, or privation; such a design must not be used if there are other procedures that would accomplish the same ends.

(h) Surgical procedures are performed under appropriate anesthesia; techniques to avoid infection and minimize pain are followed during and after surgery.

When investigators use surgical procedures as a part of the experimental design, they must use appropriate anesthesia, analgesia, and aseptic surgical procedures so as to avoid introducing pain or infectious agents. This, again, is consistent with specific NIH guidelines, as delineated in 6.20b. It also exhorts investigators to be cautious concerning these procedures, so as to avoid infection or other unnecessary complications of the procedure.

(i) When it is appropriate that the animal's life be terminated, it is done rapidly, with an effort to minimize pain, and in accordance with accepted procedures.

If an investigator terminates an animal's life as a part of the research design or upon its conclusion, he or she does so in a humane fashion. Specifically, this is done in a fashion that will minimize suffering and in conformity with standards and guidelines of the NIH and the American Veterinarian Medicine Association.

6.21 Reporting of Results

(a) Psychologists do not fabricate data or falsify results in their publications.

Competent scientific research is considered to be the cornerstone on which every area of psychology is founded. The very essence of the scientific method involves observation that can be repeated and verified by others. Therefore, violations of this standard have the potential for degrading the integrity of the profession, teaching, practice, and application of psychology on a large scale and possibly harming students, trainees, consumers, patients, and others for years to come.

In reporting research results, psychologists must never engage in fraudulent activities such as altering original data, making up data, or falsifying results in any way. Fraudulent research is considered to be a serious violation of the Ethics Code and may carry with it the most extreme sanctions and penalties (see Standard 3.03).

(b) If psychologists discover significant errors in their published data, they take reasonable steps to correct such errors in a correction, retraction, erratum, or other appropriate publication means.

Whenever an investigator encounters errors in his or her published research data, he or she must attempt to correct them by the usual publication means. It is best that such corrections be made in a timely fashion. Such errors might appear in professional journals, books, and the mass media. Reasonable steps to correct these errors include corresponding with the journal editor, publisher, or other responsible party who has had some key role in printing or presenting the erroneous information. Failure to make such an attempt would permit the proliferation of false information to other professionals or the public at large. This standard requires that reasonable steps be taken by the author; it is not a mandate for a publisher to correct the erroneous information.

6.22 Plagiarism

Psychologists do not present substantial portions or elements of another's work or data as their own, even if the other work or data source is cited occasionally.

Protecting the intellectual property rights of others is a long-standing basic principle of science and scholarship. A psychologist must not present the work of another, orally or in writing, in a way that implies authorship. It is essential to acknowledge and cite others' work when appropriate. This can be done by the use of quotation marks when the exact words of another are being used. When paraphrasing, such as making minor changes in language or rearranging the order of the words, one should always give scholarship credit by citing the source of the material each time it is used.

The prohibition of plagiarism extends to ideas, data, and other proprietary information as well. If an author models a study after one done by someone else, or if the rationale for a study or theory was suggested by someone else, that person should be given credit. Given the free exchange of ideas, which is important to the health of psychology, it is sometimes difficult to know where an idea came from. However, if the psychologist does know, he or she should acknowledge the source. This includes personal communications as well.

This rule also extends to copyrighted narrative reports based on automated scoring services and requires psychologists to clearly indicate when text is included from such a source.

6.23 Publication Credit

(a) Psychologists take responsibility and credit, including authorship credit, only for work they have actually performed or to which they have contributed.

In performing their professional work psychologists must truthfully and appropriately claim responsibility, authorship, and credit. This applies to both individual or collaborative work while performing a variety of psychological roles—author, scientific investigator, teacher, supervisor, administrator, therapist, or other role—and extends to acknowledgment in any form, including footnote or other statement of responsibility or contribution.

Authorship is reserved for persons who receive credit and hold responsibility for a published or presented work. Therefore, authorship encompasses not only those who do the actual writing, but also those who have made substantial intellectual contributions to the work. This includes conceptualizing and formulating the problem, designing the study or research protocol, organizing and conducting the statistical analyses, interpreting the results, and writing the paper. In situations in which the source or responsible party may be ambiguous or unknown, the psychologist should acknowledge this fact rather than taking credit inappropriately.

A person's consent should be obtained before placing his or her name on the byline. Furthermore, because authors are responsible for the factual accuracy of their contributions, they should carefully review their own sections as well as the entire work before it is presented or submitted for publication.

This standard is invoked by the situation of a psychologist who publishes a monthly newsletter for patients or a weekly newspaper column about various psychological topics. It is essential that the psychologist actually wrote or served as the primary contributor to the articles in order to claim authorship. This raises a question about claiming authorship when the articles were actually created by a "ghost writer." The psychologist is falsely claiming to be the author instead of acknowledging that the articles are essentially the creations of another. Certainly, claims may be made by psychologists as long as they are factual and do not violate other standards of this Ethics Code. Advertisements or publicity statements written by another, however, must be represented as such (see Standard 3.02e).

(b) Principal authorship and other publication credits accurately reflect the relative scientific or professional contributions of the individuals involved, regardless of their relative status. Mere possession of an institutional position, such as Department Chair, does not justify authorship credit. Minor contributions to the research or to the writing for publications are appropriately acknowledged, such as in footnotes or in an introductory statement.

This standard is similar in concept to the previous one and goes one step farther in providing general guidelines for authorship claims. Authors are responsible for determining authorship and for specifying the order in which two or more authors' names appear in the byline. The general rule is that the name of the principal contributor should appear first, with subsequent names in order of decreasing contribution. In a journal article, monograph, or book, the principal author would be the one who has contributed most significantly to the project in time and energy, creative ideas in format and content, organization of the work, amount of writing, or in some other relevant manner. Principal authorship carries with it the responsibility of having made scientific or professional contributions at a demonstrably higher level than the other coauthors.

In presenting research results, the principal investigator would generally be listed as the principal author and would be the individual primarily responsible for selecting the research topic, designing the research protocol, and writing up the results. Holding an institutional position, such as director or chairperson of a department, or providing a setting or laboratory in which the research can occur, does not, by itself, justify a claim of authorship credit. To be listed on the byline, that person must also make an intellectual contribution to the particular work being reported.

In other collaborative literary endeavors the same principle applies. The credit claimed must accurately reflect real differences in the publication effort. Primary authorship is reserved for the individual who has produced significantly more scientific or professional work on the project, compared with the other authors, or who has contributed significantly more in qualitative or other important ways to the project.

When authors or investigators ultimately perform much less work or do not fulfill their responsibilities in some other ways, then they may not be entitled to the originally contracted coauthorship credit. There are various ways that authors or investigators may default on their obligations and responsibilities: by failing to meet deadlines, by producing work whose quality is significantly inferior to that of collaborators, even by undermining the project in some way, or in some other way behaving inappropriately or at odds with mutual expectations.

Psychologists should also be alert to the potential for exploitation of junior authors, where there are significant power differentials. This could occur in academia, where a senior faculty member is collaborating with a junior colleague on a book and will also be voting on his or her tenure decision. The relative credit claimed on the book must not reflect the power differential, and the latter must not be used as a lever for the former.

Lesser contributions that do not warrant authorship to the research or writing effort, such as attending to the more mundane research responsibilities, testing subjects, assisting in editing, or other similar responsibilities, should be acknowledged by footnotes or elsewhere in the book. These include such supportive functions as designing or building apparatus, suggesting or advising about the statistical analyses, collecting the data, modifying or structuring a computer program, conducting therapy sessions, arranging for research participants, or assisting in editing. This is not to say that people who carry out some of these activities may not also be authors. That decision will be governed by the degree to which the person made an intellectual contribution to the work. The principal author should obtain the person's consent before including them in a note. In general, appropriate negotiation or steps should be implemented by all involved parties that reflect the spirit of these ethical principles as regards fairness in professional collaboration (see also Standards 1.09, Respecting Others; 1.13, Personal Problems and Conflicts; 1.17, Multiple Relationships; and 1.19, Exploitative Relationships).

(c) A student is usually listed as principal author on any multiple-authored article that is substantially based on the student's dissertation or thesis.

Principal authorship is usually assigned to the graduate student when several authors collaborate on a publication that is based primarily on the student's thesis or doctoral dissertation. This reflects the general concept of "credit where credit is due," even though academic advisors or chairpersons of dissertation committees may have contributed heavily in guiding the student's research and written work.

There are, however, situations in which the student would not necessarily be listed as the primary author (e.g., the student's work is part of a larger project or is based on an existing database). In these cases the order of authorship should be determined in advance of the student's work. Obviously, there are many shades of gray in assigning credit for authorship; in each case, however, the faculty member and student should openly discuss the arrangements in advance and during the ongoing project, as it might become necessary.

6.24 Duplicate Publication of Data

Psychologists do not publish, as original data, data that have been previously published. This does not preclude republishing data when they are accompanied by proper acknowledgment.

This standard addresses the practice of self-plagiarism in professional writing. It prohibits psychologists from republishing their own data as original data when it has already been published previously. In referring to one's earlier research data, it is essential to provide the usual citations, as one would do in referencing the prior research of others. Failure to do so essentially misrepresents the psychologist's efforts and creates the appearance that what is being presented is new research or otherwise innovative, when in fact it has appeared in print before. Duplicate publication distorts the knowledge base by making it appear that there is more information available than really exists or that several different studies support a view. It can also lead to copyright violations—a legal problem because an author cannot assign the copyright of the same work (data and words) to more than one publisher.

This standard does not necessarily exclude articles previously published in abstracted form, generally defined as under 1,000 words, such as the proceedings of an annual meeting or periodical with limited circulation or availability. An example might be a freely distributed report by a university department in which under 250 copies were produced. When the identical or overlapping material has appeared in a proceedings or report series that has been offered for sale to the public, however, these previous publications should be mentioned and referenced in the text, in the author footnote, and in the reference list.

Publication of a brief report in most journals is with the understanding that an extended report will not be published in another archival journal; the brief report is the archival record of the work. Therefore, if an extended report is subsequently published in a book or monograph, the brief report must be mentioned and clearly referenced. Problems of duplicate publication also may arise when material is published first by the popular press.

This standard also pertains to the prohibition against submitting the same work to more than one publisher simultaneously. If a manuscript is rejected by one editor, an author may then submit it to another. Sometimes authors may want to publish essentially the same material in different journals in order to reach different audiences. However, there is little need for this practice in the days of multidisciplinary computerized information databases and retrieval systems; duplicate publication can rarely be justified anymore. Whether publishing two or more reports based on the same or closely related research constitutes duplicate publication is sometimes a matter of editorial judgment. Certainly, the author must inform an editor of the existence of any related or similar manuscripts that have already been published or accepted for publication, or that may be submitted for concurrent consideration to the same journal or elsewhere.

Piecemeal, or fragmented, publication of several reports based on a single research project or occasion of data collection is undesirable, and it may be judged as duplicate publication unless there is a clear benefit to scientific communication rather than the author's curriculum vitae. There may be times, however, especially in multidisciplinary research, when it is necessary to break the work into parts. Such multiple reports should be made clear to editors and in the text as well, and appropriately referenced. Similarly, repeated publication from a longitudinal study may be justified if the data from different times make a scientific contribution. Again, the earlier publication should be cited, although it is usually not necessary to repeat the descriptions of the sample, instruments, data collection, and analytic procedures. Prohibiting piecemeal publication does not preclude the subsequent reanalysis of published data in light of new theories or methodologies if the reanalysis is clearly labeled as such. It also does not prevent the publication of theoretical articles that build on earlier work by the author, again if the earlier work is cited.

This standard could also have a bearing on information that is presented in resumes and curricula vitae. Multiple listings of publications or presentations should not be presented as being different when they are essentially the same. Additional information of a more detailed nature can be readily obtained from the APA Office of Publication and Communications in Washington, DC.

6.25 Sharing Data

After research results are published, psychologists do not withhold the data on which their conclusions are based from other competent professionals who seek to verify the substantive claims through analysis and who intend to use such data only for that purpose, provided that the confidentiality of the participants can be protected and unless legal rights concerning proprietary data preclude their release.

This standard elaborates the cooperative and collaborative spirit of scientific research implicit in the common goal of the pursuit of knowledge to which all scientists are committed. Under specific conditions, unless otherwise prohibited by law or institutional regulations, if data are requested for purposes of verification, psychologists have an obligation to release their own raw data following publication. They must reveal the data to competent scientific investigators who wish to test the same hypotheses or verify claims made in the original research by reanalyzing the data. This standard does not require investigators to bear the cost of locating, duplicating, and sending research data. It is reasonable to require an agreement in advance that the expenses incurred be passed on to the individual requesting the materials.

Although the standard does not specifically require this, there is an implied mandate that psychologists who obtain the data of another bear the responsibility of narrowly limiting the scope of their analysis so that no new use or applications are explored. Again, the purpose of obtaining the raw data of another is specifically to substantiate or disprove claims that have been made or to evaluate the integrity of the research; the purpose is never to perform new research on existing data unless this would be specifically agreed to by the initial researcher. In order to better monitor the use to which one's data might be put it would be useful to ask requesting researchers to state their intentions specifically in writing prior to releasing the data. In this way the original investigator may have some confidence that the data about to be released will not be subject to innovative research instead of reanalysis.

There is also an implication in this standard that one should retain research data for a reasonable length of time in order to facilitate requests for reanalysis. The period of time is not defined, but would be dictated by considerations such as feasibility and cost. Authors who publish in APA journals are required to abide by the policy of the Publications and Communications Board to retain research data for a period of 5 years following the date of publication.

The release of raw data may be refused when there are risks to the confidentiality of research participants or when participants have expressly refused to consent to such access to the data by others (see Standard 6.11). Release of data can also be refused when there are legal rights concerning data ownership. This may apply to certain institutional or industrial settings, wherein the psychologist's research may be owned in part or in full by the employing or contracting organization or corporation and such release is not granted by the agency (see Standards 1.16, 5.02, 5.04, 5.07 and 5.10).

6.26 Professional Reviewers

Psychologists who review material submitted for publication, grant, or other research proposal review respect the confidentiality of and the proprietary rights in such information of those who submitted it.

This standard is a new one, delineating some responsibilities of professional reviewers. In reviewing materials that others have submitted for a variety of scientific or publishing purposes, psychologists have a special duty to respect and maintain the confidentiality and ownership rights of any and all information contained in those documents. New information or scientific concepts contained in materials submitted for review may not be used orally or in writing by the reviewer in any way, either by direct quote, allusion, citation, reference, attribution, and so forth. These materials represent the innovative, creative, and intellectual efforts of other psychologists and should be treated with the utmost respect and highest regard for the special status that they occupy (see Standards 5.01–5.02).

Chapter 9 _____

Forensic Activities

This section of the Ethics Code is not just for the use of "forensic psychologists"; it is for all psychologists when they are performing forensic or potentially forensically relevant functions. It is a "first," for no prior APA code has specifically addressed forensic activities. Its inclusion may well reflect and be a response to the increasingly litigious character of our culture, as it was developed out of recognition of the fact that although some psychologists routinely provide services in forensic settings, many others may unexpectedly find themselves subpoenaed to produce records, having to submit to depositions, or being required to testify in court regarding a current or former student, client, or patient. This section therefore applies to the work activities of all psychologists, including academic, research, industrial/organizational, and school psychologists as well as those in the health care arena.

The forensic arena is in some respects quite different from other arenas within which most psychologists are accustomed to functioning. Significant differences include the adversarial nature of legal and judicial activity and the pressures on the psychologist to assume advocacy positions. The standards in this section are designed to provide guidance to psychologists in such circumstances.

A common confusion for those who are not forensic psychologists seems to involve making distinctions among types of witnesses. Psychologists may simply be "fact witnesses" just like any other citizens. When a psychologist testifies to what a patient told him or her about the pain caused by an auto accident, he or she may be functioning no differently from the patient's co-worker who testifies to the same point. But psychologists may *also* be called as expert witnesses. According to *Black's Law Dictionary*, an expert witness is defined as "one who by reason of education or specialized experience possesses superior knowledge respecting a subject about which persons having no particular training are incapable of forming an accurate opinion or deducing correct conclusions" (Nolan & Nolan-Haley, 1990, p. 578). Thus, as an expert, a psychologist may be asked, "In your professional judgment, was the patient's recovery such that a conversion reaction or factitious disorder may be indicated?" It should be emphasized that psychologists who render expert testimony in court are not "just giving opinions," they are providing expert opinions based on professional knowledge, skill, and techniques. Their opinions have much weight and can have great effects on the lives of the individuals concerned (see also Standard 1.15). A psychologist may be subpoenaed as an expert or as a fact witness, or may be asked questions of both types during the same testimony. However, there are times when, because of the particular roles a psychologist may be involved in, he or she may choose to not testify as an expert in a particular case or may confine testimony to "facts" and refrain from making judgments or extrapolating from data.

7. Forensic Activities

7.01 Professionalism

Psychologists who perform forensic functions, such as assessments, interviews, consultations, reports, or expert testimony, must comply with all other provisions of this Ethics Code to the extent that they apply to such activities. In addition, psychologists base their forensic work on appropriate knowledge of and competence in the areas underlying such work, including specialized knowledge concerning special populations. (See also Standards 1.06, Basis for Scientific and Professional Judgments; 1.08, Human Differences; 1.15, Misuse of Psychologists' Influence; and 1.23, Documentation of Professional and Scientific Work.)

Because this is such a specialized area, and because the forensic work of psychologists has the potential for affecting people's lives in such extremely significant ways, this standard calls to the psychologist's attention that compliance is required with other sections of the Ethics Code that relate to their forensic functions. Strict adherence to the Ethics Code decreases the likelihood of avoidable harm to the parties involved (see Standard 1.14). For example, psychologists involved in forensic situations need to know whether it is appropriate to withhold reports pending payment in full for services provided. (see Standard 5.11). They need to be aware that an incompetently performed custody evaluation and attendant testimony could lead to an individual's inappropriate loss of his or her children. It is clearly, then, of the utmost importance that assessments and tests done for the court meet the applicable standards set in this section of the Ethics Code and that the requirements of all other related standards be met.

Attention is called to Standard 1.23b, regarding documentation of professional and scientific work, when it can be anticipated that records will be used in legal proceedings. Additionally, it might be noted that it is very wise to document in the records discussions of matters such as role clarification, revelations regarding prior relationships, and other requirements as raised in the Forensic section of this Ethics Code.

Essentially, professionalism in the forensic arena means practicing in the area of one's expertise and knowing the ground rules and the system (see also Standard 7.06). Psychologists must be informed and competent in the areas in which they provide services (as required in Standard 1.04). This includes having special knowledge concerning the basic populations that they are serving: The psychologist doing child custody evaluations must have appropriate training and knowledge of children and the effects on them of divorce, as well as knowledge of adults and parenting skills. The evaluator of an 80-year-old's need for a guardian needs to know about geriatric populations. Whether doing an evaluation involving developmentally disabled individuals, chronic pain patients, criminal populations, and so forth, the psychologist needs to know the population and the problems in order to function competently in a forensic setting. In 1994, the APA Council of Representatives adopted as policy the *Guidelines for Child Custody Evaluations in Divorce Proceedings* developed by the Board of Professional Affairs. Although this document is not enforceable by the APA Ethics Committee, it does provide valuable information for psychologists involved in providing such services (APA, 1994).

Additionally, psychologists should have specialized knowledge concerning special populations such as victims of violence and underrepresented groups including ethnic minorities, persons with disabilities, and so on, for whom or about whom they provide services. They should be aware of the special vulnerability of some of those they serve and of the risks posed to victims of interpersonal violence by the disclosure of certain types of information, such as the address where a woman or man may be staying to avoid spousal or partner abuse (see also Standard 1.14).

When doing forensic work in any area, be it child custody, criminal responsibility and competency assessments, evaluation of damages in civil cases, civil commitment, guardianship and testamentary capacity, and so on, psychologists should have a reasonable degree of knowledge of the judicial system, the statutes that govern the particular area of law and relevant case law, the court rules that might apply to the presentation of evidence, and, in general, the sorts of legal procedures that might be applicable. It would also be useful to know how court procedures work and to learn courtroom etiquette. Psychologists do not need to know everything a lawyer knows. They do need to know enough about the judicial system so that they can do a competent job and avoid harm. (Mistrials have occurred as the result of forensic witnesses' inappropriate participation in evidentiary procedures.) Psychologists need to know how to handle a subpoena, how to deal with attorneys, how to conduct themselves in a deposition, and so forth.

For example, it is important to know that just because a psychologist's records are subpoenaed, that psychologist need not automatically turn over those records. There are times when the terms of even a court order should be questioned or challenged, and times when there is no problem in turning records over in response to a subpoena issued by a lawyer. If the psychologist identifies problems in providing the subpoenaed materials, then consultation with a lawyer, a forensic colleague, or the court can provide direction. Some action is required of the psychologist in response to any subpoena, although that action may be to seek to quash the subpoena or request a protective order from the court restricting the materials that must be produced or providing that they need not be produced in the absence of consent.

7.02 Forensic Assessments

(a) Psychologists' forensic assessments, recommendations, and reports are based on information and techniques (including personal interviews of the individual, when appropriate) sufficient to provide appropriate substantiation for their find-

ings. (See also Standards 1.03, Professional and Scientific Relationship; 1.23, Documentation of Professional and Scientific Work; 2.01, Evaluation, Diagnosis, and Interventions in Professional Context; and 2.05, Interpreting Assessment Results.)

In doing forensic work one needs to base one's assessments, recommendations, and reports on information and techniques that are appropriate and provide the data necessary to substantiate the findings. In some situations, personal interviews are not considered necessary, as when psychologists review records and provide reports, for example in the context of social security appeals. Such reports clearly indicate the nature of the review. And in some situations there are well-respected neuropsychologists who base their reports on test findings and standardized observations made by appropriately trained technicians.

This standard would not appear to preclude such procedures. By contrast, in doing custody evaluations, interviewing both parents is expected, with efforts made to arrange such meetings. Failure to interview a parent calls for explanation of why the interview could not be held, and that omission must be reflected in the report of and scope of findings. As discussed in the next section, a custody recommendation, for example, may not be possible in these circumstances. Although they may at times be pressured to do so, as by the parties or their lawyers, psychologists do not go beyond the data in presenting their conclusions and reports and explain any important limitations in the data.

(b) Except as noted in (c), below, psychologists provide written or oral forensic reports or testimony of the psychological characteristics of an individual only after they have conducted an examination of the individual adequate to support their statements or conclusions.

Except as provided in Standard 7.02c, this section requires an in-person examination of the individual as part of the information gathering for the preparation of written or oral forensic reports or testifying regarding an individual's psychological characteristics. In line with this standard, then, a psychologist who had been consulted only by the wife and was called into court and asked questions regarding the husband clearly would not be able to make statements regarding the psychological characteristics of the husband. The psychologist would have to indicate that the husband had not been seen and qualify any responses within that context.

Certainly, there are times when a lawyer may request that a psychologist read transcripts, look at medical records, examine test results, pore over depositions, and so on, and render a professional opinion. For the psychologist to do so would not be in conflict with this standard as long as the nature of the question addressed is such that the available data would present a meaningful response and the opinion did not include a definitive statement about the psychological characteristics of the specific individual. Statements about psychological characteristics of individuals not personally examined may not be made, in forensic situations, except as provided in 7.02c. Record reviews may also be appropriately used as the basis for responding to hypotheticals, for it is common in legal settings for statements about such data to be introduced in the form of hypothetical questions that do not relate to a specific individual. Although doing such record reviews is acceptable practice, the nature and limitations of the review must be indicated in the opinion or testimony rendered (see also 7.04b).

In applying this standard, clinical judgment is called for in order to determine what procedures constitute an adequate evaluation for particular diagnostic or evaluative statements or conclusions. Personal examination of an individual is only one possible aspect of the evaluation, although a mandatory one. Other sources of data might include, for example, testing, review of records, and contacts with school counselors; variables such as length and content of the interview, types of psychological tests conducted, and nature and extent of the history obtained all enter into determination of the adequacy of the evaluation. Psychologists are reminded that in a forensic setting their professional opinions may be sharply challenged, and they will need to provide ample justification for their conclusions.

> **(c) When, despite reasonable efforts, such an examination is not feasible, psychologists clarify the impact of their limited information on the reliability and validity of their reports and testimony, and they appropriately limit the nature and extent of their conclusions or recommendations.**

This section provides guidance in situations when, despite reasonable efforts, the psychologist may be unable to do the personal examination addressed in 7.02b. It addresses three considerations.

First, it requires that "reasonable efforts" have been made to do the examination of the individual and these have not been successful. There might be a situation in which an individual is physically incapacitated to an extent that examination is not considered feasible or the individual might be out of the country, in jail, and so on. Asking a husband to have the wife he is in the process of divorcing come in for an evaluation, and simply accepting his statement that she will not, might not appear to be a "reasonable effort." Nor might be offering a busy working person one appointment time and not offering another when told he or she cannot make it. Determining that enough steps have been taken involves assessing not only what the steps are, but whether the examination is "not feasible." One might consider calling or writing to arrange an appointment, offering alternative appointments, or working with the court or attorneys to ensure as much cooperation and understanding as possible, as reasonable efforts made. And if the examination could still not be arranged, it might then be considered as "not feasible."

Second, when the evaluations have proceeded, the data are considered to be "limited," and the psychologist, in reports and testimony, must explain how the limited evaluation affects the reliability and validity of the "reports and testimony." In other words, the qualification requirement extends to both statements of fact, which report the "data," and statements of impact, which extend to the findings and opinions as well. It is important to note that this qualification is not only regarding the "data," but extends to the findings and opinions as well. The psychologist who states "I did not see the father" is making a statement about the limitation of the procedures, but that statement does not indicate how the fact that the father was not seen qualified the conclusions drawn. This is in contrast to the psychologist who states "the validity of my opinion regarding the likely adjustment of these children is reduced by my not having evaluated the father and not obtaining his descriptions of the children's behavior" and is thereby addressing the impact of the procedure limitation on the opinions rendered, thus qualifying a finding consistent with this standard.

Third, this rule requires that when the personal examination has not occurred, the psychologist refrains from drawing conclusions and making recommendations that go beyond the limits of the data. This is, of course, required by other standards also, but is emphasized here because it is in an area fraught with problems. In other words, even if psychologists follow the stipulations, clarify that the impact of the information is limited, and limit the nature and extent of their conclusions or recommendations accordingly, there are some types of conclusions and recommendations that are precluded. Under this standard, in a child custody case in which only one parent was evaluated and it was not feasible to evaluate the other, although the psychologist may make statements about the parent who was not seen as long as he or she does not go beyond the data and does qualify conclusions by acknowledging the limitations imposed by the incompleteness of the data collected, it would generally be improper for the psychologist to offer an opinion of the missing parent's parental qualities or make a custody recommendation. If the psychologist does not evaluate a father in a custody matter but evaluates the rest of the family, whatever evidence he or she may have about the father may be presented, along with the relevant opinions. For example, if the custody matter involves a child diagnosed as having an attention deficit disorder, and the data clearly indicate that the father is a very impatient individual with two founded abuse allegations, the psychologist may use this information in the evaluation. If information ordinarily needed to render certain opinions has not been obtained, and if techniques ordinarily required to obtain this information have not been performed, then those opinions may not be offered.

7.03 Clarification of Role

In most circumstances, psychologists avoid performing multiple and potentially conflicting roles in forensic matters. When psychologists may be called on to serve in more than one role in a legal proceeding—for example, as consultant or expert for one party or for the court and as a fact witness—they clarify role expectations and the extent of confidentiality in advance to the extent feasible, and thereafter as changes occur, in order

to avoid compromising their professional judgment and objectivity and in order to avoid misleading others regarding their role.

This standard, which overlaps to a great extent with Standard 7.05, provides a norm, in forensic work, of psychologists' avoidance of multiple and potentially conflicting roles, with their attendant risks of compromising professional judgment and objectivity and of misleading others about their roles. Psychologists who participate in legal proceedings in more than one role have the responsibility to clarify those role expectations and the confidentiality limits in advance to the extent feasible and later as changes occur. It seems important to stress here that this standard is an "almost never" rule. That is, although it does allow for the possibility of exceptions, the psychologist would need to consider not only this standard but also Standard 1.17, which also addresses the matter of multiple relationships. Many forensic psychology experts believe strongly that such exceptions are fraught with risks of harm to the clients involved and strongly urge avoidance of such multiple roles.

To illustrate, consider a psychologist, Dr. Y., who is asked by an attorney to do a forensic evaluation of Ms. D., her therapy patient who has been involved in an auto accident. Ms. D. is suing for damages and requests that Dr. Y. do the assessment because of their professional relationship and the trust that she places in her. It would be incumbent on Dr. Y. to explain to Ms. D. that in her role as therapist, the client's welfare is paramount, whereas in the role of forensic assessor, objectivity and accuracy in presenting data would have to be paramount, so that the two roles might come into conflict. If Dr. Y.'s assessment findings, for example, did not reflect what the client would hope for or see as in her own best interests, that might injure or destroy the therapeutic relationship and, accordingly, it would be wiser to have Ms. D. tested by another examiner. If the request for services is repeated despite the explanation to both the client and her attorney, then Dr. Y. probably would be wise to refuse to become involved in the court case. Another option would be to decline to appear as an expert witness who will offer any opinion on the ultimate issue of damages. Dr. Y. might be unable to avoid a court appearance, if a valid subpoena and client release are provided, and in some instances might even choose to testify in her psychotherapist's role, seeing such testimony as in the patient's best welfare. Standard 7.05 addresses further Dr. Y.'s ability to testify in her role as therapist.

If one of those difficult-to-conceive-of legitimate exceptions pertained, Dr. Y. might agree to take on the assessment, but only after explaining to her client (and the attorney) the altered limits of confidentiality in doing the assessment and the different roles and expectations. Great care would have to be taken to maintain objectivity in making professional judgments while doing the assessment and report. Additionally, included in the reports, depositions, and testimony, the possibility of bias on Dr. Y.'s part because of earlier involvement as a therapist would need to be acknowledged, along with any limitation that might pertain to the opinions rendered. Psychologists are advised to document their discussions with clients and attorneys regarding confidentiality, roles, and so on.

This standard does not prohibit the therapist from testifying as an expert witness or a fact witness as described in Standards 7.05 and 1.21 in this code. In connection with this standard, see also Standards 1.17 and 7.05–7.06.

7.04 Truthfulness and Candor

(a) In forensic testimony and reports, psychologists testify truthfully, honestly, and candidly and, consistent with applicable legal procedures, describe fairly the bases for their testimony and conclusions.

Candor has been defined as openness, frankness, or fairness. This standard clearly states what is expected of psychologists in their forensic testimony and reports in terms of candor, truth, and honesty. Yet it recognizes that legal procedures may not always allow psychologists to say all that they might choose to say when testifying or being deposed. However, psychologists must always strive to remain fair and professional and not to be drawn by loyalties or emotions into becoming a biased untruthful advocate. The importance of unbiased work cannot be overemphasized, and psychologists need to guard against partisan distortion involving, for example, the omission of data incompatible with or tending to dilute the conclusions the psychologist wishes to draw (see also Standard 1.16a).

The maintenance of accurate records of the techniques used and results obtained would ordinarily be extremely important in order to facilitate a fair description of the bases of testimony and conclusions. Psychologists may expect to have their records and reports subpoenaed and should be prepared to defend their depositions or reports by documented data in their records.

(b) Whenever necessary to avoid misleading, psychologists acknowledge the limits of their data or conclusions.

In forensic matters, psychologists' control over the situations in which they are testifying is limited. Nevertheless, they do have a responsibility to volunteer any information that would prevent their testimony from being misleading and, to the extent that it is appropriate in a courtroom situation, to explain in their discussion of their findings any factors of which the judge or jury must be aware to understand the witness's opinions. At times lawyers present issues in such a manner that the testimony can be misleading, as when insisting on a yes or no answer without permitting any necessary explanation to be given. If the question cannot be answered that way, the psychologist witness must say so and explain why if asked. If the answer to the question as asked would be clearly misleading, the psychologist must say so. But the psychologist cannot reasonably be expected to control the lawyer's behavior. This standard clearly enunciates psychologists' responsibility to attempt to acknowledge the limits of their data or conclusions in order to avoid misleading, despite attempts by an attorney to truncate statements about such limitations.

In depositions, at least, there is usually sufficient opportunity for the psychologist to explain fully and completely all matters of importance regarding the opinions being offered, including the limits of the data. In other cases, such concerns usually can be made known easily to the attorney who will be soliciting the testimony or calling the psychologist at trial (see also Standards 1.15 and 2.05).

7.05 Prior Relationships

A prior professional relationship with a party does not preclude psychologists from testifying as fact witnesses or from testifying to their services to the extent permitted by applicable law. Psychologists appropriately take into account ways in which the prior relationship might affect their professional objectivity or opinions and disclose the potential conflict to the relevant parties.

This standard refers specifically to situations in which a psychologist is testifying, either in person or by providing information via a written report or deposition. The legal system works on the premise that in a democracy, one of the obligations of citizens is to participate in judicial proceedings and that the justice system has a right to factual evidence duly obtained from any witness. Psychologists can be subpoenaed to testify, willingly or against their will, and therefore, unless confidentiality, privacy, or other rights under applicable law are recognized by the court to preclude it, this standard acknowledges that psychologists can and do ethically testify as fact witnesses.

Whether qualified by the court as an expert witness or simply a fact witness (a matter over which the therapist may have no direct control), he or she might legitimately testify about the patient's therapy and about events in the therapy that he or she witnessed unless there is an applicable confidentiality rule or privilege. If designated an expert witness (i.e., a witness who is permitted to offer opinion testimony and who is not barred by hearsay rules from testifying about the statements of others), the therapist may legitimately testify about the patient's diagnosis and history, even what the patient told him or her about the issues in question, again subject to any confidentiality requirements or applicable privileges.

Although psychologists are generally qualified as expert witnesses by the courts and are equipped by education, training, and experience to make judgments based on the events or the data collected, there are times when they may decline to offer a professional opinion because of prior roles or because the type of evaluation necessary to provide a basis for a requested opinion was not done.

Dr. Y., the therapist whose patient is involved in a lawsuit stemming from an auto accident and who is called on to testify, might well refuse to make a statement about damages, for example, because she might not have the necessary objectivity in view of the therapeutic alliance with her patient. In fact, the type of testimony given by a therapist includes opinions that are distinct from opinions on the legal issues in question, such as whether the patient sustained damages as a result of the accident in question, which many forensic specialists insist call for objective evaluation unencumbered by a prior therapy relationship with the patient and one that involves different procedures from any ordinarily used in therapy.

Psychologists faced with the role boundary problems in a forensic matter may need to explore the possibility for limited testimony. One such possibility might be giving testimony in the judge's chambers rather than in an open court if that seems desirable. When in the psychologist's opinion compliance with a subpoena is in serious conflict with the ethical obligations, consideration might be given to retaining legal counsel to quash the subpoena or to requesting a protective order or some other legal remedy.

Professionally, psychologists are aware of and should disclose in their testimony the potential conflicts involved in prior relationships with patients. In a custody matter, for example, when called on to testify about Mrs. M., a former patient, the psychologist might say in essence, in response to questions regarding comparisons between Mr. and Mrs. M., "I have information only from Mrs. M. and I have no professional basis for judging Mr. M.'s mental state." Ordinarily, the adversarial process of cross-examination will in fact probe the bases of opinions, possible bias, and other relevant factors in great detail.

The psychologist who is asked by an attorney to review records, evaluate the report rendered by a colleague retained by opposing counsel, and testify concerning the findings would be expected to inform the attorney, for example, that he or she had twice served as a consultant for the opposing counsel or had once, many years ago, served with the psychologist-colleague on an American Board of Professional Psychology (ABPP) examining committee. As long as the possible conflict is revealed, and if objectivity can be retained, there is no conflict with this standard.

7.06 Compliance With Law and Rules

In performing forensic roles, psychologists are reasonably familiar with the rules governing their roles. Psychologists are aware of the occasionally competing demands placed upon them by these principles and the requirements of the court system, and attempt to resolve these conflicts by making known their commitment to this Ethics Code and taking steps to resolve the conflict in a responsible manner. (See also Standard 1.02, Relationship of Ethics and Law.)

This standard is particularly important for psychologists who do not specialize in forensic work. Psychologists are not expected to know every rule that might apply, but they do need to become reasonably familiar with the rules governing their roles in court situations. It is recommended that psychologists discuss with their lawyers what the pertinent rules and law are in the particular forensic situation in which they find themselves involved and check with them about any subpoenas they may receive. Psychologists may learn from attorneys, forensic colleagues, and available reference texts what court rules if any apply to the presentation of evidence, and, in general, the sorts of legal procedures that will be applicable. These might include, for example, how probate court or criminal court procedures occur and the basics of courtroom etiquette. Although they do not need to be legal experts, psychologists need to be familiar enough with these matters so that they can function effectively and avoid harm. They need to know the rules of comportment (e.g., whether it is proper to speak with a plaintiff in a civil case without that person's lawyer's permission, to discuss the case with opposing counsel, to contact the victim of a criminal offense, or to speak to others who are under a subpoena). In addition to the resources delineated earlier, it is also suggested that psychologists check with the APA and state psychological associations, study their own state laws and rules, and know their Ethics Code (see also Standard 7.01).

Psychologists are required to attempt to resolve conflicts between this Ethics Code and the requirements of the court system. Consider, for example, a situation in which a psychologist is ordered to provide opposing counsel with raw data in addition to the written assessment report. The psychologist is aware that Standard 2.02b of this Ethics Code prohibits release of raw data to persons (other than patients and clients, as appropriate) who are not qualified to use such information. The psychologist might consider the lawyer unqualified in this context (not all psychologists would agree) and offer to send the raw data to a professional of the counsel's choice who is qualified to interpret them appropriately. But as a caution, it should be noted that there may be a risk of incurring an Ethics Code violation if one sends raw data without being able to justify qualification of the recipient. When the court orders a release of records, and that release is seen by the psychologist as being detrimental to the welfare of the client, a consultation with the judge might result in sealing of parts of the record, a protective order limiting further disclosure, or, in some instances, a hearing in chambers.

This Ethics Code does not require heroic measures on the part of psychologists faced with such dilemmas as being cited for contempt because of refusal to comply with a subpoena. However, because of the seriousness of such a dilemma, the psychologist should seek consultation with an attorney knowledgeable about mental health law in order to resolve the conflict (see also Standard 1.02).

Chapter 10 _____

Resolving Ethical Issues

For the first time in an APA Ethics Code, the 1992 code devotes a major section to the resolution of ethical violations.

As our field grows in numbers and complexity, as our society places increasing stresses on us in the workplace, and as ours becomes an increasingly litigious culture, there are more and more complaints filed with ethics committees and licensing boards, and psychologists become more and more vulnerable. This section of this new Ethics Code is devoted to delineating psychologists' current responsibilities relative to filing or responding to ethical complaints, to providing some guidance to psychologists who become aware of possible ethical violations on the part of colleagues, and so to be of help in implementing the goals of this document: to facilitate the highest standards of ethical behavior for psychologists and in so doing to protect the public and the profession.

It should be noted that not all unethical behavior is illegal (and not all illegal behavior is unethical), although this does not necessarily keep someone who feels wronged from taking a complaint to the courts. Some behaviors may be unethical according to this Ethics Code, but not in violation of law, unless the state in which the behavior occurred had incorporated into its statutes this Ethics Code or particular ethical requirements that addressed the behavior. This is one of the reasons why ethics committees at times in considering complaints may reach different conclusions than state licensing boards and it is why, for example, Standard 8.05 includes referrals to both ethics committees and licensing boards as options.

8. Resolving Ethical Issues

8.01 Familiarity With Ethics Code

Psychologists have an obligation to be familiar with this Ethics Code, other applicable ethics codes, and their application to psychologists' work. Lack of awareness or misunderstanding of an ethical standard is not itself a defense to a charge of unethical conduct.

It is incumbent on psychologists to know the APA Ethics Code and how it applies to them professionally. The "other applicable ethics codes" alluded to in this standard might include codes in state psychology statutes, codes well recognized in law or in specialized fields (e.g., governing work with human or animal subjects) or codes adopted by hospitals at which psychologists may have staff privileges or by other institutions with which they may be affiliated, and the codes of other professional organizations of which psychologists are members. It should be noted that not following another code is not in itself a violation of this Ethics Code. The obligation is to be familiar with such codes, not to obey every pronoun of every such "code."

The second sentence simply indicates that, when defending against a charge of unethical conduct, ignorance is no excuse. Indeed, ignorance is in itself a violation of the Ethics Code.

8.02 Confronting Ethical Issues

When a psychologist is uncertain whether a particular situation or course of action would violate this Ethics Code, the psychologist ordinarily consults with other psychologists knowledgeable about ethical issues, with state or national psychology ethics committees. or with other appropriate authorities in order to choose a proper response.

No code of ethics can give explicit answers to all problem situations, and ethical issues often present complex dilemmas. This rule addresses the resolution of dilemmas in which the uncertainty is whether a contemplated action would be a "violation" of the code. The same procedures are also applicable to resolving dilemmas regarding "aspirational" ethics. It is not infrequent for psychologists to talk about problems with close colleagues or friends, but remain uncertain about what to do. In the face of such uncertainty, this standard calls attention to the wisdom of consultation, specifically consultation with colleagues knowledgeable regarding ethical issues, not just with colleagues selected solely on the basis of their proximity or friendship. Psychologists who do not know whom to consult might do well to contact state or local psychological association ethics chairpersons, the APA Ethics Office, their APA divisional ethics committee, or their state psychology board for guidance.

8.03 Conflicts Between Ethics and Organizational Demands

If the demands of an organization with which psychologists are affiliated conflict with this Ethics Code, psychologists clarify the nature of the conflict, make known their commitment to the Ethics Code, and to the extent feasible, seek to resolve the conflict in a way that permits the fullest adherence to the Ethics Code.

This standard indicates that psychologists are not ordinarily expected to resign from their professional positions in order to comply with the stipulations of this Ethics Code. (A personal code of ethics might so dictate, but this Ethics Code does not. Also in rare instances the entire employment situation might be so obviously illegal and unethical as to require withdrawal, such as if the psychologist finds that he or she has been hired solely to "develop" and sell bogus, totally unvalidated "diagnostic" tests.) But psychologists are required to identify conflicts between this Ethics Code and the requirements placed on them by the organization, to communicate those concerns to their commanding officer, hospital administrator, supervisor, or employer, and to otherwise seek a solution that will permit compliance with the code to the fullest extent possible.

Presenting the issues regarding ethical responsibilities to one's supervisor or the administrator of a program who is not a psychologist may result in a change of policy to bring the procedures into conformity with proper practice. Professionals, including psychologists who work in institutional settings as part of a treatment team, may have limited power individually to affect decisions regarding such matters as format of the hospital's informed consent forms or the termination of treatment resulting from hospital discharge. But they would need to exercise the power they do have to try to effect changes in line with this Ethics Code. The psychologist who is pressured by his or her hospital administrator to hospitalize patients who do not really need inpatient care in order to fill hospital beds would be required to make his or her objections to such a policy known. Psychologists must take reasonable steps to try to resolve the conflict and such steps must include explaining the Ethics Code requirement. Additionally, suggesting possible solutions tailored to accommodate the Ethics Code without placing unacceptable burdens on the institution might be made. It is recognized that in some situations as, for example, in the military, the psychologist is not likely to be able to change the system. But note that failing to *resolve* the conflict is not an ethical violation. Failing to *attempt* resolution is.

8.04 Informal Resolution of Ethical Violations

When psychologists believe that there may have been an ethical violation by another psychologist, they attempt to resolve the issue by bringing it to the attention of the individual if an informal resolution appears appropriate and the intervention does not violate any confidentiality rights that may be involved.

It is recommended that Standards 8.04 and 8.05 be studied together in order to provide the best understanding of what is expected of psychologists regarding the handling of situations if they become aware of what appear to be ethical violations on the part of other psychologists. Jointly, the standards make it clear that in such situations, the psychologist is required to do something, to the extent permitted by confidentiality restrictions.

Instead of the requirement of prior codes that one differentiate between "major" and "minor" violations in order to determine appropriate action, the focus in the new code is on deciding when to attempt informal resolution of possible violations (as in this standard) and, when such attempts are either inappropriate, unsuccessful, or even risky, to consider other actions (as in Standard 8.05).

Both Standards 8.04 and 8.05 also now state, contrary to previous rules, that maintaining confidentiality is a superior responsibility to reporting ethical violations only if the confidentiality problems cannot be resolved after trying to do so. Also, with state mandatory reporting laws, the psychologist may not have the option of doing nothing. The commentary in Standard 8.05 discusses reporting further.

Psychologists who believe an ethical violation by a colleague may have occurred are not required by Standard 8.04 (or 8.05) to file reports with a state licensing board or a professional ethics committee if the matter appears appropriate for an informal resolution *and* one has been achieved. This is a matter of judgment; certainly, consultations with ethics committees, in which the anonymity of the potential complainee is protected, could help the psychologist arrive at a reasonable course of action.

It would generally seem inappropriate to try to address as informal resolutions under Standard 8.04 exclusively such complex situations as possible sexual misconduct violations or significant financial investment dealings with clients. Psychologists need to give careful thought to the range of actions available to them. In the course of evaluating the possible choices, psychologists may wish to consider the following variables: (a) the credibility and seriousness of the allegation, (b) the nature of the relationship with the colleague, (c) the likelihood of successful resolution, (d) the personal risks involved (such as the possibility of suit, job loss, etc.), (e) the likelihood of repetitions of the violation even if informal resolutions were achieved, and (f) the seriousness of future violations.

Consider some examples. Suppose a female psychologist is walking down the hall in her office and notes that a colleague's file cabinets, which are in a corner near the patients' restroom, are kept unlocked and open during office hours and are accessible to curious eyes. After considering the options, as above, she calls this to the attention of her office associate, who says that he had not realized and immediately corrects the problem. This is an appropriate way to handle a problem and protect clients.

The psychologist who sees an ad placed by a colleague that contains seriously erroneous and misleading information about credentials may choose to contact that individual and talk about it. If the next ad reflects a correction, informal resolution has been achieved. If the ads continue unchanged, in apparent violation of Standard 3.03(a), further action would be indicated and might include filing a complaint in accordance with Standard 8.05.

If a psychologist learns of a possible violation in the course of doing therapy with a patient, confidentiality would preclude taking action unless privilege is waived. But suppose a patient describes behavior on the part of the former male therapist, which sounds as though that therapist, initially very effective, had changed markedly and become agitated, preoccupied, and nonresponsive during sessions, allowing personal issues to interfere with professional performance. With the permission of the patient, the former therapist is approached, acknowledges his distress, and states that he has gone into treatment. But that is not necessarily considered sufficient, because he is still seeing patients and his performance is not being monitored in any way. The psychologist is aware that there is an effective local impaired psychologists committee, and he agrees to contact the committee and to place himself under supervision. When he has done so, the psychologist who initiated the discussion with him feels that a satisfactory informal resolution of the problem has been reached, and he has discharged his responsibilities as reflected in this standard.

Another example might be that of a psychologist who has seen a male colleague, Dr. D., with whom he shares offices, drink one too many martinis at professional dinner meetings on multiple occasions, wondered whether Dr. D. had a drinking problem, but decided it was not appropriate for him to say anything about it. Then, one day, he sees Dr. D. come into the office for patient appointments, with an unsteady gait and the odor of bourbon on his breath. He talks to him about what is going on, and Dr. D. enters an alcoholism treatment program. His behavior is being monitored, and the public is being protected, without the filing of a complaint. In actuality, local groups are often in a better position to monitor than are state and national ethics committees.

Other situations might involve skill deficiency on the part of a psychologist that may interfere with professional effectiveness. In cases in which the psychologist acknowledges the difficulty and is willing to follow through with remedial measures, an alternative to filing a complaint might involve seeing that the psychologist entered into appropriate supervision. For example, suppose that a female psychologist, Dr. A., receives a forensic report from Dr. C. that appears to be grossly flawed and in violation of the Ethics Code. She calls Dr. C. to discuss the report and learns that this is the first such case he has ever been involved in. In the course of their conversation, he expresses genuine concern about his lack of knowledge and requests that Dr. A. provide him with consultation and supervision. Dr. A. is unable to take on another commitment, but suggests the names of several individuals in the area with expertise in forensic psychology who might be able to provide a tutorial and subsequent consultation and supervision. Dr. C. calls to let her know that he has followed through and is enthusiastic about the help he is receiving. This would appear to have been a constructive approach for Dr. A. to pursue.

8.05 Reporting Ethical Violations

If an apparent ethical violation is not appropriate for informal resolution under Standard 8.04 or is not resolved properly in that fashion, psychologists take further action appropriate to the situation, unless such action conflicts with confidentiality rights in ways that cannot be resolved. Such action might include referral to state or national committees on ethics or to state licensing boards.

It is suggested that Standard 8.04 and the commentary provided be reviewed before considering Standard 8.05 here.

In Standard 8.05, psychologists are mandated to follow up on possible violations they do not consider amenable to informal resolution attempts or that they do not succeed in resolving informally. In all instances, the confidentiality rights of others take precedence, and unless the necessary waivers have been secured or the law mandates otherwise, taking action on the possible violation is precluded. The standard requires action and provides examples, but not an exhaustive list of options.

Although this standard does not unilaterally require that a complaint be filed, acknowledging as it does that confidentiality issues, if they cannot be resolved in a way that permits disclosure, take precedence over the mandate to file complaints, psychologists are required to take action in situations to which this exception does not pertain and to consider thoughtfully what actions might or might not be appropriate to take and whether to take them. In this decision-making process, it is important to review carefully the provisions of this Ethics Code and to remember that consultation with objective and learned colleagues as appropriate can be extremely helpful. Psychologists also need to be aware that their state laws may mandate reporting to designated governmental agencies.

If informal attempts to rectify an apparent Ethics Code violation do not succeed, the psychologist identifying the possible violation must take further action if appropriate to the situation and not precluded by confidentiality issues. This might include filing a complaint with a state ethics committee, the APA Ethics Committee, or the appropriate licensing board. The psychologist seeing a patient who claims to have been sexually exploited by a former therapist but withholds permission for the psychologist to reveal this is not required, under this standard, to file a complaint. But the subsequent treating psychologist might wish to explore with the patient the possibility of reporting the exploitation, thereby resolving the confidentiality issue. If the patient is not willing to do so at that time, the psychologist does not have the right to breach confidentiality unless mandated by law. Of course, the psychologist might continue to try to help the patient reach a point where he or she is able to file a complaint personally or might refer the patient to a therapist who specializes in such problems, if such referral is warranted.

If a psychologist spots what appears to be plagiarism on the part of a fellow researcher, and the latter denies that such is the case, a referral to the Ethics Committee might be considered in view of the seriousness of the possible violation, which could erode the credibility of the scientific basis of the discipline of psychology and do individual harm to those colleagues whose work is not cited appropriately. There are situations in which consultation with the APA Publications and Communications Board might be of help in addressing corrections to the literature.

In the case of the alcohol-abusing psychologist who denies having a problem and refuses to obtain appropriate help, a referral to an ethics committee or state board would be appropriate for the protection of both the profession and the public.

8.06 Cooperating With Ethics Committees

Psychologists cooperate in ethics investigations, proceedings, and resulting requirements of the APA or any affiliated state psychological association to which they belong. In doing so, they make reasonable efforts to resolve any issues as to confidentiality. Failure to cooperate is itself an ethics violation.

When an ethical complaint is filed against a psychologist, that individual is required to cooperate with the investigatory process of the APA and any affiliated state psychological association of which he or she is a member. Requests for information must be responded to in a timely fashion, as set forth in the rules and procedures of the investigating body, and pertinent material must be provided as appropriate. Many potential confidentiality concerns may be allayed by the fact that the APA Ethics Committee does not pursue a complaint if the individual filing the complaint does not provide appropriate releases, freeing the psychologist being complained about to defend his or her actions within the context of the APA ethics process. Reasonable efforts to resolve confidentiality issues might involve such actions as asking a patient whose treatment is at issue to permit disclosure of records or trying to locate, by letter or other means, an individual who could waive confidentiality and permit certain documents to be submitted. The psychologist in all cases must be afforded an opportunity to present a defense against any allegations of unethical conduct.

Cooperation with the Ethics Committee is mandated not only in reference to investigative procedures, but also, for example, as a means of complying with the committee's directives regarding sanctions, consistent with the APA Ethics Committee's Rules and Procedures (see Appendix C). Failure to complete tutorials or supervision requirements would be illustrative of noncooperation. Failure to cooperate is considered a serious violation of this code, and, as noted in the APA Ethics Committee's Rules and Procedures, "Failure to cooperate shall not prevent continuation of any proceedings and itself constitutes a violation of the Ethics Code that may warrant being dropped from membership" (APA, 1992b, p. 1619; see Appendix C in this volume, pp. 222–223).

8.07 Improper Complaints

Psychologists do not file or encourage the filing of ethics complaints that are frivolous and are intended to harm the respondent rather than to protect the public.

This is a new standard for an APA ethics code, although the idea of rejecting frivolous complaints has been embedded in the APA Ethics Committee's Rules and Procedures.

The ultimate purposes of this Ethics Code are the education of psychologists, the delineation of sound scientific and professional performance by psychologists, and the protection of the public. A frivolous complaint filed solely to injure is an abuse of the Ethics Code and the ethics process. In addition to the time, expense, and anxiety associated with an ethics complaint, some insurance applications or applications for employment or hospital privileges may ask whether a complaint has ever been filed, and the information becomes part of the psychologist's record, even if the complaint was dismissed. Thus, filing an ethics complaint against a colleague is a serious matter, with potentially serious consequences.

In view of the very serious issues involved, the Ethics Code includes a prohibition against psychologists participating in the filing of frivolous complaints that are intended to harm the complainee rather than to protect the public. Of course, even though a complaint may be motivated in part by hostility toward a disliked coworker, if it is well founded and raises a serious ethical issue, it would not be considered an improper complaint, as characterized in this standard. The public is benefited as a by-product of complaints that correct unethical behavior, even those filed for the "wrong" reasons. One might compare this to the complaint filed by the "whistle-blower" who identifies fraud by a government contractor, not because he or she is patriotic but because federal laws provide monetary rewards for true revelations of fraud that wastes taxpayers' money. And even if a complaint is frivolous, it does not violate this standard unless it was improperly motivated. The standard does not punish a complainant who makes an honest mistake. This standard prohibits only complaints that are both frivolous *and* intended to harm rather than protect the public.

An example of a frivolous complaint might be one in which plagiarism is charged by a jealous colleague, but the two documents, although on the same topic, have very different approaches and no evidence of plagiarism can be detected. Another example of using the Ethics Code and Rules and Procedures in a self-serving manner might be the filing of a complaint against a competitor who aggressively markets his or her services in a manner that is clearly not in violation of the Ethics Code. In assessing whether a complaint is frivolous, or intended to harm, one might consider such factors as whether harm to the public or the profession can be identified, whether the ethical violation is clear or ambiguous, whether a reasonable colleague would have supposed that any ethical violation might exist, whether the "evidence" is or is not there or is present for the absence of violation, whether successful pursuit of the allegation would have an impact on one's own self-interest, and whether people have been informed of the complaint in the absence of any emergency need for them to know. The stipulations regarding the processing of complaints, delineated in the Rules and Procedures of the APA Ethics Committee, provide a way to deal with frivolous complaints.

Part III

Conclusion

Chapter 11 _____

Putting Ethics Into Context

Regulation of the Practice of Psychology

The profession of psychology is regulated by a series of state and federal laws, case law decisions, regulations, and codes of ethics and standards of practice adopted by recognized state and national professional organizations. It is important that psychologists be aware of the various kinds of regulations that affect the profession of psychology as well as the rationale for the regulation of professions and the specific methods by which professions are regulated. In addition, psychologists must be aware of the negative consequences that violations of the Ethics Code, statutes, or regulations will have on their professional career.

In this chapter, we describe the broad process of professional regulation. Next, in summarizing several new or expanded areas of the 1992 code, we stress that the Ethics Code may best be perceived as both a guide to proper ethical behavior and as a living document that mirrors the growth of our profession and the evolution of social and political mores.

Purpose of Statutory Regulation

The ultimate purpose for regulation of a profession is to protect the public. To accomplish this, there are two primary goals embodied in regulatory statutes. The first is to establish minimal education and training requirements for entry into the profession. In almost all jurisdictions, a doctoral degree in psychology as defined in the state statute is necessary to meet the education requirements for practice. Most states also require that the individual have 2 years of supervised experience, one of which must be postdoctoral, and pass a written and sometimes an oral examination before being granted the right to practice the profession. In effect, these requirements tend to narrow the pool of providers and ideally increase the quality of services provided by those who are recognized by the state to provide services. The higher the requirements for practice, the fewer the practitioners. If the criteria are set far too high, it can unreasonably restrict competition and interfere with consumer choice. If the criteria are too low, the regulatory scheme will not differentiate the uneducated, the quacks, or the charlatans from those who meet the minimal standards for practice.

The second purpose of regulation is to provide a mechanism to police and discipline members of the profession for such things as unethical conduct, incompetence, or practicing outside one's area of expertise. The state has the power to suspend, revoke, place a psychologist's license on probation, or otherwise discipline a practitioner for violations of the licensing act. Many state regulatory statutes make specific reference to violations of the APA Ethics Code as reasons for disciplinary action.

Regulation by Statute

The foundation of the economic system of the United States is built on the principle that there should be a competitive and open marketplace in which citizens are able to engage in free trade with each other. State constitutions, however, permit the state to regulate certain professions when such regulation is in the best interest of the citizens of the state. Therefore, the state may exercise its police power over the members of certain professions when it has determined that to do so would protect the public health, safety, and welfare and that to leave the profession unregulated might lead to harm to citizens. State and federal statutes that regulate professions place restrictions on who may belong to the profession and may delineate or place restrictions on how members of that profession may conduct business. As such, these regulatory schemes appear to be antithetical to the fundamental principle of an open marketplace. Because the regulation of the professions may limit the number or distribution of available service providers and interfere with consumer choice in a free economy, any regulatory scheme should generally be implemented with care. The necessity to regulate a profession must be greater than the possible negative consequences such regulation has for consumer freedom and other economic considerations. It should also be noted that some forms of regulation serve to enhance consumer choice, for example, by restraining private monopolies that themselves may constrain consumer choice. The federal antitrust laws are examples of powerful mechanisms to assure open competition in the marketplace. However, because state regulation of professions protects the public, reasonable systems of regulation are given a wide berth by the antitrust enforcement agencies and the courts.

In the health care arena, professionals are generally regulated to assure that the public seeking services will be assured that the service provider meets minimal established standards for education and training to practice the profession. The primary means of regulation occurs at the state level through regulatory schemes designed to protect the pubic health, safety, and welfare.

State statutes vary considerably from jurisdiction to jurisdiction, and psychologists are advised to become familiar with the particular laws that regulate the profession in their state. The statutes regulating psychologists generally establish a regulatory board to implement the provisions of the law. Among other functions, the board is empowered to investigate charges of unprofessional or unethical conduct on the part of a regulated practitioner and to take action against the practitioner in order to protect the public health, safety, and welfare. In addition to these laws, psychologists should also be aware of relevant federal statutes and rules that regulate the delivery of psychological services, including both health care services as well as the conduct of research.

Relationship of Statutes and Regulations

Regulatory statutes are augmented by a set of rules and regulations to implement the statute. These rules are generally much more detailed and spell out the specifics of the statute. They also may contain elaborations on acceptable or unethical behaviors and procedures used to investigate allegations of improper practice. Psychologists need to be aware of the provisions contained in both the law as well as the implementing rules and regulations that have the force of law.

Institutional Regulations

In addition to statutory regulation, the delivery of psychological services may be regulated by institutional rules and regulations, such as hospital by-laws relating to privileging and staff membership; policies adopted by organizations and companies that employ psychologists; state regulations governing corporations, partnerships, and group practices; rules and procedures implemented by federal, state, county, and private health care payers; or policies and regulations adopted by academic institutions.

Professional Associations

State and national associations play a major role in the regulation of the practice of psychology. At the national level the APA, with more than 118,000 members and affiliates, is the largest membership group of psychologists. APA members and associate members may be investigated for alleged violations of this Ethics Code by the APA Ethics Committee. The state and provincial psychological associations (SPPAs), although affiliated with the APA in certain ways, are entirely independent corporate entities with independent membership lists and independent ethics processes even if they chose to adopt the APA Ethics Code as their own. Most of these SPPAs, however, generally adhere to important APA standards as well as the APA Ethics Code and have ethics committees that may also investigate complaints against members of the organization.

Psychologists who have membership in the APA or an SPPA that has adopted the APA Ethics Code will be subject to the provisions of the APA Ethics Code. Psychologists who do not belong to a professional association may also be subject to the APA Ethics Code if it is referenced in the state statute regulating the profession.

A consumer who believes that a psychologist has acted improperly may report the alleged violation to (a) the ethics committee of the SPPA if that SPPA investigates complaints and the psychologist is a member of the association, (b) the Ethics Committee of the APA if the psychologist is an APA member, (c) the state or provincial psychology regulatory board if the psychologist is licensed, and (d) the complaint or review committees of institutions or agencies. In addition, the consumer may also file a malpractice action against the psychologist.

Consequences of Ethics Complaints

Violations of state board rules, of course, may result in loss of psychologist's license. But psychologists also should not underestimate the seriousness of an allegation of a violation of the Ethics Code made to the APA or a state association. Even a complaint that the psychologist perceives as frivolous may be cause for concern and such a complaint may not be perceived as frivolous by the person complaining. Once a complaint has been filed, it may become part of the psychologist's professional history and, if asked about, must be reported on insurance forms for application or renewal of professional liability insurance, on applications for hospital privileges, on applications for membership on provider panels of managed care companies, and perhaps on applications for membership in state or national psychological associations or other professional associations. Needless to say, a serious ethics violation may well have tremendous consequences for a psychologist's career.

Summary

There were several goals in drafting the new Ethics Code, including (a) addressing the issues that were emerging in the field of psychology; (b) providing strong educative value (i.e., a code that is comprehensive yet specific enough to provide direct guidance to psychologists in a variety of settings); and (c) providing clear mandates of acceptable and unacceptable behavior in more areas of psychology.

The new Ethics Code facilitates psychologists' understanding of what is expected of them in a variety of roles. For one thing, having a clear demarcation between aspirational and mandatory aspects of the document aids learning and applying the various concepts. Furthermore, the use of indexing and cross-referencing makes it easy for consumers, students, and others to thread their way through the enforceable standards. Also, by mandating such behaviors as avoiding unfair discrimination and using appropriately intelligible language with their patients, students, and so on, the Ethics Code provides enforceable statements that closely reflect the overarching goals described by the General Principles.

The new content areas bring this code into closer conformity with the realities of psychological research, teaching, and practice of the 1990s. For example, forensic activities have long been part of the formal obligations of psychologists, but were never fully addressed in an ethics code before. This code puts psychologists on notice to recognize their obligations when either invited or required to testify.

This Ethics Code clearly addresses the limits of concurrent multiple roles that psychologists may develop with others. It also addresses the specific changes in informing potential research participants and clients about experiences they will have. By including the use of barter for psychological services and its inherent risks, the Ethics Code formally provides guidance in an area that has already been explored informally and with some liability by many psychologists for years. Advertising practices also underwent some changes, including loosening some of the restrictive practices in comparing one's own services and products with those of another. The changes in the standards involving research provide greater specificity and perhaps a greater measure of protection to research participants than before. And the changes in the rules governing the claiming of publication credit are more thoroughly explicated than before, providing clearer guidelines for coauthors. And finally, the changes in those standards pertaining to individuals in academic settings emphasize fair treatment of students as well as colleagues.

Learning and applying a new Ethics Code may make it easy to think of it, as any regulatory document, as written in stone, filled with what is perceived by their creators as immutable truths arrived at with the wisdom of Solomon and comprising commandments from above. That "above" can be the APA Council of Representatives or the policy-making body of another organization, a state legislature, the Congress of the United States, or a governmental or organizational entity empowered to derive the rules and regulations that implement the primary documents and have the force of law. Even as we know that the documents can be revised, their here-and-now demands for compliance add to the illusion of steadfastness of belief and unwavering values and attitudes.

In fact, however, regulatory documents are not written in stone. Rather, for psychology, as for other disciplines, they need to reflect our evolving science and profession. And they need to be responsive to the increasingly complex technology available and the ongoing changes in our culture that in turn change and shape our field. This is not to say that nothing stays the same. In the APA Ethical Principles for Psychologists and Code of Conduct, the aspirational ideas have been with us for many decades, reflecting as they do some basic values such as competence, integrity, responsibility, and respect for others. These aspirational elements are not likely to change. But the operationalized, enforceable standards that guide us as we go about our work as psychologists do change. They change as we learn more, for example, about the impact of cultural differences on testing and therapy or the problems implicit in delivery of service under some managed care contracts. They change as we understand more about problems of psychologists and patients living and working in rural areas. They change as we learn more. Often the changes involve the addition of standards to cover situations newly generated, such as those that present themselves when families are treated as the client. Sometimes the changes may involve modifications or deletions of standards, as in the FTC's Consent Agreement. But there will always be change, continual review and refinement, sometimes minor changes, and periodically changes that are major in scope. And should the Ethics Code fail to be of assistance to the profession and those we serve, it could even be completely replaced. However, it is important to note that although some of the current standards will surely change, over time, as long as they are part of the Ethics Code they must be interpreted as written and applied to current conduct and proceedings. They are, in fact, "cast in concrete" in that they are the "law"—unless and until they change.

Even as we write, we are aware that plans are being implemented to review the Ethics Code with an eye toward possible minor revision within the next 2–3 years, and a review will begin in 1995 to determine the method for the next major revision. We do not know when that revision will occur, but we do know that there will be one. For the Ethics Code is a living document that cannot possibly cover all issues to be confronted by psychologists and, like all laws and regulatory documents, this Ethics Code, too, will continue to evolve through adjudication and as laws change. Ultimately, it will be evaluated in the light of legal and societal values, of case law built on the interpretation of statutes, and the changing tenor of the times.

Appendix A

Ethical Principles of Psychologists and Code of Conduct

CONTENTS

Introduction

The American Psychological Association's (APA's) Ethical Principles of Psychologists and Code of Conduct (hereinafter referred to as the Ethics Code) consists of an Introduction, a Preamble, six General Principles (A–F), and specific Ethical Standards. The Introduction discusses the intent, organization, procedural considerations, and scope of application of the Ethics Code. The Preamble and General Principles are *aspirational* goals to guide psychologists toward the highest ideals of psychology. Although the Preamble and General Principles are not themselves enforceable rules, they should be considered by psychologists in arriving at an ethical course of action and may be considered by ethics bodies in interpreting the Ethical Standards. The Ethical Standards set forth *enforceable* rules for conduct as psychologists. Most of the Ethical Standards are written broadly, in order to apply to psychologists in varied roles, although the application of an Ethical Standard may vary depending on the context. The Ethical Standards are not exhaustive. The fact that a given conduct is not specifically addressed by the Ethics Code does not mean that it is necessarily either ethical or unethical.

Reprinted from *American Psychologist*, Vol. 47, pp. 1597–1611. Copyright 1992 by the American Psychological Association.

This version of the APA Ethics Code was adopted by the American Psychological Association's Council of Representatives during its meeting, August 13 and 16, 1992, and effective beginning December 1, 1992. Inquiries concerning the substance or interpretation of the APA Ethics Code should be addressed to the Director, Office of Ethics, American Psychological Association, 750 First Street, NE, Washington, DC 20002-4242.

This Code will be used to adjudicate complaints brought concerning alleged conduct occurring on or after the effective date. Complaints regarding conduct occurring prior to the effective date will be adjudicated on the basis of the version of the Code that was in effect at the time the conduct occurred, except that no provisions repealed in June 1989 will be enforced even if an earlier version contains the provision. The Ethics Code will undergo continuing review and study for future revisions; comments on the Code may be sent to the above address.

The APA has previously published its Ethical Standards as follows:

American Psychological Association. (1953). *Ethical standards of psychologists*. Washington, DC: Author.

American Psychological Association. (1958). Standards of ethical behavior for psychologists. *American Psychologist, 13*, 268–271.

American Psychological Association. (1963). Ethical standards of psychologists. *American Psychologist, 18*, 56–60.

American Psychological Association. (1968). Ethical standards of psychologists. *American Psychologist, 23*, 357–361.

American Psychological Association. (1977, March). Ethical standards of psychologists. *APA Monitor*, pp. 22–23.

American Psychological Association. (1979). *Ethical standards of psychologists*. Washington, DC: Author.

American Psychological Association. (1981). Ethical principles of psychologists. *American Psychologist, 36*, 633–638.

American Psychological Association. (1990). Ethical principles of psychologists (Amended June 2, 1989). *American Psychologist, 4*, 390–395.

Request copies of the APA's Ethical Principles of Psychologists and Code of Conduct from the APA Order Department, 750 First Street, NE, Washington, DC 20002-4242, or phone (202) 336-5510.

Membership in the APA commits members to adhere to the APA Ethics Code and to the rules and procedures used to implement it. Psychologists and students, whether or not they are APA members, should be aware that the Ethics Code may be applied to them by state psychology boards, courts, or other public bodies.

This Ethics Code applies only to psychologists' work-related activities, that is, activities that are part of the psychologists' scientific and professional functions or that are psychological in nature. It includes the clinical or counseling practice of psychology, research, teaching, supervision of trainees, development of assessment instruments, conducting assessments, educational counseling, organizational consulting, social intervention, administration, and other activities as well. These work-related activities can be distinguished from the purely private conduct of a psychologist, which ordinarily is not within the purview of the Ethics Code.

The Ethics Code is intended to provide standards of professional conduct that can be applied by the APA and by other bodies that choose to adopt them. Whether or not a psychologist has violated the Ethics Code does not by itself determine whether he or she is legally liable in a court action, whether a contract is enforceable, or whether other legal consequences occur. These results are based on legal rather than ethical rules. However, compliance with or violation of the Ethics Code may be admissible as evidence in some legal proceedings, depending on the circumstances.

In the process of making decisions regarding their professional behavior, psychologists must consider this Ethics Code, in addition to applicable laws and psychology board regulations. If the Ethics Code establishes a higher standard of conduct than is required by law, psychologists must meet the higher ethical standard. If the Ethics Code standard appears to conflict with the requirements of law, then psychologists make known their commitment to the Ethics Code and take steps to resolve the conflict in a responsible manner. If neither law nor the Ethics Code resolves an issue, psychologists should consider other professional materials[1] and the dictates of their own conscience, as well as seek consultation with others within the field when this is practical.

The procedures for filing, investigating, and resolving complaints of unethical conduct are described in the current Rules and Procedures of the APA

---

[1]Professional materials that are most helpful in this regard are guidelines and standards that have been adopted or endorsed by professional psychological organizations. Such guidelines and standards, whether adopted by the American Psychological Association (APA) or its Divisions, are not enforceable as such by this Ethics Code, but are of educative value to psychologists, courts, and professional bodies. Such materials include, but are not limited to, the APA's *General Guidelines for Providers of Psychological Services* (1987), *Specialty Guidelines for the Delivery of Services by Clinical Psychologists, Counseling Psychologists, Industrial/Organizational Psychologists, and School Psychologists* (1981), *Guidelines for Computer Based Tests and Interpretations* (1987), *Standards for Educational and Psychological Testing* (1985), *Ethical Principles in the Conduct of Research With Human Participants* (1982), *Guidelines for Ethical Conduct in the Care and Use of Animals* (1986), *Guidelines for Providers of Psychological Services to Ethnic, Linguistic, and Culturally Diverse Populations* (1990), and *Publication Manual of the American Psychological Association* (3rd ed., 1983). Materials not adopted by APA as a whole include the APA Division 41 (Forensic Psychology)/American Psychology–Law Society's *Specialty Guidelines for Forensic Psychologists* (1991).

Ethics Committee. The actions that APA may take for violations of the Ethics Code include actions such as reprimand, censure, termination of APA membership, and referral of the matter to other bodies. Complainants who seek remedies such as monetary damages in alleging ethical violations by a psychologist must resort to private negotiation, administrative bodies, or the courts. Actions that violate the Ethics Code may lead to the imposition of sanctions on a psychologist by bodies other than APA, including state psychological associations, other professional groups, psychology boards, other state or federal agencies, and payors for health services. In addition to actions for violation of the Ethics Code, the APA Bylaws provide that APA may take action against a member after his or her conviction of a felony, expulsion or suspension from an affiliated state psychological association, or suspension or loss of licensure.

Preamble

Psychologists work to develop a valid and reliable body of scientific knowledge based on research. They may apply that knowledge to human behavior in a variety of contexts. In doing so, they perform many roles, such as researcher, educator, diagnostician, therapist, supervisor, consultant, administrator, social interventionist, and expert witness. Their goal is to broaden knowledge of behavior and, where appropriate, to apply it pragmatically to improve the condition of both the individual and society. Psychologists respect the central importance of freedom of inquiry and expression in research, teaching, and publication. They also strive to help the public in developing informed judgments and choices concerning human behavior. This Ethics Code provides a common set of values upon which psychologists build their professional and scientific work.

This Code is intended to provide both the general principles and the decision rules to cover most situations encountered by psychologists. It has as its primary goal the welfare and protection of the individuals and groups with whom psychologists work. It is the individual responsibility of each psychologist to aspire to the highest possible standards of conduct. Psychologists respect and protect human and civil rights, and do not knowingly participate in or condone unfair discriminatory practices.

The development of a dynamic set of ethical standards for a psychologist's work-related conduct requires a personal commitment to a lifelong effort to act ethically; to encourage ethical behavior by students, supervisees, employees, and colleagues, as appropriate; and to consult with others, as needed, concerning ethical problems. Each psychologist supplements, but does not violate, the Ethics Code's values and rules on the basis of guidance drawn from personal values, culture, and experience.

General Principles

Principle A: Competence

Psychologists strive to maintain high standards of competence in their work. They recognize the boundaries of their particular competencies and the limitations of their expertise. They provide only those services and use only those techniques for which they are qualified by education, training, or experience. Psychologists are cognizant of the fact that the competencies required in serving, teaching, and/or studying groups of people vary with the distinctive characteristics of those groups. In those areas in which recognized professional standards do not yet exist, psychologists exercise careful judgment and take appropriate precautions to protect the welfare of those with whom they work. They maintain knowledge of relevant scientific and professional information related to the services they render, and they recognize the need for ongoing education. Psychologists make appropriate use of scientific, professional, technical, and administrative resources.

Principle B: Integrity

Psychologists seek to promote integrity in the science, teaching, and practice of psychology. In these activities psychologists are honest, fair, and respectful of others. In describing or reporting their qualifications, services, products, fees, research, or teaching, they do not make statements that are false, misleading, or deceptive. Psychologists strive to be aware of their own belief systems, values, needs, and limitations and the effect of these on their work. To the extent feasible, they attempt to clarify for relevant parties the roles they are performing and to function appropriately in accordance with those roles. Psychologists avoid improper and potentially harmful dual relationships.

Principle C: Professional and Scientific Responsibility

Psychologists uphold professional standards of conduct, clarify their professional roles and obligations, accept appropriate responsibility for their behavior, and adapt their methods to the needs of different populations. Psychologists consult with, refer to, or cooperate with other professionals and institutions to the extent needed to serve the best interests of their patients, clients, or other recipients of their services. Psychologists' moral standards and conduct are personal matters to the same degree as is true for any other person, except as psychologists' conduct may compromise their professional responsibilities or reduce the public's trust in psychology and psychologists. Psychologists are concerned about the ethical compliance of their colleagues' scientific and professional conduct. When appropriate, they consult with colleagues in order to prevent or avoid unethical conduct.

Principle D: Respect for People's Rights and Dignity

Psychologists accord appropriate respect to the fundamental rights, dignity, and worth of all people. They respect the rights of individuals to privacy, confidentiality, self-determination, and autonomy, mindful that legal and other obligations may lead to inconsistency and conflict with the exercise of these rights. Psychologists are aware of cultural, individual, and role differences, including those due to age, gender, race, ethnicity, national origin, religion, sexual orientation, disability, language, and socioeconomic status. Psychologists try to eliminate the effect on their work of biases based on those factors, and they do not knowingly participate in or condone unfair discriminatory practices.

Principle E: Concern for Others' Welfare

Psychologists seek to contribute to the welfare of those with whom they interact professionally. In their professional actions, psychologists weigh the welfare and rights of their patients or clients, students, supervisees, human research participants, and other affected persons, and the welfare of animal subjects of research. When conflicts occur among psychologists' obligations or concerns, they attempt to resolve these conflicts and to perform their roles in a responsible fashion that avoids or minimizes harm. Psychologists are sensitive to real and ascribed differences in power between themselves and others, and they do not exploit or mislead other people during or after professional relationships.

Principle F: Social Responsibility

Psychologists are aware of their professional and scientific responsibilities to the community and the society in which they work and live. They apply and make public their knowledge of psychology in order to contribute to human welfare. Psychologists are concerned about and work to mitigate the causes of human suffering. When undertaking research, they strive to advance human welfare and the science of psychology. Psychologists try to avoid misuse of their work. Psychologists comply with the law and encourage the development of law and social policy that serve the interests of their patients and clients and the public. They are encouraged to contribute a portion of their professional time for little or no personal advantage.

Ethical Standards

1. General Standards

These General Standards are potentially applicable to the professional and scientific activities of all psychologists.

1.01 Applicability of the Ethics Code

The activity of a psychologist subject to the Ethics Code may be reviewed under these Ethical Standards only if the activity is part of his or her work-related functions or the activity is psychological in nature. Personal activities having no connection to or effect on psychological roles are not subject to the Ethics Code.

1.02 Relationship of Ethics and Law

If psychologists' ethical responsibilities conflict with law, psychologists make known their commitment to the Ethics Code and take steps to resolve the conflict in a responsible manner.

1.03 Professional and Scientific Relationship

Psychologists provide diagnostic, therapeutic, teaching, research, supervisory, consultative, or other psychological services only in the context of a defined professional or scientific relationship or role. (See also Standards 2.01, Evaluation, Diagnosis, and Interventions in Professional Context, and 7.02, Forensic Assessments.)

1.04 Boundaries of Competence

(a) Psychologists provide services, teach, and conduct research only within the boundaries of their competence, based on their education, training, supervised experience, or appropriate professional experience.

(b) Psychologists provide services, teach, or conduct research in new areas or involving new techniques only after first undertaking appropriate study, training, supervision, and/or consultation from persons who are competent in those areas or techniques.

(c) In those emerging areas in which generally recognized standards for preparatory training do not yet exist, psychologists nevertheless take reasonable steps to ensure the competence of their work and to protect patients, clients, students, research participants, and others from harm.

1.05 Maintaining Expertise

Psychologists who engage in assessment, therapy, teaching, research, organizational consulting, or other professional activities maintain a reasonable level of awareness of current scientific and professional information in their fields of activity, and undertake ongoing efforts to maintain competence in the skills they use.

1.06 Basis for Scientific and Professional Judgments

Psychologists rely on scientifically and professionally derived knowledge when making scientific or professional judgments or when engaging in scholarly or professional endeavors.

1.07 Describing the Nature and Results of Psychological Services

(a) When psychologists provide assessment, evaluation, treatment, counseling, supervision, teaching, consultation, research, or other psychological services to an individual, a group, or an organization, they provide, using language that is reasonably understandable to the recipient of those services, appropriate information beforehand about the nature of such services and appropriate information later about results and consultations. (See also Standard 2.09, Explaining Assessment Results.)

(b) If psychologists will be precluded by law or by organizational roles from providing such information to particular individuals or groups, they so inform those individuals or groups at the outset of the service.

1.08 Human Differences

Where differences of age, gender, race, ethnicity, national origin, religion, sexual orientation, disability, language, or socioeconomic status significantly affect psychologists' work concerning particular individuals or groups, psychologists obtain the training, experience, consultation, or supervision necessary to ensure the competence of their services, or they make appropriate referrals.

1.09 Respecting Others

In their work-related activities, psychologists respect the rights of others to hold values, attitudes, and opinions that differ from their own.

1.10 Nondiscrimination

In their work-related activities, psychologists do not engage in unfair discrimination based on age, gender, race, ethnicity, national origin, religion, sexual orientation, disability, socioeconomic status, or any basis proscribed by law.

1.11 Sexual Harassment

(a) Psychologists do not engage in sexual harassment. Sexual harassment is sexual solicitation, physical advances, or verbal or nonverbal conduct that is sexual in nature, that occurs in connection with the psychologist's activities or roles as a psychologist, and that either: (1) is unwelcome, is offensive, or creates a hostile workplace environment, and the psychologist knows or is told this; or (2) is sufficiently severe or intense to be abusive to a reasonable person in the context. Sexual harassment can consist of a single intense or severe act or of multiple persistent or pervasive acts.

(b) Psychologists accord sexual-harassment complaints and respondents dignity and respect. Psychologists do not participate in denying a person academic admittance or advancement, employment, tenure, or promotion, based solely upon their having made, or their being the subject of, sexual-harassment charges. This does not preclude taking action based upon the outcome of such proceedings or consideration of other appropriate information.

1.12 Other Harassment

Psychologists do not knowingly engage in behavior that is harassing or demeaning to persons with whom they interact in their work based on factors such as those persons' age, gender, race, ethnicity, national origin, religion, sexual orientation, disability, language, or socioeconomic status.

1.13 Personal Problems and Conflicts

(a) Psychologists recognize that their personal problems and conflicts may interfere with their effectiveness. Accordingly, they refrain from undertaking an activity when they know or should know that their personal problems are likely to lead to harm to a patient, client, colleague, student, research participant, or other person to whom they may owe a professional or scientific obligation.

(b) In addition, psychologists have an obligation to be alert to signs of, and to obtain assistance for, their personal problems at an early stage, in order to prevent significantly impaired performance.

(c) When psychologists become aware of personal problems that may interfere with their performing work-related duties adequately, they take appropriate measures, such as obtaining professional consultation or assistance, and determine whether they should limit, suspend, or terminate their work-related duties.

1.14 Avoiding Harm

Psychologists take reasonable steps to avoid harming their patients or clients, research participants, students, and others with whom they work, and to minimize harm where it is foreseeable and unavoidable.

1.15 Misuse of Psychologists' Influence

Because psychologists' scientific and professional judgments and actions may affect the lives of others, they are alert to and guard against personal, financial, social, organizational, or political factors that might lead to misuse of their influence.

1.16 Misuse of Psychologists' Work

(a) Psychologists do not participate in activities in which it appears likely that their skills or data will be misused by others, unless corrective mechanisms are available. (See also Standard 7.04, Truthfulness and Candor.)

(b) If psychologists learn of misuse or misrepresentation of their work, they take reasonable steps to correct or minimize the misuse or misrepresentation.

1.17 Multiple Relationships

(a) In many communities and situations, it may not be feasible or reasonable for psychologists to avoid social or other nonprofessional contacts with persons such as patients, clients, students, supervisees, or research participants. Psychologists must always be sensitive to the potential harmful effects of other contacts on their work and on those persons with whom they deal. A psychologist refrains from entering into or promising another personal, scientific, professional, financial, or other relationship with such persons if it appears likely that such a relationship reasonably might impair the psychologist's objectivity or otherwise interfere with the psychologist's effectively performing his or her function as a psychologist, or might harm or exploit the other party.

(b) Likewise, whenever feasible, a psychologist refrains from taking on professional or scientific obligations when preexisting relationships would create a risk of such harm.

(c) If a psychologist finds that, due to unforeseen factors, a potentially harmful multiple relationship has arisen, the psychologist attempts to resolve it with due regard for the best interests of the affected person and maximal compliance with the Ethics Code.

1.18 Barter (With Patients or Clients)

Psychologists ordinarily refrain from accepting goods, services, or other nonmonetary remuneration from patients or clients in return for psychological services because such arrangements create inherent potential for conflicts, exploitation, and distortion of the professional relationship. A psychologist may participate in bartering only if (1) it is not clinically contraindicated, and (2) the relationship is not exploitative. (See also Standards 1.17, Multiple Relationships, and 1.25, Fees and Financial Arrangements.)

1.19 Exploitative Relationships

(a) Psychologists do not exploit persons over whom they have supervisory, evaluative, or other authority such as students, supervisees, employees, research participants, and clients or patients. (See also Standards 4.05–4.07 regarding sexual involvement with clients or patients.)

(b) Psychologists do not engage in sexual relationships with students or supervisees in training over whom the psychologist has evaluative or direct authority, because such relationships are so likely to impair judgment or be exploitative.

1.20 Consultations and Referrals

(a) Psychologists arrange for appropriate consultations and referrals based principally on the best interests of their patients or clients, with appropriate consent, and subject to other relevant considerations, including applicable law and contractual obligations. (See also Standards 5.01, Discussing the Limits of Confidentiality, and 5.06, Consultations.)

(b) When indicated and professionally appropriate, psychologists cooperate with other professionals in order to serve their patients or clients effectively and appropriately.

(c) Psychologists' referral practices are consistent with law.

1.21 Third-Party Requests for Services

(a) When a psychologist agrees to provide services to a person or entity at the request of a third party, the psychologist clarifies to the extent feasible, at the outset of the service, the nature of the relationship with each party. This clarification includes the role of the psychologist (such as therapist, organizational consultant, diagnostician, or expert witness), the probable uses of the services provided or the information obtained, and the fact that there may be limits to confidentiality.

(b) If there is a foreseeable risk of the psychologist's being called upon to perform conflicting roles because of the involvement of a third party, the psychologist clarifies the nature and direction of his or her responsibilities, keeps all parties appropriately informed as matters develop, and resolves the situation in accordance with this Ethics Code.

1.22 Delegation to and Supervision of Subordinates

(a) Psychologists delegate to their employees, supervisees, and research assistants only those responsibilities that such persons can reasonably be expected to perform competently, on the basis of their education, training, or experience, either independently or with the level of supervision being provided.

(b) Psychologists provide proper training and supervision to their employees or supervisees and take reasonable steps to see that such persons perform services responsibly, competently, and ethically.

(c) If institutional policies, procedures, or practices prevent fulfillment of this obligation, psychologists attempt to modify their role or to correct the situation to the extent feasible.

1.23 Documentation of Professional and Scientific Work

(a) Psychologists appropriately document their professional and scientific work in order to facilitate provision of services later by them or by other professionals, to ensure accountability, and to meet other requirements of institutions or the law.

(b) When psychologists have reason to believe that records of their professional services will be used in legal proceedings involving recipients of or participants in their work, they have a responsibility to create and maintain documentation in the kind of detail and quality that would be consistent with reasonable scrutiny in an adjudicative forum. (See also Standard 7.01, Professionalism, under Forensic Activities.)

1.24 Records and Data

Psychologists create, maintain, disseminate, store, retain, and dispose of records and data relating to their research, practice, and other work in accordance with law and in a manner that permits compliance with the requirements of this Ethics Code. (See also Standard 5.04, Maintenance of Records.)

1.25 Fees and Financial Arrangements

(a) As early as is feasible in a professional or scientific relationship, the psychologist and the patient, client, or other appropriate recipient of psychological services reach an agreement specifying the compensation and the billing arrangements.

(b) Psychologists do not exploit recipients of services or payors with respect to fees.

(c) Psychologists' fee practices are consistent with law.

(d) Psychologists do not misrepresent their fees.

(e) If limitations to services can be anticipated because of limitations in financing, this is discussed with the patient, client, or other appropriate recipient of services as early as is feasible. (See also Standard 4.08, Interruption of Services.)

(f) If the patient, client, or other recipient of services does not pay for services as agreed, and if the psychologist wishes to use collection agencies or legal measures to collect the fees, the psychologist first informs the person that such measures will be taken and provides that person an opportunity to make prompt payment. (See also Standard 5.11, Withholding Records for Nonpayment.)

1.26 Accuracy in Reports to Payors and Funding Sources

In their reports to payors for services or sources of research funding, psychologists accurately state the nature of the research or service provided, the fees or charges, and where applicable, the identity of the provider, the findings, and the diagnosis. (See also Standard 5.05, Disclosures.)

1.27 Referrals and Fees

When a psychologist pays, receives payment from, or divides fees with another professional other than in an employer–employee relationship, the payment to each is based on the services (clinical, consultative, administrative, or other) provided and is not based on the referral itself.

2. Evaluation, Assessment, or Intervention

2.01 Evaluation, Diagnosis, and Interventions in Professional Context

(a) Psychologists perform evaluations, diagnosis services, or interventions only within the context of a defined professional relationship. (See also Standard 1.03, Professional and Scientific Relationship.)

(b) Psychologists' assessments, recommendations, reports, and psychological diagnostic or evaluative statements are based on information and techniques (including personal interviews of the individual when appropriate) sufficient to provide appropriate substantiation for their findings. (See also Standard 7.02, Forensic Assessments.)

2.02 Competence and Appropriate Use of Assessments and Interventions

(a) Psychologists who develop, administer, score, interpret, or use psychological assessment techniques, interviews, tests, or instruments do so in a manner and for purposes that are appropriate in light of the research on or evidence of the usefulness and proper application of the techniques.

(b) Psychologists refrain from misuse of assessment techniques, interventions, results, and interpretations and take reasonable steps to prevent others from misusing the information these techniques provide. This includes refraining from releasing raw test results or raw data to persons, other than to patients or clients as appropriate, who are not qualified to use such information. (See also Standards 1.02, Relationship of Ethics and Law, and 1.04, Boundaries of Competence.)

2.03 Test Construction

Psychologists who develop and conduct research with tests and other assessment techniques use specific procedures and current professional knowledge for test design, standardization, validation, reduction or elimination of bias, and recommendations for use.

2.04 Use of Assessment in General and With Special Populations

(a) Psychologists who perform interventions or administer, score, interpret, or use assessment techniques are familiar with the reliability, validation, and related standardization or outcome studies of, and proper applications and uses of, the techniques they use.

(b) Psychologists recognize limits to the certainty with which diagnoses, judgments, or predictions can be made about individuals.

(c) Psychologists attempt to identify situations in which particular interventions or assessment techniques or norms may not be applicable or may require adjustment in administration or interpretation because of factors such as individuals' gender, age, race, ethnicity, national origin, religion, sexual orientation, disability, language, or socioeconomic status.

2.05 Interpreting Assessment Results

When interpreting assessment results, including automated interpretations, psychologists take into account the various test factors and characteristics of the person being assessed that might affect psychologists' judgments or reduce the accuracy of their interpretations. They indicate any significant reservations they have about the accuracy or limitations of their interpretations.

2.06 Unqualified Persons

Psychologists do not promote the use of psychological assessment techniques by unqualified persons. (See also Standard 1.22, Delegation to and Supervision of Subordinates.)

2.07 Obsolete Tests and Outdated Test Results

(a) Psychologists do not base their assessment or intervention decisions or recommendations on data or test results that are outdated for the current purpose.

(b) Similarly, psychologists do not base such decisions or recommendations on tests and measures that are obsolete and not useful for the current purpose.

2.08 Test Scoring and Interpretation Services

(a) Psychologists who offer assessment or scoring procedures to other professionals accurately describe the purpose, norms, validity, reliability, and applications of the procedures and any special qualifications applicable to their use.

(b) Psychologists select scoring and interpretation services (including automated services) on the basis of evidence of the validity of the program and procedures as well as on other appropriate considerations.

(c) Psychologists retain appropriate responsibility for the appropriate application, interpretation, and use of assessment instruments, whether they score and interpret such tests themselves or use automated or other services.

2.09 Explaining Assessment Results

Unless the nature of the relationship is clearly explained to the person being assessed in advance and precludes provision of an explanation of results (such as in some organizational consulting, preemployment or security screenings, and forensic evaluations), psychologists ensure that an explanation of the results is provided using language that is reasonably understandable to the person assessed or to another legally authorized person on behalf of the client. Regardless of whether the scoring and interpretation are done by the psychologist, by assistants, or by automated or other outside services, psychologists take reasonable steps to ensure that appropriate explanations of results are given.

2.10 Maintaining Test Security

Psychologists make reasonable efforts to maintain the integrity and security of tests and other assessment techniques consistent with law, contractual obligations, and in a manner that permits compliance with the requirements of this Ethics Code. (See also Standard 1.02, Relationship of Ethics and Law.)

3. *Advertising and Other Public Statements*

3.01 Definition of Public Statements

Psychologists comply with this Ethics Code in public statements relating to their professional services, products, or publications or to the field of psychology. Public statements include but are not limited to paid or unpaid advertising, brochures, printed matter, directory listings, personal resumes or curricula vitae, interviews or comments for use in media, statements in legal proceedings, lectures and public oral presentations, and published materials.

3.02 Statements by Others

(a) Psychologists who engage others to create or place public statements that promote their professional practice, products, or activities retain professional responsibility for such statements.

(b) In addition, psychologists make reasonable efforts to prevent others whom they do not control (such as employers, publishers, sponsors, organizational clients, and representatives of the print or broadcast media) from making deceptive statements concerning psychologists' practice or professional or scientific activities.

(c) If psychologists learn of deceptive statements about their work made by others, psychologists make reasonable efforts to correct such statements.

(d) Psychologists do not compensate employees of press, radio, television, or other communication media in return for publicity in a news item.

(e) A paid advertisement relating to the psychologist's activities must be identified as such, unless it is already apparent from the context.

3.03 Avoidance of False or Deceptive Statements

(a) Psychologists do not make public statements that are false, deceptive, misleading, or fraudulent, either because of what they state, convey, or suggest or because of what they omit, concerning their research, practice, or other work activities or those of persons or organizations with which they are affiliated. As examples (and not in limitation) of this standard, psychologists do not make false or deceptive statements concerning (1) their training, experience, or competence; (2) their academic degrees; (3) their credentials; (4) their institutional or association affiliations; (5) their services; (6) the scientific or clinical basis for, or results or degree of success of, their services; (7) their fees; or (8) their publications or research findings. (See also Standards 6.15, Deception in Research, and 6.18, Providing Participants With Information About the Study.)

(b) Psychologists claim as credentials for their psychological work, only degrees that (1) were earned from a regionally accredited educational institution or (2) were the basis for psychology licensure by the state in which they practice.

3.04 Media Presentations

When psychologists provide advice or comment by means of public lectures, demonstrations, radio or television programs, prerecorded tapes, printed articles, mailed material, or other media, they take reasonable precautions to ensure that (1) the statements are based on appropriate psychological literature and practice, (2) the statements are otherwise consistent with this Ethics Code, and (3) the recipients of the information are not encouraged to infer that a relationship has been established with them personally.

3.05 Testimonials

Psychologists do not solicit testimonials from current psychotherapy clients or patients or other persons who because of their particular circumstances are vulnerable to undue influence.

3.06 In-Person Solicitation

Psychologists do not engage, directly or through agents, in uninvited in-person solicitation of business from actual or potential psychotherapy patients or clients or other persons who because of their particular circumstances are vulnerable to undue influence. However, this does not preclude attempting to implement appropriate collateral contacts with significant others for the purpose of benefiting an already engaged therapy patient.

4. _Therapy_

4.01 Structuring the Relationship

(a) Psychologists discuss with clients or patients as early as is feasible in the therapeutic relationship appropriate issues, such as the nature and anticipated course of therapy, fees, and confidentiality. (See also Standards 1.25, Fees and Financial Arrangements, and 5.01, Discussing the Limits of Confidentiality.)

(b) When the psychologist's work with clients or patients will be supervised, the above discussion includes that fact, and the name of the supervisor, when the supervisor has legal responsibility for the case.

(c) When the therapist is a student intern, the client or patient is informed of that fact.

(d) Psychologists make reasonable efforts to answer patients' questions and to avoid apparent misunderstandings about therapy. Whenever possible, psychologists provide oral and/or written information, using language that is reasonably understandable to the patient or client.

4.02 Informed Consent to Therapy

(a) Psychologists obtain appropriate informed consent to therapy or related procedures, using language that is reasonably understandable to participants. The content of informed consent will vary depending on many circumstances; however, informed consent generally implies that the person (1) has the capacity to consent, (2) has been informed of significant information concerning the procedure, (3) has freely and without undue influence expressed consent, and (4) consent has been appropriately documented.

(b) When persons are legally incapable of giving informed consent, psychologists obtain informed permission from a legally authorized person, if such substitute consent is permitted by law.

(c) In addition, psychologists (1) inform those persons who are legally incapable of giving informed consent about the proposed interventions in a manner commensurate with the persons' psychological capacities, (2) seek their assent to those interventions, and (3) consider such persons' preferences and best interests.

4.03 Couple and Family Relationships

(a) When a psychologist agrees to provide services to several persons who have a relationship (such as husband and wife or parents and children), the psychologist attempts to clarify at the outset (1) which of the individuals are patients or clients and (2) the relationship the psychologist will have with each person. This clarification includes the role of the psychologist and the probable uses of the services provided or the information obtained. (See also Standard 5.01, Discussing the Limits of Confidentiality.)

(b) As soon as it becomes apparent that the psychologist may be called on to perform potentially conflicting roles (such as marital counselor to husband and wife, and then witness for one party in a divorce proceeding), the psychologist attempts to clarify and adjust, or withdraw from, roles appropriately. (See also Standard 7.03, Clarification of Role, under Forensic Activities.)

4.04 Providing Mental Health Services to Those Served by Others

In deciding whether to offer or provide services to those already receiving mental health services elsewhere, psychologists carefully consider the treatment issues and the potential patient's or client's welfare. The psychologist discusses these issues with the patient or client, or another legally authorized person on behalf of the client, in order to minimize the risk of confusion and conflict, consults with the other service providers when appropriate, and proceeds with caution and sensitivity to the therapeutic issues.

4.05 Sexual Intimacies With Current Patients or Clients

Psychologists do not engage in sexual intimacies with current patients or clients.

4.06 Therapy With Former Sexual Partners

Psychologists do not accept as therapy patients or clients persons with whom they have engaged in sexual intimacies.

4.07 Sexual Intimacies With Former Therapy Patients

(a) Psychologists do not engage in sexual intimacies with a former therapy patient or client for at least two years after cessation or termination of professional services.

(b) Because sexual intimacies with a former therapy patient or client are so frequently harmful to the patient or client, and because such intimacies undermine public confidence in the psychology profession and thereby deter the public's use of needed services, psychologists do not engage in sexual intimacies with former therapy patients and clients even after a two-year interval except in the most unusual circumstances. The psychologist who engages in such activity after the two years following cessation or termination of treatment bears the burden of demonstrating that there has been no exploitation, in light of all relevant factors, including (1) the amount of time that has passed since therapy terminated, (2) the nature and duration of the therapy, (3) the circumstances of termination, (4) the patient's or client's personal history, (5) the patient's or client's current mental status, (6) the likelihood of adverse impact on the patient or client and others, and (7) any statements or actions made by the therapist during the course of therapy suggesting or inviting the possibility of a posttermination sexual or romantic relationship with the patient or client. (See also Standard 1.17, Multiple Relationships.)

4.08 Interruption of Services

(a) Psychologists make reasonable efforts to plan for facilitating care in the event that psychological services are interrupted by factors such as the psychologist's illness, death, unavailability, or relocation or by the client's relocation or financial limitations. (See also Standard 5.09, Preserving Records and Data.)

(b) When entering into employment or contractual relationships, psychologists provide for orderly and appropriate resolution of responsibility for patient or client care in the event that the employment or contractual relationship ends, with paramount consideration given to the welfare of the patient or client.

4.09 Terminating the Professional Relationship

(a) Psychologists do not abandon patients or clients. (See also Standard 1.25e, under Fees and Financial Arrangements.)

(b) Psychologists terminate a professional relationship when it becomes reasonably clear that the patient or client no longer needs the service, is not benefiting, or is being harmed by continued service.

(c) Prior to termination for whatever reason, except where precluded by the patient's or client's conduct, the psychologist discusses the patient's or client's views and needs, provides appropriate pretermination counseling, suggests alternative service providers as appropriate, and takes other reasonable steps to facilitate transfer of responsibility to another provider if the patient or client needs one immediately.

5. *Privacy and Confidentiality*

These Standards are potentially applicable to the professional and scientific activities of all psychologists.

5.01 Discussing the Limits of Confidentiality

(a) Psychologists discuss with persons and organizations with whom they establish a scientific, or professional relationship (including, to the extent feasible, minors and their legal representatives) (1) the relevant limitations on confidentiality, including limitations where applicable in group, marital, and family therapy or in organizational consulting, and (2) the foreseeable uses of the information generated through their services.

(b) Unless it is not feasible or is contraindicated, the discussion of confidentiality occurs at the outset of the relationship and thereafter as new circumstances may warrant.

(c) Permission for electronic recording of interviews is secured from clients and patients.

5.02 Maintaining Confidentiality

Psychologists have a primary obligation and take reasonable precautions to respect the confidentiality rights of those with whom they work or consult, recognizing that confidentiality may be established by law, institutional rules, or professional or scientific relationships. (See also Standard 6.26, Professional Reviewers.)

5.03 Minimizing Intrusions on Privacy

(a) In order to minimize intrusions on privacy, psychologists include in written and oral reports, consultations, and the like, only information germane to the purpose for which the communication is made.

(b) Psychologists discuss confidential information obtained in clinical or consulting relationships, or evaluative data concerning patients, individual or organizational clients, students, research participants, supervisees, and employees, only for appropriate scientific or professional purposes and only with persons clearly concerned with such matters.

5.04 Maintenance of Records

Psychologists maintain appropriate confidentiality in creating, storing, accessing, transferring, and disposing of records under their control, whether these are written, automated, or in any other medium. Psychologists maintain and dispose of records in accordance with law and in a manner that permits compliance with the requirements of this Ethics Code.

5.05 Disclosures

(a) Psychologists disclose confidential information without the consent of the individual only as mandated by law, or where permitted by law for a valid purpose, such as (1) to provide needed professional services to the patient or the individual or organizational client, (2) to obtain appropriate professional consultations, (3) to protect the patient or client or others from harm, or (4) to obtain payment for services, in which instance disclosure is limited to the minimum that is necessary to achieve the purpose.

(b) Psychologists also may disclose confidential information with the appropriate consent of the patient or the individual or organizational client (or of another legally authorized person on behalf of the patient or client), unless prohibited by law.

5.06 Consultations

When consulting with colleagues, (1) psychologists do not share confidential information that reasonably could lead to the identification of a patient, client, research participant, or other person or organization with whom they have a confidential relationship unless they have obtained the prior consent of the person or organization or the disclosure cannot be avoided, and (2) they share information only to the extent necessary to achieve the purposes of the consultation. (See also Standard 5.02, Maintaining Confidentiality.)

5.07 Confidential Information in Databases

(a) If confidential information concerning recipients of psychological services is to be entered into databases or systems of records available to persons whose access has not been consented to by the recipient, then psychologists use coding or other techniques to avoid the inclusion of personal identifiers.

(b) If a research protocol approved by an institutional review board or similar body requires the inclusion of personal identifiers, such identifiers are deleted before the information is made accessible to persons other than those of whom the subject was advised.

(c) If such deletion is not feasible, then before psychologists transfer such data to others or review such data collected by others, they take reasonable steps to determine that appropriate consent of personally identifiable individuals has been obtained.

5.08 Use of Confidential Information for Didactic or Other Purposes

(a) Psychologists do not disclose in their writings, lectures, or other public media, confidential, personally identifiable information concerning their patients, individual or organizational clients, students, research participants, or other recipients of their services that they obtained during the course of their work, unless the person or organization has consented in writing or unless there is other ethical or legal authorization for doing so.

(b) Ordinarily, in such scientific and professional presentations, psychologists disguise confidential information concerning such persons or organizations so that they are not individually identifiable to others and so that discussions do not cause harm to subjects who might identify themselves.

5.09 Preserving Records and Data

A psychologist makes plans in advance so that confidentiality of records and data is protected in the event of the psychologist's death, incapacity, or withdrawal from the position or practice.

5.10 Ownership of Records and Data

Recognizing that ownership of records and data is governed by legal principles, psychologists take reasonable and lawful steps so that records and data remain available to the extent needed to serve the best interests of patients, individual or organizational clients, research participants, or appropriate others.

5.11 Withholding Records for Nonpayment

Psychologists may not withhold records under their control that are requested and imminently needed for a patient's or client's treatment solely because payment has not been received, except as otherwise provided by law.

6. Teaching, Training Supervision, Research, and Publishing

6.01 Design of Education and Training Programs

Psychologists who are responsible for education and training programs seek to ensure that the programs are competently designed, provide the proper experiences, and meet the requirements for licensure, certification, or other goals for which claims are made by the program.

6.02 Descriptions of Education and Training Programs

(a) Psychologists responsible for education and training programs seek to ensure that there is a current and accurate description of the program content, training goals and objectives, and requirements that must be met for satisfactory completion of the program. This information must be made readily available to all interested parties.

(b) Psychologists seek to ensure that statements concerning their course outlines are accurate and not misleading, particularly regarding the subject matter to be covered, bases for evaluating progress, and the nature of course experiences. (See also Standard 3.03, Avoidance of False or Deceptive Statements.)

(c) To the degree to which they exercise control, psychologists responsible for announcements, catalogs, brochures, or advertisements describing workshops, seminars, or other non-degree-granting educational programs ensure that they accurately describe the audience for which the program is intended, the educational objectives, the presenters, and the fees involved.

6.03 Accuracy and Objectivity in Teaching

(a) When engaged in teaching or training, psychologists present psychological information accurately and with a reasonable degree of objectivity.

(b) When engaged in teaching or training, psychologists recognize the power they hold over students or supervisees and therefore make reasonable efforts to avoid engaging in conduct that is personally demeaning to students or supervisees. (See also Standards 1.09, Respecting Others, and 1.12, Other Harassment.)

6.04 Limitation on Teaching

Psychologists do not teach the use of techniques or procedures that require specialized training, licensure, or expertise, including but not limited to hypnosis, biofeedback, and projective techniques, to individuals who lack the prerequisite training, legal scope of practice, or expertise.

6.05 Assessing Student and Supervisee Performance

(a) In academic and supervisory relationships, psychologists establish an appropriate process for providing feedback to students and supervisees.

(b) Psychologists evaluate students and supervisees on the basis of their actual performance on relevant and established program requirements.

6.06 Planning Research

(a) Psychologists design, conduct, and report research in accordance with recognized standards of scientific competence and ethical research.

(b) Psychologists plan their research so as to minimize the possibility that results will be misleading.

(c) In planning research, psychologists consider its ethical acceptability under the Ethics Code. If an ethical issue is unclear, psychologists seek to resolve the issue through consultation with institutional review boards, animal care and use committees, peer consultations, or other proper mechanisms.

(d) Psychologists take responsible steps to implement appropriate protections for the rights and welfare of human participants, other persons affected by the research, and the welfare of animal subjects.

6.07 Responsibility

(a) Psychologists conduct research competently and with due concern for the dignity and welfare of the participants.

(b) Psychologists are responsible for the ethical conduct of research conducted by them or by others under their supervision or control.

(c) Researchers and assistants are permitted to perform only those tasks for which they are appropriately trained and prepared.

(d) As part of the process of development and implementation of research projects, psychologists consult those with expertise concerning any special population under investigation or most likely to be affected.

6.08 Compliance With Law and Standards

Psychologists plan and conduct research in a manner consistent with federal and state law and regulations, as well as professional standards governing the conduct of research, and particularly those standards governing research with human participants and animal subjects.

6.09 Institutional Approval

Psychologists obtain from host institutions or organizations appropriate approval prior to conducting research, and they provide accurate information about their research proposals. They conduct the research in accordance with the approved research protocol.

6.10 Research Responsibilities

Prior to conducting research (except research involving only anonymous surveys, naturalistic observations, or similar research), psychologists enter into an agreement with participants that clarifies the nature of the research and the responsibilities of each party.

6.11 Informed Consent to Research

(a) Psychologists use language that is reasonably understandable to research participants in obtaining their appropriate informed consent (except as provided in Standard 6.12, Dispensing With Informed Consent). Such informed consent is appropriately documented.

(b) Using language that is reasonably understandable to participants, psychologists inform participants of the nature of the research; they inform participants that they are free to participate or to decline to participate or to withdraw from the research; they explain the foreseeable consequences of declining or withdrawing; they inform participants of significant factors that may be expected to influence their willingness to participate (such as risks, discomfort, adverse effects, or limitations on confidentiality, except as provided in Standard 6.15, Deception in Research); and they explain other aspects about which the prospective participants inquire.

(c) When psychologists conduct research with individuals such as students or subordinates, psychologists take special care to protect the prospective participants from adverse consequences of declining or withdrawing from participation.

(d) When research participation is a course requirement or opportunity for extra credit, the prospective participant is given the choice of equitable alternative activities.

(e) For persons who are legally incapable of giving informed consent, psychologists nevertheless (1) provide an appropriate explanation, (2) obtain the participant's assent, and (3) obtain appropriate permission from a legally authorized person, if such substitute consent is permitted by law.

6.12 Dispensing With Informed Consent

Before determining that planned research (such as research involving only anonymous questionnaires, naturalistic observations, or certain kinds of archival research) does not require the informed consent of research participants, psychologists consider applicable regulations and institutional review board requirements, and they consult with colleagues as appropriate.

6.13 Informed Consent in Research Filming or Recording

Psychologists obtain informed consent from research participants prior to filming or recording them in any form, unless the research involves simply naturalistic observations in public places and it is not anticipated that the recording will be used in a manner that could cause personal identification or harm.

6.14 Offering Inducement for Research Participants

(a) In offering professional services as an inducement to obtain research participants, psychologists make clear the nature of the services, as well as the risks, obligations, and limitations. (See also Standard 1.18 Barter [With Patients or Clients].)

(b) Psychologists do not offer excessive or inappropriate financial or other inducements to obtain research participants, particularly when it might tend to coerce participation.

6.15 Deception in Research

(a) Psychologists do not conduct a study involving deception unless they have determined that the use of deceptive techniques is justified by the study's prospective scientific, educational, or applied value and that equally effective alternative procedures that do not use deception are not feasible.

(b) Psychologists never deceive research participants about significant aspects that would affect their willingness to participate, such as physical risks, discomfort, or unpleasant emotional experiences.

(c) Any other deception that is an integral feature of the design and conduct of an experiment must be explained to participants as early as is feasible, preferably at the conclusion of their participation, but no later than at the conclusion of the research. (See also Standard 6.18, Providing Participants With Information About the Study.)

6.16 Sharing and Utilizing Data

Psychologists inform research participants of their anticipated sharing or further use of personally identifiable research data and of the possibility of unanticipated future uses.

6.17 Minimizing Invasiveness

In conducting research, psychologists interfere with the participants or milieu from which data are collected only in a manner that is warranted by an appropriate research design and that is consistent with psychologists' roles as scientific investigators.

6.18 Providing Participants With Information About the Study

(a) Psychologists provide a prompt opportunity for participants to obtain appropriate information about the nature, results, and conclusions of the research, and psychologists attempt to correct any misconceptions that participants may have.

(b) If scientific or humane values justify delaying or withholding this information, psychologists take reasonable measures to reduce the risk of harm.

6.19 Honoring Commitments

Psychologists take reasonable measures to honor all commitments they have made to research participants.

6.20 Care and Use of Animals in Research

(a) Psychologists who conduct research involving animals treat them humanely.

(b) Psychologists acquire, care for, use, and dispose of animals in compliance with current federal, state, and local laws and regulations, and with professional standards.

(c) Psychologists trained in research methods and experienced in the care of laboratory animals supervise all procedures involving animals and are responsible for ensuring appropriate consideration of their comfort, health, and humane treatment.

(d) Psychologists ensure that all individuals using animals under their supervision have received instruction in research methods and in the care, maintenance, and handling of the species being used, to the extent appropriate to their role.

(e) Responsibilities and activities of individuals assisting in a research project are consistent with their respective competencies.

(f) Psychologists make reasonable efforts to minimize the discomfort, infection, illness, and pain of animal subjects.

(g) A procedure subjecting animals to pain, stress, or privation is used only when an alternative procedure is unavailable and the goal is justified by its prospective scientific, educational, or applied value.

(h) Surgical procedures are performed under appropriate anesthesia; techniques to avoid infection and minimize pain are followed during and after surgery.

(i) When it is appropriate that the animal's life be terminated, it is done rapidly, with an effort to minimize pain, and in accordance with accepted procedures.

6.21 Reporting of Results

(a) Psychologists do not fabricate data or falsify results in their publications.

(b) If psychologists discover significant errors in their published data, they take reasonable steps to correct such errors in a correction, retraction, erratum, or other appropriate publication means.

6.22 Plagiarism

Psychologists do not present substantial portions or elements of another's work or data as their own, even if the other work or data source is cited occasionally.

6.23 Publication Credit

(a) Psychologists take responsibility and credit, including authorship credit, only for work they have actually performed or to which they have contributed.

(b) Principal authorship and other publication credits accurately reflect the relative scientific or professional contributions of the individuals involved, regardless of their relative status. Mere possession of an institutional position, such as Department Chair, does not justify authorship credit. Minor contributions to the research or to the writing for publications are appropriately acknowledged, such as in footnotes or in an introductory statement.

(c) A student is usually listed as principal author on any multiple-authored article that is substantially based on the student's dissertation or thesis.

6.24 Duplicate Publication of Data

Psychologists do not publish, as original data, data that have been previously published. This does not preclude republishing data when they are accompanied by proper acknowledgment.

6.25 Sharing Data

After research results are published, psychologists do not withhold the data on which their conclusions are based from other competent professionals who seek to verify the substantive claims through reanalysis and who intend to use such data only for that purpose, provided that the confidentiality of the participants can be protected and unless legal rights concerning proprietary data preclude their release.

6.26 Professional Reviewers

Psychologists who review material submitted for publication, grant, or other research proposal review respect the confidentiality of and the proprietary rights in such information of those who submitted it.

7. Forensic Activities

7.01 Professionalism

Psychologists who perform forensic functions, such as assessments, interviews, consultations, reports, or expert testimony, must comply with all other provisions of this Ethics Code to the extent that they apply to such activities. In addition, psychologists base their forensic work on appropriate knowledge of and competence in the areas underlying such work, including specialized knowledge concerning special populations. (See also Standards 1.06, Basis for Scientific and Professional Judgments; 1.08, Human Differences; 1.15, Misuse of Psychologists' Influence; and 1.23, Documentation of Professional and Scientific Work.)

7.02 Forensic Assessments

(a) Psychologists' forensic assessments, recommendations, and reports are based on information and techniques (including personal interviews of the individual, when appropriate) sufficient to provide appropriate substantiation for their findings. (See also Standards 1.03, Professional and Scientific Relationship; 1.23, Documentation of Professional and Scientific Work; 2.01, Evaluation, Diagnosis, and Interventions in Professional Context; and 2.05, Interpreting Assessment Results.)

(b) Except as noted in (c), below, psychologists provide written or oral forensic reports or testimony of the psychological characteristics of an individual only after they have conducted an examination of the individual adequate to support their statements or conclusions.

(c) When, despite reasonable efforts, such an examination is not feasible, psychologists clarify the impact of their limited information on the reliability and validity of their reports and testimony, and they appropriately limit the nature and extent of their conclusions or recommendations.

7.03 Clarification of Role

In most circumstances, psychologists avoid performing multiple and potentially conflicting roles in forensic matters. When psychologists may be called on to serve in more than one role in a legal proceeding—for example, as consultant or expert for one party or for the court and as a fact witness—they clarify role expectations and the extent of confidentiality in advance to the extent feasible, and thereafter as changes occur, in order to avoid compromising their professional judgment and objectivity and in order to avoid misleading others regarding their role.

7.04 Truthfulness and Candor

(a) In forensic testimony and reports, psychologists testify truthfully, honestly, and candidly and, consistent with applicable legal procedures, describe fairly the bases for their testimony and conclusions.

(b) Whenever necessary to avoid misleading, psychologists acknowledge the limits of their data or conclusions.

7.05 Prior Relationships

A prior professional relationship with a party does not preclude psychologists from testifying as fact witnesses or from testifying to their services to the extent permitted by applicable law. Psychologists appropriately take into account ways in which the prior relationship might affect their professional objectivity or opinions and disclose the potential conflict to the relevant parties.

7.06 Compliance With Law and Rules

In performing forensic roles, psychologists are reasonably familiar with the rules governing their roles. Psychologists are aware of the occasionally competing demands placed upon them by these principles and the requirements of the court system, and attempt to resolve these conflicts by making known their commitment to this Ethics Code and taking steps to resolve the conflict in a responsible manner. (See also Standard 1.02, Relationship of Ethics and Law.)

8. *Resolving Ethical Issues*

8.01 *Familiarity With Ethics Code*

Psychologists have an obligation to be familiar with this Ethics Code, other applicable ethics codes, and their application to psychologists' work. Lack of awareness or misunderstanding of an ethical standard is not itself a defense to a charge of unethical conduct.

8.02 *Confronting Ethical Issues*

When a psychologist is uncertain whether a particular situation or course of action would violate this Ethics Code, the psychologist ordinarily consults with other psychologists knowledgeable about ethical issues, with state or national psychology ethics committees, or with other appropriate authorities in order to choose a proper response.

8.03 *Conflicts Between Ethics and Organizational Demands*

If the demands of an organization with which psychologists are affiliated conflict with this Ethics Code, psychologists clarify the nature of the conflict, make known their commitment to the Ethics Code, and to the extent feasible, seek to resolve the conflict in a way that permits the fullest adherence to the Ethics Code.

8.04 *Informal Resolution of Ethical Violations*

When psychologists believe that there may have been an ethical violation by another psychologist, they attempt to resolve the issue by bringing it to the attention of that individual if an informal resolution appears appropriate and the intervention does not violate any confidentiality rights that may be involved.

8.05 *Reporting Ethical Violations*

If an apparent ethical violation is not appropriate for informal resolution under Standard 8.04 or is not resolved properly in that fashion, psychologists take further action appropriate to the situation, unless such action conflicts with confidentiality rights in ways that cannot be resolved. Such action might include referral to state or national committees on professional ethics or to state licensing boards.

8.06 Cooperating With Ethics Committees

Psychologists cooperate in ethics investigations, proceedings, and resulting requirements of the APA or any affiliated state psychological association to which they belong. In doing so, they make reasonable efforts to resolve any issues as to confidentiality. Failure to cooperate is itself an ethics violation.

8.07 Improper Complaints

Psychologists do not file or encourage the filing of ethics complaints that are frivolous and are intended to harm the respondent rather than to protect the public.

Appendix B

Record Keeping Guidelines

*Drafted by the Committee on Professional Practice &
Standards, A Committee of the
Board of Professional Affairs
Adopted by the Council of Representatives,
February 1993*

Introduction[1]

The guidelines that follow are based on the General Guidelines, adopted by the American Psychological Association (APA) in July 1987 (APA, 1987). The guidelines receive their inspirational guidance from specific APA *Ethical Principles of Psychologists and Code of Conduct* (APA, 1992).

These guidelines are aspirational and professional judgment must be used in specific applications. They are intended for use by providers of health care

---

Reprinted from the *American Psychologist, 48,* 984–986. Copyright 1993 by the American Psychological Association.

[1]In 1988 the Board of Professional Affairs (BPA) directed the Committee on Professional Practice and Standards (COPPS) to determine whether record keeping guidelines would be appropriate. COPPS was informed that these guidelines would supplement the provisions contained in the *General Guidelines for Providers of Psychological Services*, which had been amended two years earlier. The Council of Representatives approved the General Guidelines records provisions after extended debate on the minimum recordation concerning the nature and contents of psychological services. The General Guidelines reflect a compromise position that psychologists hold widely varying views on the wisdom of recording the content of the psychotherapeutic relationship. In light of the Council debate on the content of psychological records and the absence of an integrated document, BPA instructed COPPS to assess the need for such guidelines, and, if necessary, the likely content.

COPPS undertook a series of interviews with psychologists experienced in this area. The consensus of the respondents indicated that practicing psychologists could benefit from guidance in this area. In addition, an APA legal intern undertook a 50-state review of laws governing psychologists with respect to record keeping provisions. The survey demonstrated that while some states have relatively clear provisions governing certain types of records, many questions are often left unclear. In addition, there is a great deal of variability among the states, so that consistent treatment of records as people move from state to state, or as records are sought from other states, may not be easy to achieve.

Based on COPPS' survey and legal research, BPA in 1989 directed COPPS to prepare an initial set of record keeping guidelines. This document resulted.

services.[2,3] The language of these guidelines must be interpreted in light of their aspirational intent, advancements in psychology and the technology of record keeping, and the professional judgment of the individual psychologist. It is important to highlight that professional judgment is not preempted by these guidelines: rather, the intent is to enhance it.

Underlying Principles and Purpose

Psychologists maintain records for a variety of reasons, the most important of which is the benefit of the client. Records allow a psychologist to document and review the delivery of psychological services. The nature and extent of the record will vary depending upon the type and purpose of psychological services. Records can provide a history and current status in the event that a user seeks psychological services from another psychologist or mental health professional.

Conscientious record keeping may also benefit psychologists themselves, by guiding them to plan and implement an appropriate course of psychological services, to review work as a whole, and to self-monitor more precisely.

Maintenance of appropriate records may also be relevant for a variety of other institutional, financial, and legal purposes. State and federal laws in many cases require maintenance of appropriate records of certain kinds of psychological services. Adequate records may be a requirement for receipt of third party payment for psychological services.

In addition, well documented records may help protect psychologists from professional liability, if they become the subject of legal or ethical proceedings. In these circumstances, the principal issue will be the professional action of the psychologist, as reflected in part by the records.

At times, there may be conflicts between the federal, state or local laws governing record keeping, the requirements of institutional rules, and these guidelines. In these circumstances, psychologists bear in mind their obligations to conform to applicable law. When laws or institutional rules appear to conflict with the principles of these guidelines, psychologists use their education, skills and training to identify the relevant issues, and to attempt to resolve it in a way that, to the maximum extent feasible, conforms both to law and to professional practice, as required by ethical principles.

Psychologists are justifiably concerned that, at times, record keeping information will be required to be disclosed against the wishes of the psychologist or client, and may be released to persons unqualified to interpret such records.

---

[2]These guidelines apply to Industrial/Organizational psychologists providing health care services but generally not to those providing non-health care I/O services. For instance, in I/O psychology, written records may constitute the primary work product, such as a test instrument or a job analysis, while psychologists providing health care services may principally use records to document non-written services and to maintain continuity.

[3]Rather than keeping their own record system, psychologists practicing in institutional settings comply with the institution's policies on record keeping, so long as they are consistent with legal and ethical standards.

These guidelines assume that no record is free from disclosure all of the time, regardless of the wishes of the client or the psychologist.

1. Content of Records

a. Records include any information (including information stored in a computer) that may be used to document the nature, delivery, progress, or results of psychological services. Records can be reviewed and duplicated.

b. Records of psychological services minimally include (a) identifying data, (b) dates of services, (c) types of services, (d) fees, (e) any assessment, plan for intervention, consultation, summary reports, and/or testing reports and supporting data as may be appropriate, and (f) any release of information obtained.

c. As may be required by their jurisdiction and circumstances, psychologists maintain to a reasonable degree accurate, current, and pertinent records of psychological services. The detail is sufficient to permit planning for continuity in the event that another psychologist takes over delivery of services, including, in the event of death, disability, and retirement. In addition, psychologists maintain records in sufficient detail for regulatory and administrative review of psychological service delivery.

d. Records kept beyond the minimum requirements are a matter of professional judgment for the psychologist. The psychologist takes into account the nature of the psychological services, the source of the information recorded, the intended use of the records, and his or her professional obligation.

e. Psychologists make reasonable efforts to protect against the misuse of records. They take into account the anticipated use by the intended or anticipated recipients when preparing records. Psychologists adequately identify impressions and tentative conclusions as such.

2. Construction and Control of Records

a. Psychologists maintain a system that protects the confidentiality of records. They must take reasonable steps to establish and maintain the confidentiality of information arising from their own delivery of psychological services, or the services provided by others working under their supervision.

b. Psychologists have ultimate responsibility for the content of their records and the records of those under their supervision. Where appropriate, this requires that the psychologist oversee the design and implementation of record keeping procedures, and monitor their observance.

c. Psychologists maintain control over their clients' records, taking into account the policies of the institutions in which they practice. In situations where psychologists have control over their clients' records and where circumstances change such that it is no longer feasible to maintain control over such records, psychologists seek to make appropriate arrangements for transfer.

d. Records are organized in a manner that facilitates their use by the psychologist and other authorized persons. Psychologists strive to assure that record entries are legible. Records are to be completed in a timely manner.

e. Records may be maintained in a variety of media, so long as their utility, confidentiality and durability are assured.

3. Retention of Records

a. The psychologist is aware of relevant federal, state and local laws and regulations governing record retention. Such laws and regulations supersede the requirements of these guidelines. In the absence of such laws and regulations, complete records are maintained for a minimum of 3 years after the last contact with the client. Records, or a summary, are then maintained for an additional 12 years before disposal.[4] If the client is a minor, the record period is extended until 3 years after the age of majority.

b. All records, active and inactive, are maintained safely, with properly limited access, and from which timely retrieval is possible.

4. Outdated Records

a. Psychologists are attentive to situations in which record information has become outdated, and may therefore be invalid, particularly in circumstances where disclosure might cause adverse effects. Psychologists ensure that when disclosing such information that its outdated nature and limited utility are noted using professional judgment and complying with applicable law.

b. When records are to be disposed of, this is done in an appropriate manner that ensures nondisclosure (or preserves confidentiality) (see Section 3a).

5. Disclosure of Record Keeping Procedures

a. When appropriate, psychologists may inform their clients of the nature and extent of their record keeping procedures. This information includes a statement on the limitations of the confidentiality of the records.

b. Psychologists may charge a reasonable fee for review and reproduction of records. Psychologists do not withhold records that are needed for valid healthcare purposes solely because the client has not paid for prior services.

---

[4]These time limits follow the APA's specialty guidelines. If the specialty guidelines should be revised, a simple 7 year requirement for the retention of the complete record is preferred, which would be a more stringent requirement than any existing state statute.

Appendix C

Rules and Procedures

Introduction

The revised Rules and Procedures of the Ethics Committee of the American Psychological Association, which are set forth below, were approved by the APA Board of Directors on August 15, 1992, with an effective date of October 1, 1992. The rules will be applied prospectively to all complaints and cases pending on the effective date, except, as provided in Part II, Subsection 1.2, "no amendment shall adversely affect the rights of a member of the Association whose conduct is being investigated by the Ethics Committee or against whom the Ethics Committee has filed formal charges" as of the effective date. In the event application of the revised Rules and Procedures would adversely affect such rights, the pertinent provisions of the former Rules and Procedures will be applied. Failure by the Committee or APA to follow these rules and procedures shall be cause to set aside action taken pursuant thereto only in the event such failure has resulted in genuine prejudice to the compliance or member.

The revised Rules and Procedures are divided into five parts, which are further subdivided by sections and subsections.

Overview

This brief overview is intended only to orient the reader to the overall structure of the Rules. The overview is not binding on the Committee or participants in the ethics process, and is not an independent source of authority.

General Provisions

Part I describes the objectives and authority of the Ethics Committee.

Part II sets forth the Committee's general operating rules. These include, among others, rules governing confidentiality and disclosures of information concerning ethics cases; rules governing the maintenance and disposition of Ethics Committee records; rules governing the Committee's jurisdiction, including the time limits within which ethics complaints must be filed; rules governing applications to reopen a closed case; rules describing the various sanctions and directives that may be imposed; and procedures pursuant to which at the outset of the ethics process a member may admit the alleged violation and resign from the Association.

Reprinted from *American Psychologist*, Vol. 47, pp. 1612–1628. Copyright 1992 by the American Psychological Association.

The Board of Directors adopted, in August 1992, these Rules and Procedures to replace its earlier set (which were published in the June 1985 issue of the *American Psychologist*, pp. 685–694, with a minor amendment added in June 1991). They are available from the APA Ethics Office.

Provisions Bearing on Membership Applications

Part III sets forth the procedures governing Ethics Committee review of applications or reapplications for membership in APA, and procedures governing Ethics Committee review of allegations that membership was obtained based upon false pretenses.

Provisions Governing "Show Cause" Proceedings in Response to Prior Serious Adverse Actions by Other Tribunals

Part IV establishes procedures available to the Committee in cases in which other tribunals—including criminal courts, licensing boards, and state psychological associations—have already taken specified serious adverse actions against a member pursuant to presumptively valid procedures. If a member has been convicted of a felony or commensurate criminal offense; has been expelled or suspended by a state psychological association; or has been decertified or unlicensed or had a certificate or license revoked or suspended by a state or local board, the Committee may notify the member that he or she has 60 days to set forth, in writing, why APA should not expel the member from membership on the basis of that prior action. Based solely on the available record leading to the prior action, the member's written response and any evidence developed by the Committee, the Committee may recommend to the Board whether the member should be expelled, some lesser sanction should be applied, or the charges dismissed. The Committee may also choose to adjudicate the matter pursuant to the plenary procedures of Part V, or to offer the member the option of resigning pursuant to stipulated conditions in lieu of other actions, subject to approval by the Board of Directors. The member may file a written response to the recommendation to the Board, which will act based upon the written record in the case.

Provisions Governing Submission and Resolution of Complaints Against Members

Part V establishes the procedures used in resolving and adjudicating complaints of unethical conduct against members. Complaints may be submitted by members or nonmembers of the Association, or may be initiated by the Ethics Committee acting on its own (*sua sponte* complaints). Complaints must be submitted within the time periods set forth in Part II, Section 5, or fall within the exceptions set forth in that section.

Complaints are evaluated initially by the Chair of the Ethics Committee and Director of the Ethics Office to determine whether the Committee has jurisdiction and whether there is cause for action by the Committee (defined in Part V, Subsection 5.1). If necessary, the Chair and Director will conduct a preliminary investigation to assist in making these threshold determinations. If the Committee has no jurisdiction, or if cause for action does not exist, the complaint will be dismissed at this stage. If the Committee has jurisdiction and cause for action exists, the Director will open a formal case and conduct an investigation.

A formal case is initiated with a charge letter, sent to the complainee. The complainee is afforded an opportunity to review all materials submitted to the Committee and upon which the Committee may rely in adjudicating the complaint. At the conclusion of the investigation, the formal case is referred to the Committee for review and resolution.

In resolving a case, the Committee may dismiss it, recommend that it be resolved with sanctions less than formal charges (i.e., recommend a censure or reprimand, with or without supplemental directives), or issue formal charges (a recommendation to the Board of Directors that the complainee be dropped from membership). The Committee may also offer the member the option of resigning pursuant to stipulated conditions in lieu of other actions, subject to approval by the Board of Directors.

If the Committee votes to recommend resolution without formal charges or issues formal charges, the complainee has a right to an Independent Adjudication or Formal Hearing, respectively. If the Committee has voted to recommend resolution without formal charges, the adjudicatory mechanism is via written submissions to an Independent Adjudication Panel. The decision of the Independent Adjudication Panel is the final adjudication. If the complainee elects *not* to seek an independent adjudication of the Committee's recommendation, the Director implements the recommendation as the accepted adjudication.

If the Committee has issued formal charges, the adjudicatory mechanism is an in-person hearing before a Formal Hearing Committee, which makes an independent recommendation to the Board of Directors. The Board reviews the recommendation of the Hearing Committee, and must adopt that recommendation unless specified defects require the matter to be remanded for further actions. In the event of formal charges, if the complainee elects not to seek adjudication, the Board of Directors reviews the Ethics Committee's recommendation upon the same terms as it would review the recommendation of a Hearing Committee.

Part I. Objectives and Authority of the Committee

1. Objectives

The fundamental objectives of the Ethics Committee (hereinafter the Committee) shall be to maintain ethical conduct by psychologists at the highest professional level, to educate psychologists concerning ethical standards, to endeavor to protect the public against harmful conduct by psychologists, and to aid the Association in achieving its objectives as reflected in its Bylaws.[1]

2. Authority

The Committee is authorized to:

2.1 Formulate rules or principles of ethics for adoption by the Association;

2.2 Investigate allegations of unethical conduct of Fellows, Members, and Associates (hereinafter members) and, in certain instances, applicants for membership;

2.3 Resolve allegations of unethical conduct and/or recommend such action as is necessary to achieve the objectives of the Association;

2.4 Report on types of complaints investigated with special description of difficult cases;

2.5 Adopt rules and procedures governing the conduct of all the matters within its jurisdiction;

2.6 Take such other actions as are consistent with the Bylaws of the Association, the Rules of Council, the Association's Ethics Code, and these Rules and Procedures, and as are necessary and appropriate to achieving the objectives of the Committee; and

2.7 Delegate appropriate tasks to subcommittees of the Ethics Committee or to agents or employees of the Association, such subcommittees, agents, and employees in such event to be fully bound by these Rules and Procedures.

Part II. General Operating Rules

1. General Provisions

1.1 APA Documents.   The Committee shall base its actions on applicable governmental laws and regulations, the Bylaws of the Association,[2] the Association Rules,[3] the Association's Ethics Code, and these Rules and Procedures.

1.2 Rules and Procedures.   The Committee may adopt rules and procedures governing the conduct of all matters within its jurisdiction, and may amend such rules from time to time upon a two-thirds vote of the Committee members, provided that no amendment shall adversely affect the rights of a

---

[1]The Ethics Committee seeks to protect the public by deterring unethical conduct by psychologists; by taking appropriate action when an ethical violation has been proved according to these Rules and Procedures; and by setting standards to aid psychologists in understanding their ethical obligations. Of course, in no circumstances can or does the Committee or the Association guarantee that unethical behavior will not occur or that members of the public will never be harmed by the actions of individual psychologists.

[2]APA Bylaws (1991), Article II, Sections 18 and 19, and Article X, Section 5, pertain to the Committee specifically.

[3]Association Rules (1991) 10-11, 10-12, 10-13, 20-1, 20-2, 20-3, and 20-4 pertain to the Committee specifically.

member of the Association whose conduct is being investigated by the Ethics Committee or against whom the Ethics Committee has filed formal charges at the time of amendment. Changes to the Rules and Procedures must be ratified by the Board of Directors acting for the Council of Representatives.

1.3 Compliance With Time Requirements. The Committee and complainee shall use their best efforts to adhere strictly to the time requirements specified in these Rules and Procedures. Failure to do so will not prohibit final resolution unless such failure was unduly prejudicial.

1.4 Computation of Time. In computing any period of time prescribed or allowed by these rules, the day of the act, event, or default from which the designated period of time begins to run shall not be included. The last day of the period shall be included unless it is a Saturday, a Sunday, or a legal holiday, in which event the period runs until the end of the next day which is not one of the aforementioned days.

2. Meetings and Officers

2.1 Frequency and Quorum. The Committee shall meet at reasonable intervals as needed. A quorum at such meetings shall consist of the majority of the elected members of the Committee.

2.2 Selection of Officers. The Chair and Vice Chair shall be elected annually at a duly constituted meeting. The Chief Executive Officer of the Association shall designate a staff member to serve as Director of the Ethics Office. Whenever they appear in these rules, "Chair," "Vice Chair," and "Director" shall mean these individuals or their designees.

2.3 Vice Chair. The Vice Chair shall have the authority to perform all the duties of the Chair when the latter is unavailable or unable to perform them, and shall perform such other tasks as are delegated by the Chair or by these rules.

2.4 Majority Rule. Except as otherwise noted in the Rules and Procedures, all decisions shall be by majority vote of those members present or, in the case of a vote by mail, a majority of those members qualified to vote.

2.5 Attendance. Attendance at the Ethics Committee's deliberation of cases is restricted to elected members of the Committee, the Director of the Ethics Office, the Ethics Office staff, members of the Board of Directors, Legal Counsel of the Association, and other duly appointed persons authorized by the Committee to assist it in carrying out its functions, except when the Committee, by two-thirds vote, authorizes the presence of other persons.

3. Confidentiality and Disclosures

3.1 Requirement of Confidentiality. All information concerning complaints against members shall be confidential, except that the Committee may disclose such information when compelled by a valid subpoena, when otherwise required by law, or as otherwise provided in these Rules and Procedures.

3.2 Access by Staff, Legal Counsel, and Other Duly Appointed Per-

sons. Information may be shared with Legal Counsel of the Association, with the Chief Executive Officer of the Association, with staff of the Association's Central Office designated by the Chief Executive Officer to assist the Committee with its work, and with other duly appointed persons authorized by the Committee to assist it in carrying out its functions.

3.3 Notification of Final Disposition of Case by the Board of Directors

3.3.1 Complainee. The Board of Directors shall inform the complainee or member of its final action, including which Ethical Standard(s)[4] were judged to have been violated, should there be any, and the rationale for the Association's actions. The Director of the Ethics Office (hereinafter Director) shall be provided a copy of the letter to the complainee.

3.3.2 Complainant. The Director shall inform the complainant of the Board of Directors' final action, including which Ethical Standard(s) were judged to have been violated, should there by any, and, if the Board of Directors deems it appropriate, the rationale therefor.

3.3.3 Membership. The Board shall report annually and in confidence to the membership the names of members who have been expelled or dropped from membership and the Ethical Standard(s) involved.

3.3.4 Council of Representatives. The Board shall report annually and in executive session to the Council the names of members who have been allowed to resign under stipulated conditions or who have been dropped or expelled from membership and the Ethical Standard(s) involved.

3.3.5 Other Entities. When the Board of Directors deems it necessary for the protection of the Association or the public or to maintain the standards of the Association, the Board shall direct the Committee to notify of its final action (a) affiliated state and regional associations,[5] (b) the American Board of Professional Psychology (ABPP), (c) state or local licensing and certification boards,[6] (d) the Association of State and Provincial Psychology Boards (ASPPB), (e) the Council for the National Register of Health Service Providers in Psychology (CNRHSPP), and/or (f) other appropriate parties.

3.4 Notification of Final Disposition of Case by the Ethics Committee and/or Independent Adjudication Panel

3.4.1 Complainee. The Committee shall inform the complainee of the final disposition of the case and the rationale therefor, including the Ethical Standard(s) violated, if any.

3.4.2 Complainant. The Committee shall inform the complainant of the final disposition of the case, including the Ethical Standard(s) violated, if any, and, if the Committee deems it appropriate, the rationale therefor.

---

[4]In this document "Ethical Standard(s)" refers to the Ethical Standard(s) in the *Ethical Principles of Psychologists and Code of Conduct* or the Ethical Principle(s) in the *Ethical Principles of Psychologists.*

[5]For purposes of these Rules and Procedures, a state association shall include territorial, local, or county psychological associations, and in cases of Canadian members of the Association, provincial psychological associations.

[6]For purposes of these Rules and Procedures, state boards shall include boards in Canadian provinces or state or provincial boards of examiners or education in those cases where the pertinent licensing or certification is secured from such entities, or in states or provinces with no licensing authority, nonstatutory boards established for such purpose.

3.4.3 Other Parties Informed of the Complaint. The Committee may inform such other parties as have been informed of the complaint of the final disposition of the case, including the Ethical Standard(s) violated, if any, and the rationale therefor.

3.4.4 Further Disclosure of Cases Resulting in Probation. In cases that have resulted in a member's probation, the Committee may communicate these actions to: (a) members; (b) governance groups, committees, and divisions of the Association; (c) affiliated state and regional associations; (d) ABPP and state licensing and certification boards; (e) the ASPPB; (f) the CNRHSPP; and/or (g) such other individuals or organizations as the Committee shall deem necessary to protect the public.

3.4.5 Disclosure of Fact of Investigation. The Committee may disclose to any of the entities enumerated in Subsection 3.4.4(a)–(g) of this part the fact that an individual is under ethical investigation in cases deemed to be serious threats to the public welfare (as determined by a two-thirds vote of the Committee at a regularly scheduled meeting), but only when to do so before final adjudication appears necessary to protect the public.

3.4.6 Notification of Additional Parties at the Request of Complainee. The Ethics Office may notify such additional parties of the final disposition as are requested by the complainee.

3.4.7 Initiation of Legal Action Constitutes Waiver. Initiation of a legal action against the Association or any of its agents, officers, directors, or employees concerning any matters considered or actions taken by the Ethics Committee or Ethics Office shall constitute a waiver by the person initiating such action of an interest in confidentiality recognized in these Rules or other organic documents of the Association with respect to the subject matter of the legal action.

3.5 Communication for Investigation or Other Functions.   Nothing in this section shall be construed to prevent the Committee from communicating with the complainee, complainant, witnesses, or other sources of information necessary to enable the Committee to carry out its functions.

4. Records

4.1 Confidential Permanent Files.   Files of the Committee related to investigation and adjudication of cases shall be confidential, within the limitations of Section 3 of this part, and shall be maintained, consistent with these Rules and Procedures.

4.2 Preliminary Investigation Files.   If a preliminary investigation is closed for no cause for action, records containing personally identifiable information shall be maintained for at least one year after the matter is closed.

4.3 Formal Case and Show Cause Records

4.3.1 Closure for Nonviolation. In cases closed due to finding of nonviolation, records shall be maintained for at least five years after closure.

4.3.2 Closure for Insufficient Evidence. In cases closed due to evidence insufficient to support a finding of an ethical violation, records shall be maintained for at least five years after closure.

4.3.3 Censure and Reprimand. In cases resulting in censure or reprimand, records shall be maintained for at least five years after closure.

4.3.4 Dropped Membership and Expulsion. In cases in which members have been dropped from membership or expelled, records shall be maintained indefinitely.

4.3.5 Stipulated Resignation. In cases in which members have been permitted a stipulated resignation and the complainee does not reapply for membership, records shall be maintained indefinitely. In cases where the complainee is subsequently readmitted, records shall be maintained for at least five years after readmission.

4.4 Death of a Member. Records concerning members whom the Association has determined to be deceased shall be maintained for at least one year after that determination was made.

4.5 Records for Educative Purposes. Nothing in these Rules and Procedures shall preclude the Committee from maintaining records in a secure place for archival or record keeping purposes, or from using or publishing information concerning ethics matters for educative purposes without identifying individuals involved.

5. Jurisdiction

5.1 Persons. The Committee has jurisdiction over individual members, associate members, fellows, and applicants for membership in the American Psychological Association.[7]

5.2 Subject Matter. The Committee has jurisdiction to achieve its objectives and perform those functions for which it is authorized in these Rules and Procedures and other organic documents of the Association.[8]

5.3 Time Limits for Complaints and Show Cause Notices

5.3.1 Complaints by Members. Except as provided in Subsections 5.3.5 and 5.3.6 of this part, the Committee may consider complaints brought by members of the Association against other members only if the complaint is received less than one year after the alleged conduct either occurred or was discovered by the complainant.

5.3.2 Complaints by Nonmembers. Except as provided in Subsections 5.3.5 and 5.3.6 of this part, the Committee may consider complaints brought by nonmembers only if the complaint is received less than five years after the alleged conduct either occurred or was discovered by the complainant.

5.3.3 Sua Sponte Complaints. The Committee may initiate a *sua sponte* complaint under Part V of these Rules and Procedures only if it does so less

---

[7]Whether an individual is a member of the Association is determined according to the Bylaws, Association Rules, and other pertinent organic documents of the Association. Under the current rules, nonpayment of dues results in discontinuation of membership only after two consecutive calendar years during which dues to the Association have remained unpaid. See Bylaws, Article XVIII, Section 3; Association Rules 10-12.1. For purposes of these Rules and Procedures, an affiliate is not a member of the Association.

[8]Conduct complained of pursuant to this part is subject to the Ethics Code in effect at the time it occurs.

than one year after it discovered the alleged unethical conduct and less than 10 years after the alleged conduct occurred, except that whether or not such periods have expired, the Committee may initiate a *sua sponte* complaint less than one year after it discovered that any of the following actions had become final: (a) a felony conviction, (b) a finding of malpractice by a duly authorized tribunal, (c) expulsion or suspension from a state association for unethical conduct, or (d) revocation, suspension, or surrender of a license or certificate for ethical violations by a state board or while ethical proceedings before such board were pending.

5.3.4 Show Cause Notices. The Committee may initiate a show cause notice under Part IV of these Rules and Procedures only if it does so less than one year after the date it discovered that the applicable predicate for use of show cause procedures (i.e., an event described in Part IV, Section 1) has become final.

5.3.5 Exceptions to Time Limits for Complaints by Members and Non-members

5.3.5.1 Threshold Criteria. Any complaint not received within the time limits set forth in this section shall not be considered unless, with respect to complaints subject to Subsections 5.3.1 and 5.3.2 of this part, at least two thirds of the Committee members voting determine that each of the following criteria are met:

5.3.5.1.1 Considering the version of the Ethics Code under which the case would be judged, the alleged offense is serious enough that the Committee would be likely to recommend that the complainee be dropped from membership in the Association if it is substantiated;

5.3.5.1.2 There is significant supporting evidence for the allegations;

5.3.5.1.3 There is good cause demonstrated for the complaint not having been filed within the applicable time limit; and

5.3.5.1.4 The complaint was received less than 10 years after the alleged conduct occurred.

5.3.5.2 Determination to Supersede Applicable Time Limit. Where, pursuant to Subsection 5.3.5.1 of this part, the Committee has determined that the threshold criteria are met, the applicable limit shall be superseded if two thirds of the Committee (excluding recused or otherwise unavailable members), in their sole discretion, vote to do so.

5.3.6 Absolute Time Limit for Member and Nonmember Complaints. Subsections 5.3.1, 5.3.2, and 5.3.5 of this part notwithstanding, the Committee may not proceed pursuant to any member or nonmember complaint received more than 10 years after the alleged conduct occurred. This rule shall not be construed as prohibiting the Committee from considering the information contained in such a complaint in determining whether to initiate a *sua sponte* action or issuing a show cause notice, where such action would otherwise be consistent with the time limits set forth in Subsections 5.3.3 or 5.3.4 of this part.

5.4 Resignation Barred. Except as provided in Subsection 11.4 of this part or Parts IV and V of these Rules, no one under the scrutiny of the Committee will be allowed to resign either by letter of resignation, by nonpayment of dues, or otherwise.

5.5 Litigation Not a Bar to Action by Committee; Ethics Committee Authorized to Stay Ethics Process Pending Resolution. Civil or criminal litigation involving members shall not bar action by the Committee; the Committee may proceed during the course of litigation or may stay the ethics process pending its completion. Delay in conducting the investigation by the Committee during the pendency of civil or criminal proceedings shall not constitute waiver of jurisdiction.

5.6 Other Disciplinary Proceedings Not a Bar to Action by Committee; Ethics Committee Authorized to Stay Ethics Process Pending Resolution. Disciplinary proceedings or action by another body or tribunal shall not bar action by the Committee; the Committee may proceed during the course of such proceedings or stay the ethics process pending their completion. Delay in conducting the investigation by the Committee during the pendency of such proceedings shall not constitute a waiver of jurisdiction. Where the Committee learns that disciplinary action by another authorized tribunal has been stayed, such stay shall neither require nor preclude action by the Committee.

5.7 Referral and Retention of Jurisdiction. The Committee may at any time refer a matter to another recognized tribunal for appropriate action. If a case is referred to another tribunal, the Committee may retain jurisdiction and consider the complaint independently pursuant to these Rules and Procedures.

6. Reopening a Closed Case

If the complainant presents significant new evidence of unethical conduct after a matter has been closed, the case may be reopened and acted upon under regular procedures. To be considered under this rule, evidence must meet each of the following criteria:

6.1 The evidence was discovered after the Committee closed the case;

6.2 The evidence could not with reasonable diligence have been discovered before the case was closed; and

6.3 The evidence would probably produce a different result.

7. Choice and Conversion of Procedures

7.1 Choice of Procedures. Where a case might be adjudicated pursuant to the show cause procedures set forth in Part IV of these Rules and Procedures, the Committee shall determine whether to proceed pursuant to Part IV or Part V of these Rules and Procedures. The Committee shall also be the sole judge whether a matter shall be disposed of without formal charges, whether a stipulated resignation shall be sought, or whether formal charges shall be brought.

7.2 Conversion of Show Cause Case. In its sole discretion, the Committee may convert a proceeding begun by show cause procedures under Part IV hereof to a plenary case under Part V hereof. In event of such conversion, the complaint shall be deemed timely filed if the show cause proceeding had been initiated in timely fashion.

7.3 *Conversion of Plenary Case.*   In its sole discretion, where the predicates for use of show cause procedures set forth in Part IV, Section 1 are present, the Committee may convert a plenary proceeding begun by *sua sponte*, member, or nonmember complaint under Part V hereof to a show cause proceeding under Part IV. In such event, the show cause proceeding shall be deemed timely initiated if at the time of conversion it satisfies the provisions of Subsection 5.3.4 of this part.

8. Correspondence and Documentation

8.1 *Use of Correspondence.*   The Committee shall conduct as much of its business as is practical through correspondence.

8.2 *Personal Response Required.*   Although the complainee has the right to consult with an attorney concerning all phases of the ethics process, the complainee must respond to charges of unethical conduct personally and not through legal counsel or another third party. If the complainee shows good cause as to why he or she cannot respond personally, the Director may waive this requirement.

8.3 *Transcription of Audiotapes, Videotapes, and Similar Data Compilations Required.*   It shall be the responsibility of the individual or entity submitting to the Committee an audiotape, videotape, or similar data compilation, to provide an accurate transcription of the information contained thereon. In the sole discretion of the Director, any audiotape, videotape, or similar data compilation provided unaccompanied by a transcription as required in this subsection may be rejected unless and until such transcription is provided.

8.4 *Service.*   For purposes of notice, service shall be made by delivery to the complainee or the complainee's attorney or by mail or common carrier to the complainee or the complainee's attorney at the complainee's or attorney's last known address. Delivery within this rule means handing it to the complainee or the attorney or leaving it at the complainee's office or place of abode or the attorney's office with a receptionist, secretary, clerk, or other person in charge thereof, or, if there is no one in charge, leaving it in a conspicuous place therein. Service by mail is complete upon mailing. Where, after good faith efforts, the Committee has been unable to locate the complainee, it may give notice by causing to be published in a newspaper of general circulation in the complainee's last known place of domicile a notice to contact the Ethics Office concerning an important matter.

9. Failure to Cooperate With Ethics Process

Members are required to cooperate fully and in a timely fashion with the ethics process. Failure to cooperate shall not prevent continuation of any proceedings and itself constitutes a violation of the Ethics Code that may warrant being dropped from membership.

10. Board of Directors' Standing Hearing Panel

The President of the Association shall appoint members of the Standing Hearing Panel. Standing Hearing Panel members shall serve a three-year term. The Standing Hearing Panel shall consist of at least 30 members at least 5 of whom shall be public members, and the remainder shall be members of the Association in good standing, and shall not include any present members of the Ethics Committee.

11. Available Sanctions

On the basis of circumstances that aggravate or mitigate the culpability of the member, a sanction more or less severe, respectively, than would be warranted on the basis of the factors set forth below, may be appropriate.

11.1 Reprimand. Reprimand is the appropriate sanction if there has been an ethics violation but the violation was not of a kind likely to cause harm to another person or to cause substantial harm to the profession, and was not otherwise of sufficient gravity as to warrant a more severe sanction.

11.2 Censure. Censure is the appropriate sanction if there has been an ethics violation, and the violation was of a kind likely to cause harm to another person, but the violation was not of a kind likely to cause substantial harm to another person or to the profession, and was not otherwise of sufficient gravity as to warrant a more severe sanction.

11.3 Drop From Membership or Expulsion. Dropping from membership or expulsion from membership is the appropriate sanction if there has been an ethics violation, and the violation was of a kind likely to cause substantial harm to another person or the profession, or was otherwise of sufficient gravity as to warrant such action.

11.4 Stipulated Resignation. Stipulated resignation may be offered by the Committee:

11.4.1 Pursuant to Member/Complainee's Initial Response to the Show Cause Notice, contingent upon execution of an acceptable affidavit admitting responsibility for the violations charged, under Part IV, Subsection 10.1; or

11.4.2 Pursuant to a Committee Finding That the Member/Complainee Has Committed a Violation of the Ethics Code, contingent on execution of an acceptable affidavit and approval by the Board of Directors, under Part IV, Subsection 10.2, or Part V, Subsection 7.5.

12. Available Directives

12.1 Cease and Desist Order. Such a directive requires the complainee to cease and desist specified unethical behavior(s).

12.2 Supervision Requirement.   Such a directive requires that the complainee engage in supervision.

12.3 Education, Training, or Tutorial Requirement.   Such a directive requires that the complainee engage in education, training, or a tutorial.

12.4 Evaluation and/or Treatment Requirement.   Such a directive requires that the complainee be evaluated to determine the possible need for treatment and/or, if dysfunction has been established, obtain treatment appropriate to that dysfunction.

12.5 Probation.   Such a directive requires monitoring of the complainee by the Committee to ensure compliance with Ethics Committee-mandated directives.

13. Matters Requiring the Concurrence of the Chair of the Committee and Director of the Ethics Office

Whenever matters entrusted by these Rules and Procedures to the Chair and Director require the concurrence of those officers before certain action may be taken, either officer in the event of disagreement may refer to the matter to the Vice Chair, who together with the Chair and Director make a final determination by majority vote.

Part III. Membership

1. Applications

1.1 Specific Jurisdiction.   The Committee has the power to investigate the preadmission scientific and professional ethics and conduct of all applicants for membership in the Association and to make recommendations whether an individual shall become a member or be readmitted to membership.

1.2 Initial Application.   The Committee shall review applications for membership upon referral by the Membership Committee where there are questions of unethical conduct or false or fraudulent information.

1.3 Procedures for Review.   The Director shall transmit to the Committee a copy of the membership application and any other materials pertinent to the case. The Ethics Office shall take such steps, including contacting the applicant or other sources of information, as necessary and appropriate to making a fair determination. Upon review, the Committee may recommend to the Board of Directors that membership be denied.

2. Application for Readmission

The Director shall receive from the Membership Committee all applications for readmission by persons who have been (a) expelled or dropped from membership or (b) permitted to resign under stipulated conditions.

2.1 Elapsed Time for Review.   Applications for readmission by members who have been expelled or dropped from membership shall be considered by the Committee only after five years have elapsed from the date of that action. Applications for readmission by members who have been permitted to resign shall be considered only after the stipulated period or, where no period has been stipulated, three years have elapsed.

2.2 Procedures for Review.   The Director shall transmit to the Committee a summary of the application for readmission and the record of the previous case against the former member. In all cases, the ex-member must show that he or she is technically and ethically qualified, and has satisfied any conditions upon readmission established by the Board. The Committee shall make one of the following recommendations:

2.2.1 Readmission. Recommend to the Membership Committee that the former member be readmitted; or

2.2.2 Denied Readmission. Recommend to the Membership Committee that readmission be denied; or

2.2.3 Deferred Readmission. Recommend to the Membership Committee that the application for readmission be deferred for a stated period of time; or

2.2.4 Further Investigation. Charge the Director to investigate issues specified by the Committee and to place the matter before the Committee at a future date.

3. Allegations That Membership Was Obtained Under False Pretenses

3.1 Specific Jurisdiction.   The Committee has the power to investigate allegations that membership was obtained on the basis of false or fraudulent information, and to take appropriate action with respect thereto.

3.2 Procedures for Review.   The Director shall transmit to the Committee a copy of the membership application and any other materials pertinent to the case. The Ethics Office shall take such steps, including contacting the member or other sources of information, conducting or authorizing a hearing for the purpose of ascertaining pertinent facts, etc., as necessary and appropriate to making a fair determination in the circumstances of the case.

3.3 Sanctions.   Upon completion of this review, the Committee may recommend to the Board of Directors that it void the election to membership in the Association of any person who obtained membership on the basis of false or fraudulent information.

Part IV. Show Cause Procedures Based Upon Actions by Other Recognized Tribunals

1. Predicates for Use of Show Cause Procedures

1.1 Felony or Commensurate Offense.   The Committee may elect to utilize the process authorized by this part if (a) the Committee finds that a member has been convicted of a felony (as defined by state or provincial law or otherwise a criminal offense with possible term of incarceration exceeding one year) and such conviction is not under appeal, and (b) after review of the publicly available record leading to such conviction, the Committee determines that use of this process appears necessary for the protection of the public.

1.2 Expulsion, Suspension, Unlicensure, or Decertification. The Committee may elect to utilize the process authorized by this part if (a) the Committee finds that a member has been expelled or suspended from an affiliated state or regional psychological association or decertified or unlicensed or had a certificate or license revoked or suspended by a state or local board, and such action is not under appeal, and (b) after review of the publicly available record leading to such action, the Committee determines that use of this process appears necessary for the protection of the public.

2. Notice by the Committee and Response by Member

The member shall be notified by the Committee that he or she has been barred from resigning membership in the Association (subject only to the terms of Section 10 of this part) and, on the basis of Part IV of these Rules and Procedures, will be afforded 60 days in which to show good cause as to why he or she should not be expelled from membership in the Association.

3. Showing by Member That Prior Proceeding Lacked Due Process

In addition to a response to the substance of the charges pursuant to Section 2 of this part, the member may seek within the 60-day period to show that the procedures followed by the other recognized tribunal did not follow fair procedure. If the Committee finds merit to this contention, it may exercise its discretion pursuant to Part II, Subsection 7.2 of these Rules and convert the matter to a *sua sponte* plenary case under Part V hereof or dismiss the complaint.

4. Investigation

The Committee may conduct a further investigation, including seeking additional information from the member or others or requesting that the member appear in person. Any evidence not obtained directly from the member and relied upon by the Committee in connection with adjudication shall first have been provided to the member, who shall have an opportunity to respond in person or shall have been afforded not less than 15 days to respond thereto in writing.

5. Review and Recommendation by the Committee

Upon receipt of the member's response and upon conclusion of any necessary further investigation, or the expiration of 60 days without response, the Committee may vote to recommend one of the following courses of action to the Board of Directors:

5.1 Dismissal of Charges.   The Committee may recommend that the case be dismissed, with or without an educative letter.

5.2 Censure or Reprimand, With or Without Directives.   The Committee may recommend that the member be censured or reprimanded, with or without one or more directives.

5.3 Expulsion.   The Committee may recommend that the member be expelled from the Association; In the alternative, the Committee may elect to recommend the sanction of stipulated resignation, pursuant to the procedure set forth in subsection 10.2 of this part.

6. Notification of Member

The Committee shall notify the member of its recommendation, and shall inform the member of his or her opportunity to file a written statement with the Board of Directors.

7. Member's Statements in Response to Recommendation

Within 15 days of receipt of notification of the Committee's recommendation, the member may file a written statement with the Board of Directors. The statement should be mailed care of the Ethics Office.

8. Committee Response

The Ethics Committee shall have 15 days from the time it receives the member's written statement to file a written response, if any. A copy will be provided to the member.

9. Review by the Board of Directors

Within 180 days after receiving the record, the Committee's recommendation, any written statement by the complainee and any written response by the Committee, the Board of Directors shall vote whether to expel the member from the Association or to issue a lesser sanction. The Board may select a sanction more or less severe than that recommended by the Committee.

10. Stipulated Resignation

10.1 Stipulated Resignation With Admission of Violation Pursuant to Member's Initial Response to the Show Cause Notice

10.1.1 Member Officer of Stipulated Resignation With Admission of Violation. In his or her initial response to the Committee's notice to show cause under Section 2 of this part, the member may offer to resign membership in the Association with admission of violation. Such an offer must include a statement of intent to execute an affidavit, acceptable to the Committee, (a) admitting the violation underlying the criminal conviction, expulsion, unlicensure or decertification, and (b) resigning membership in the Association.

10.1.2 Committee Response and Proposed Affidavit of Stipulated Resignation. Where the member makes such an offer, the Committee in due course will forward to the member a proposed affidavit of stipulated resignation.

10.1.3 Acceptance by Member. Within 30 days of receipt, the member may resign membership in the Association by executing and having notarized the proposed affidavit and returning it to the Committee. Resignation shall be effective upon the Committee's timely receipt of the executed notarized affidavit.

10.1.4 Rejection by Member. If the member fails to execute, have notarized, and return an acceptable affidavit within 30 days, or formally notifies the Committee of rejection of the proposed affidavit, the offer of stipulated resignation shall be deemed rejected. The member shall be afforded an additional 30 days within which to supplement his or her response to the Committee's show cause notice. The matter shall thereafter be resolved according to the applicable procedures set forth in this part. All materials submitted by the member shall be part of the file to be considered by the Committee and/or the Board of Directors, in connection with the case.

10.1.5 Stipulated Resignation With Admission of Violation Pursuant to This Section Is Available Only at the Time and in the Manner Set Forth in This Section. Unless stipulated resignation with admission of violation is accomplished at the time and in the manner set forth in this section, members may not resign while under scrutiny of the Ethics Committee except as set forth in Subsection 10.2 of this part.

10.2 Stipulated Resignation Pursuant to Review and Recommendation by the Committee. In lieu of the recommendations set forth in Section 5 of this part, with the agreement of the member, the Committee in its sole discretion may recommend that the member be permitted to resign from the Association under stipulations set forth by the Committee, pursuant to the following procedure:

10.2.1 Offer of Stipulated Resignation by Committee. When the Committee finds that the member has committed a violation of the Ethics Code, the Committee, in its sole discretion, may offer to enter into an agreement with the member, contingent upon approval by the Board of Directors, that the member shall resign from the Association pursuant to mutually agreed upon stipulations. Such stipulations shall include the extent to which the stipulated resignation and underlying ethics violations shall be disclosed and a minimum period of time, after resignation, during which the resigned member shall be ineligible to reapply for membership. The Committee may, in its discretion, also vote to impose, and inform the member of, an alternative recommended sanction, chosen from among Subsections 11.1–11.3 of Part II of these Rules, it would recommend in the event the member does not accept the offer of stipulated resignation.

10.2.2 Notification of Member. In such cases, the member shall be notified, in writing, of the Committee's recommended resolution of stipulated resignation and that he or she may accept the Committee's recommended resolution within 30 days of receipt. The member shall also be notified of any alternative recommended sanction.

10.2.3 Acceptance by Member. Within 30 days, the member may accept the recommended resolution of stipulated resignation by executing a notarized affidavit of resignation acceptable to both the member and the Committee and forwarding the executed notarized affidavit to the Committee. Such resignation shall become effective only with the approval of the Board, as set forth in this section.

10.2.4 Transmittal to Board of Directors. If the member accepts the recommended resolution of stipulated resignation, the Committee shall submit a copy of the affidavit of resignation, together with the record in the matter and the rationale for recommending stipulated resignation on the terms set forth in the affidavit, to the Board of Directors.

10.2.5 Action by Board of Directors. Within 180 days, the Board of Directors shall accept the member's resignation on the terms stated in the affidavit of resignation, unless it is persuaded that to do so would not be in the best interest of the Association and/or of the public. If the resignation is accepted by the Board, the Ethics Office shall notify the member of the resolution of the case.

10.2.6 Rejection of Stipulated Resignation by Member. If the member fails within 30 days to accept the recommended resolution, or formally notifies the Committee of rejection of the offer of stipulated resignation within the 30 day period, the offer of stipulated resignation shall be deemed rejected. The Committee shall reconsider the matter pursuant to these Rules and Procedures or, in the event an alternative recommended sanction has previously been identified by the Committee, such alternative recommended sanction shall automatically become the recommended sanction pursuant to Section 5 of this part. The Committee shall notify the member of the recommendation and of his or her opportunity to file a written statement with the Board of Directors, as set forth in Section 6 of this part. Sections 7–9 of this part shall also apply.

10.2.7 Rejection of Stipulated Resignation by Board. If the Board rejects the affidavit of resignation pursuant to Subsection 10.2.5 of this part, the Committee shall notify the member and reconsider the matter pursuant to these Rules and Procedures.

Part V. Plenary Procedures For Complaints Against Members

1. Initiation of Plenary Procedures

Plenary ethics proceedings against a member are initiated by the filing of a complaint or, in the case of a *sua sponte* action, by the issuance of a charge letter pursuant to Subsection 6.1.1 of this part.

2. Complaints

2.1 Complaints Submitted by Members or Nonmembers.   Complaints may be submitted by members or nonmembers of the Association. Upon receipt of an inquiry concerning filing a complaint, the Committee shall provide a copy of the Association's Ethics Code, the ethics complaint form, and these Rules and Procedures.

2.2 Sua Sponte Action.   When a member appears to have violated the Association's Ethics Code, the Committee may proceed on its own initiative.

2.3 Sua Sponte Action Based Upon Member's Filing of Capricious or Malicious Complaint.   To prevent abuse of the ethics process, the Committee is empowered to bring charges itself against a complainant if the initial complaint is judged by two thirds of Committee members present to be (a) frivolous and (b) intended to harm the complainee rather than to protect the public. The filing of such a complaint constitutes a violation of the Ethics Code. Such charges shall be investigated and adjudicated under the terms of this part.

2.4 Countercomplaints.   The Committee will not consider a complaint from a complainee member against a complainant member during the course of its investigation and resolution of the initial complaint. Rather, the Committee shall study all sides of the matter leading to the first complaint, and consider countercharges only after the initial complaint is finally resolved.

2.5 Anonymous Complaints.   The Committee shall not act upon anonymous complaints. If material in the public domain is provided anonymously, the Committee may choose to employ such material in support of a *sua sponte* complaint.

2.6 Complaints Against Nonmembers.   If the complaint does not involve a member, the Ethics Office shall inform the complainant and may suggest that the complainant contact another agency or association that may have jurisdiction.

2.7 Consecutive Complaints.   When a complaint is lodged against a member with respect to whom a case involving similar alleged behavior was previously closed, materials in the prior case may be considered in determining whether to open a case.

2.8 Simultaneous Complaints.   When more than one complaint is simultaneously pending against the same member, the Committee may choose to combine the cases or to keep them separate. In the event the cases are combined, the Committee shall take reasonable steps to ensure that the legitimate confidentiality interests of any complainant, witness, or complainee are not compromised by combination.

3. Procedures for Filing Complaints

A Complaint by a member or nonmember shall comprise:

3.1   A completed APA Ethics Complaint Form;

3.2   Such releases as are required by the Committee;

3.3   A waiver by the complainant of any right to subpoena from the

Committee or its agents for the purposes of private civil litigation any documents or information concerning the case[9]; and

3.4   A request that the applicable time limit be waived, if necessary.

4. Preliminary Evaluation of Complaints by Ethics Office

The Ethics Office shall review each complaint to determine if jurisdictional criteria are met and if it can be determined whether cause for action exists.

4.1 Lack of Jurisdiction.   If jurisdictional criteria are not satisfied, the matter shall be closed and the complainant so notified.

4.2 Information Insufficient to Determine Jurisdiction

4.2.1 Request for Supplementation of Complaint. If there is not information sufficient to determine whether jurisdictional criteria are met, or if it appears that the complaint is outside the applicable time limit, the Ethics Office shall so inform the complainant, who will be given 30 days from receipt of the request to supplement the complaint and/or ask for a waiver of the applicable time limit.

4.2.2 Consequences of Failure to Supplement Complaint. If no response is received from the complainant within 30 days from receipt of the request, the matter may be closed. If at a later date the complainant shows good cause for delay and demonstrates that jurisdictional criteria can be met, the supplemented complaint shall be considered.

4.3 Process With Respect to Superseding Applicable Time Limit

4.3.1 Consideration by Chair and Director. If a complaint otherwise within the jurisdiction of the Ethics Committee appears to have been filed outside the applicable time limit, and the complainant asks the Committee to supersede the time limit, that request will be considered initially by the Chair and the Director pursuant to the criteria set forth in Part II, Subsection 5.3.5. If they do not agree that those criteria appear to be satisfied, the case will be closed pursuant to Subsection 4.1 of this part.

4.3.2 Response by Complainee Where Standards Appear to Be Met. If the Chair and Director agree that the standards of Part II, Subsection 5.3.5 may be satisfied, the Director shall notify the complainee, provide the complainee with a copy of the complaint, the complainant's submission with respect to the time limit, and any other materials the Director deems appropriate. The complainee shall have 30 days from receipt of these materials to address whether the criteria of Part II, Subsection 5.3.5 are met, or reasons, apart from the criteria, why the applicable limit should not be superseded.

4.3.3 Determination by Committee. In any case not closed pursuant to Subsection 4.3.1 above, the Committee shall consider the request that the time limit be superseded under the standards of Part II, Subsection 5.3.5, based upon any materials provided by the complainant and complainee, and any other information available to or obtained by the Committee. If the Committee

---

[9]This waiver is required to help assure participants in the APA ethics process, including complainants, that the process will not be inappropriately used to gain an advantage in other fora.

votes to supersede the time limit, the matter shall then be considered pursuant to Section 5 of this part. If the Committee does not vote to supersede the time limit, the matter shall be closed pursuant to Subsection 4.1 of this part.

4.4 Information Insufficient to Determine Cause for Action

4.4.1 Request for Supplementation of Complaint. If there is not information sufficient to determine whether cause for action exists, the Ethics Office shall so inform the complainant, who will be given 30 days from receipt of the request to supplement the complaint.

4.4.2 Consequences of Failure to Supplement Complaint. If no response is received from the complainant within 30 days, the matter may be closed. If at a later date the complainant shows good cause for delay and responds to the request for supplementation, the supplemented complaint shall be considered.

5. Evaluation of Complaints by Chair and Director

All complaints not closed by the Ethics Office pursuant to Section 4 of this part shall be reviewed by the Chair and the Director to determine whether cause for action by the Ethics Committee has been shown to exist.

5.1 Cause for Action Defined. Cause for action shall exist when the complainee's alleged actions and/or omissions, if proved, would in the judgment of the decision maker constitute a breach of ethics. For purposes of determining whether cause for action exists, incredible, speculative, and/or internally inconsistent allegations may be disregarded.

5.2 Preliminary Investigation Due to Insufficient Information. If, after supplementation of the complaint by the complainant pursuant to Subsection 4.4.1 of this part, the Chair and the Director determine that they still lack evidence sufficient to determine whether a case should be opened, a preliminary investigation may be initiated.

5.2.1 Notification to Complainee. If a preliminary investigation is opened, the Director shall so inform the complainee in writing. The Director will include a copy of the completed Ethics Complaint Form and all materials submitted by the complainant or on the complainant's behalf; a copy of the APA Ethics Code; the Committee's Rules and Procedures; and a statement that information submitted by the complainee shall become a part of the record, and could be used if further proceedings ensue.

5.2.2 Time for Complainee Response. The complainee shall have 30 days after receipt of the complaint to file an initial response to the complaint. When requested in writing, within the 30 days to respond and when good cause is shown, the Director may extend the time for responding to the complaint.

5.2.3 Response From Complainee. The complainee is required to respond as completely as possible, in writing, personally, and within specified time limits. The complainee is free to consult legal counsel, but correspondence must be from the complainee and not from legal counsel or another third party acting for the complainee. If the complainee shows good cause as to why he or she can not respond personally, the Director may waive this requirement.

5.2.4 Information From Other Sources. The Director, Chair, or the Committee may request additional information from the complainant and/or any other appropriate source. The Committee will not rely upon information submitted by such sources unless it has been shared with the complainee, and the complainee has been afforded an opportunity to respond thereto.

5.2.5 Action if There Continues to Be Insufficient Information. At the conclusion of the preliminary investigation, if the Director and Chair determine that they still lack evidence sufficient to determine whether cause for action exists, the matter shall be closed and the complainant notified.

5.3 Finding of Cause for Action by Committee. If the Director and the Chair agree that cause for action exists, they shall open a formal case, unless they also agree that the allegations even if substantiated are trivial or likely to be corrected.

5.4 Finding of No Cause for Action by Committee. If the Director and Chair do not agree that there is cause for action by the Committee, the matter shall be closed. The matter shall also be closed if the Director and Chair agree that, although cause for action otherwise exists, the allegations even if substantiated would constitute a trivial violation or one likely to be corrected. In the event of closure, the Director shall so inform the complainant in writing. A case closed pursuant to this subsection may be reopened only if the complainant presents significant new evidence, as defined in Part II, Section 6.

5.5 Supplementary or Alternative Action by Committee. The Director and Chair may recommend that the complainant refer the complaint to a relevant state psychological association, state board, appropriate regulatory agency, any subsidiary body of the Association, or other appropriate entity, or they may make such referral on their own initiative. Such referral does not constitute a waiver of jurisdiction over the complaint provided that the Committee opens a formal case within 24 months from the date of referral.

6. Formal Case Investigation

6.1 Issuance of Charge Letter and Response From Complainee

6.1.1 Charge Letter. If a formal case is opened, the Director shall so inform the complainee in a charge letter. The charge letter shall contain a concise description of the alleged behaviors at issue and identify the specific section(s) of the Ethics Code that the complainee is alleged to have violated. The Director shall enclose a copy of any completed Ethics Complaint Form and any materials submitted to date by the complainant or on the complainant's behalf that will be included in the record before the Committee; a copy of the APA Ethics Code and the Committee's Rules and Procedures; and a statement that information submitted by the complainee shall become a part of the record, and could be used if further proceedings ensue.

6.1.2 Significance of Charge Letter. A charge letter does not constitute or represent a finding that any unethical behavior has taken place, or that any allegations of the complaint are or are not likely to be found to be true.

6.1.3 Issuance of Charge Letter to Conform to Evidence Discovered During Investigation. At any time prior to final resolution by the Committee, in order to conform the charges to the evidence developed during the investigation, the Director and Chair may issue a new charge letter setting forth Ethical Standard(s) and/or describing alleged behaviors different from or in addition to those contained in the initial charge letter. In a *sua sponte* case, the date of issuance shall, for purposes of applicable time limits, be deemed to relate back to the date of the initial charge letter. The new charge letter shall in all other respects be treated exactly as an initial charge letter issue pursuant to Subsection 6.1.1 of this part.

6.1.4 Time for Compliance Response. The complainee shall have 30 days after receipt of the charge letter to file an initial response. Any request to extend the time for responding to the charge letter must be made in writing, within the 30 days to respond, and must show good cause for an extension. Based upon such request, the Director may extend the time for responding to the charge letter.

6.1.5 Response From Complainee. The complainee is required to respond as completely as possible, in writing, personally, and within specified time limits. The complainee is free to consult legal counsel, but the response must be from the complainee and not through legal counsel or another third party acting for the complainee. If the complainee shows good cause as to why he or she cannot respond personally, the Director may waive this requirement.

6.1.6 Personal Appearance. The Director and Chair may request the complainee to appear personally before the Committee. The complainee has no right to such an appearance.

6.2 Information From Other Sources. The Director, Chair, or the Committee may request additional information from the complainant, complainee, or any other appropriate source.

6.3 Referral to Committee. When in the sole judgment of the Chair and Director the investigation is complete, the case will be referred to the Committee for review and resolution. The Ethics Office shall notify the complainant and complainee that the matter has been referred to the Committee.

6.4 Documentation Subsequent to Investigation and Prior to Resolution by the Committee. Within 30 days after receipt of notification that the case is being referred to the Ethics Committee for review and resolution, the complainant and complainee may submit any additional information or documentation. Any materials timely submitted by the complainant or on the complainant's behalf will be forwarded to the complainee. Within 15 days from receipt of those materials, the complainee may submit any additional information or documentation. All such materials submitted within these time limitations shall be included in the file to be reviewed by the Ethics Committee. Materials submitted out of time will not be included in the file materials relative to the ethics case and will not be reviewed by the Ethics Committee. In the sole discretion of the Director, where good cause for noncompliance with these time limits is shown by the complainant or the complainee, the resolution of the case may be postponed until the next scheduled meeting of the Ethics Committee and the information or documentation provided out of time may be included in the file materials to be reviewed by the Committee at that later time. In the sole discretion of the Director, in the event the complainee fails to comply with these time limits, the information or documentation provided out of time may be included in the file materials to be reviewed by the Committee and the matter maintained for resolution by the Committee as originally scheduled.

7. Review and Resolution by the Committee

Upon conclusion of the investigation, the Committee shall take one of the actions listed below. The Complainee shall then be notified of the Committee's action, the Ethical Standard(s) involved if any, the rationale for the Committee's decision, any sanction, and any directives.

7.1 Remand. The Committee may remand the matter to the Ethics Office for continued investigation or issuance of a new charge letter pursuant to Subsection 6.1.3 of this part.

7.2 Dismiss the Charges

7.2.1 No Violation. The Committee may dismiss the complaint if it finds the complainee has not violated the Ethical Standard(s) as charged.

7.2.2 Trivial or Corrected Violation. The Committee may dismiss the complaint if it concludes that any violation it might find would be trivial or has been or is likely to be corrected.

7.2.3 Insufficient Evidence. The Committee may dismiss the complaint if it finds insufficient evidence to support a finding of an ethics violation.

7.2.4 Educative Letter. Where the Committee deems it appropriate, it may dismiss the complaint and issue an educative letter, to be shared only with the complainee, concerning the behaviors charged.

7.3 Recommend a Sanction Less Than Formal Charges. If the Committee finds that the complainee has violated the Ethics Code, but decides that the nature of the complainee's behavior is such that the matter would be most appropriately resolved without bringing formal charges, the Committee will recommend censure or reprimand of the complainee, with or without one or more available directives. See Part II, Subsections 11.1, 11.2, and Section 12.

7.4 Issue Formal Charges. The Committee may issue formal charges if it concludes that there has been an ethics violation, that it was of a kind likely to cause substantial harm to another person or the profession, or that it was otherwise of such gravity as to warrant this action.[10] Formal charges consist of a statement submitted by the Committee to the Board of Directors recommending that the Board of Directors drop the complainee from membership in the Association.

7.5 Stipulated Resignation. In lieu of the other resolutions set forth in this section, with the agreement of the member, the Committee, in its sole discretion, may recommend to the Board that the member be permitted to resign under stipulations set forth by the Committee, pursuant to the following procedure:

7.5.1 Offer of Stipulated Resignation by the Committee. When the Committee finds that the complainee has committed a violation of the Ethics Code, the Committee, in its sole discretion, may offer to enter into an agreement

---

[10]Noncooperation with the APA ethics process is a violation of sufficient gravity, posting danger of substantial harm to the profession, to warrant formal charges.

with the complainee, contingent upon approval by the Board of Directors, that the complainee shall resign from the Association pursuant to mutually agreed upon stipulations. Such stipulations shall include the extent to which the stipulated resignation and underlying ethics violation shall be disclosed, and a minimum period of time, after resignation, during which the complainee shall be ineligible to reapply for membership. The Committee may, in its discretion, also vote to impose, and inform the member of, an alternative recommended sanction, chosen from among Subsections 11.1–11.3 of Part II of these Rules, that it would recommend in the event the member does not accept the offer of stipulated resignation.

7.5.2 Notification of Complainee. In such cases, the complainee shall be notified, in writing, of the Committee's recommended resolution of stipulated resignation and that he or she may accept the Committee's recommended resolution within 30 days of receipt. The complainee shall also be notified of any alternative recommended sanction.

7.5.3 Acceptance by Complainee. Within 30 days, the complainee may accept the recommended resolution of stipulated resignation by executing a notarized affidavit of resignation acceptable both to the complainee and the Committee and forwarding the executed notarized affidavit to the Committee. Such resignation shall become effective only with the approval of the Board, as set forth in Subsection 7.5 of this part.

7.5.4 Transmittal to Board of Directors. If the complainee accepts the recommended resolution of stipulated resignation, the Committee shall in due course submit a copy of the affidavit of resignation, together with the record in the matter and the rationale for recommending stipulated resignation on the terms set forth in the affidavit, to the Board of Directors.

7.5.5 Action by Board of Directors. Within 180 days, the Board of Directors shall accept the complainee's resignation on the terms stated in the affidavit of resignation, unless it is persuaded that to do so would not be in the best interest of the Association and/or of the public. If the resignation is accepted by the Board, the Ethics Office shall notify the complainant and complainee of the resolution of the case. A copy of the affidavit of resignation shall be provided to the complainant.

7.5.6 Rejection of Stipulated Resignation by Complainee. If the complainee fails to accept the determination within 30 days, or formally notifies the Committee of rejection of the offer of stipulated resignation within the 30-day period, the offer of stipulated resignation shall be deemed rejected. The Committee shall reconsider the matter pursuant to these Rules and Procedures or, in the event an alternative recommended sanction has previously been identified by the Committee, such alternative recommended resolution shall automatically become the recommended sanction pursuant to Subsection 7.3 or 7.4 of this part.

7.5.7 Rejection of Stipulated Resignation by Board. If the Board rejects the affidavit of resignation pursuant to Subsection 7.5.5 of this part, the Committee shall notify the complainee and reconsider the matter pursuant to these Rules and Procedures.

RULES AND PROCEDURES   237

8. *Procedures Subsequent to Committee Action: Dismissal*

The complainant may seek reconsideration when the Committee dismisses a case pursuant to Subsection 7.2 of this part only if the complainant furnishes the Committee significant new evidence, consistent with Part II, Section 6. If, in the judgment of the Director, such information is furnished, at its next meeting the Committee will consider whether to reopen the case. If the complainant seeks reconsideration on these grounds within 30 days of notification of dismissal, a reopened complaint shall be deemed to have been filed on the date the original complaint was received. If the complainant seeks reconsideration on these grounds more than 30 days after notification of dismissal, a reopened complaint shall be deemed to have been filed on the date the request for reconsideration was received.

9. *Procedures Subsequent to Committee Recommendation: Sanction Less Than Formal Charges*

If the Committee proceeds pursuant to Subsection 7.3 of this part, the following procedures shall govern:

9.1 Acceptance of Sanction Less Than Formal Charges.   If the complainee accepts the Committee's recommended sanction and directives, if any, the right of independent adjudication shall be waived, any stipulations will be implemented by the Director, and the case will remain open until the directives are met. The complainee's failure to respond within 30 days of notification shall be deemed acceptance of the Committee's recommended sanction and directives.

9.2 Independent Adjudication Pursuant to Recommended Sanction Less Than Formal Charges.   The adjudicatory mechanism for a recommended sanction less than formal charges is an independent adjudication before a three-person Independent Adjudication Panel.

9.2.1 Request for Independent Adjudication and Rationale for Nonacceptance. The complainee may exercise his or her right to independent adjudication by furnishing the Committee within 30 days after notification of the Committee's recommendation a written request for independent adjudication and rationale for nonacceptance of the recommendation.

9.2.2 Personal and Prompt Response. During the independent adjudication process, the complainee is required to respond personally and not through an agent or representative, as completely as possible, in writing, and within specified time limits. The complainee is free to consult legal counsel. If the complainee shows good cause as to why he or she cannot respond personally, the Director may permit him or her to respond through counsel.

9.2.3 Response by Committee. Within 30 days of receipt of the complainee's rationale for nonacceptance, the Committee may prepare a response and provide a copy to the complainee. No response by the Committee is required.

9.2.4 Selection of Independent Adjudication Panel

9.2.4.1 Provision of Standing Hearing Panel List. Within 60 days after the request for an independent adjudication, the Director shall provide the complainee with the names and curricula vitae of six members of the Board of Directors' Standing Hearing Panel, of whom at least one shall be a public member. The Director shall make inquiry and ensure that proposed panel members do not have a conflict of interest as defined by applicable law and appear otherwise able to apply fairly the APA Ethics Code based solely on the record in the particular case.

9.2.4.2 Designation of Panel Members. Within 15 days after receipt of the six-member list, the complainee shall select three of the six to constitute the Independent Adjudication Panel. The Panel shall include not fewer than two members of the Association. Whenever feasible, the complainee's selection will be honored. If at any time prior to conclusion of the appeal an individual selected by the complainee cannot serve on the Independent Adjudication Panel for any reason, the complainee shall be notified promptly and afforded the opportunity within 10 days of receipt of notification to replace that individual from among a list of not fewer than four members of the Board of Directors' Standing Hearing Panel. In the event the complainee fails to notify the Director of his or her initial or replacement selections in a timely fashion, the right to do so is waived and the President of the Association or designee (hereinafter President) shall select the member(s), whose name(s) shall then be made known to the complainee.

9.2.4.3 Designation of Chair of Independent Adjudication Panel. The President shall designate one of the three Panel members to serve as Chair. The Chair of the Panel shall ensure that the Panel fulfills its obligations pursuant to these Rules and Procedures.

9.2.5 Provision of Case File to Independent Adjudication Panel. Within 15 days of selection of the Independent Adjudication Panel, receipt of the Committee's response pursuant to Subsection 9.2.3 of this part, or, if no Committee response is received, the expiration of the time period for such response, whichever occurs latest, the Director will provide the case file to the members of the Independent Adjudication Panel.

9.2.6 Consideration and Vote by Independent Adjudication Panel. Within 60 days of the receipt of the case file and the rationale for nonacceptance, the members of the Panel shall confer with each other and, solely on the basis of the documentation provided and deliberations among themselves, shall vote to:

9.2.6.1 Adopt the Committee's Recommended Sanction and Directives; or

9.2.6.2 Adopt a Lesser Sanction and/or Less Burdensome Directives; or

9.2.6.3 Dismiss the Case.

9.2.7 Decision of the Independent Adjudication Panel. Decisions of the Independent Adjudication Panel will be made by majority vote, and at least two reviewers must agree to written findings, a sanction, if any, and a directive or directives, if any. The Committee bears the burden to prove the charges by a preponderance of the evidence. The panelists' votes and the majority's written decision must be submitted to the Ethics Office within the 60-day period set forth in Subsection 9.2.6 of this part. If no two panelists can agree as to the appropriate outcome or a written decision, the case will be referred to the

Committee for further action. The decision of the Independent Adjudication Panel is unappealable and binding on the Committee and the complainee. A decision either to impose a sanction and/or directive(s) or to dismiss the case will be implemented by the Committee as the final adjudication.

9.2.8 Notification. The Committee shall inform the complainee and complainant of the final adjudication. The complainee shall be provided a copy of the majority's written decision.

10. Procedures Subsequent to Committee Recommendations: Formal Charges

If the Committee proceeds pursuant to Subsection 7.4 of this part, the following procedures shall govern:

10.1 Acceptance of Formal Charges. If the complainee accepts the Committee's recommendation to the Board of Directors that he or she be dropped from membership (formal charge), the right to a formal hearing shall be waived, and the Committee shall proceed with its recommendation to the Board of Directors pursuant to Subsection 10.3.4 and other subsections of this part. In such event, the recommendation of the Ethics Committee shall be treated as the equivalent of the recommendation of a Formal Hearing Committee that the complainee be dropped from membership. The complainee's failure to respond within 30 days after notification shall be deemed acceptance of the Committee's recommendation.

10.2 Adjudication Procedures: Formal Charges. The adjudicatory mechanism for formal charges issued pursuant to Subsection 7.4 of this part is a formal hearing before a three-member Hearing Committee.

10.2.1 Request for Formal Hearing. The complainee may exercise her or his right to a formal hearing by furnishing the Committee within 30 days of notification of the Committee's action a written request.

10.2.2 Personal and Prompt Response. During the adjudicatory process and prior to the formal hearing, the complainee is required to respond personally and not through an agent or representative, as completely as possible, in writing, and within specified time limits. The complainee is free to consult legal counsel. If the complainee shows good cause as to why he or she cannot respond personally, the Director may permit him or her to respond through counsel.

10.2.3 Selection of the Formal Hearing Date and Hearing Committee

10.2.3.1 Establishment of Hearing Date and Provision of Standing Hearing Panel List. Within 60 days after the complainee requests a formal hearing, the President shall establish the date of the hearing and provide the complainee with the date and the names and curricula vitae of six members of the Board of Directors' Standing Hearing Panel. The six identified members of the Board of Directors' Standing Hearing Panel shall include at least one public member. The Director shall make inquiry and ensure that proposed panel members do not have a conflict of interest as defined by applicable law and appear otherwise able to apply fairly the Ethics Code based solely on the record in the particular case.

10.2.3.2 Designation of Hearing Committee Members. The formal hearing shall be heard by a Hearing Committee of three individuals, selected from among the six individuals from the Board of Directors' Standing Hearing Panel identified pursuant to Subsection 10.2.3.1 of this part. The Hearing Committee shall include not fewer than two members of the Association. Within 15 days after the receipt of the names and curricula vitae pursuant to Subsection 10.2.3.1 of this part, the complainee shall notify the Director of his or her selections for the Hearing Committee. Whenever feasible, the complainee's selections will be honored. In the event an individual timely selected by the complainee cannot serve on the Hearing Committee for any reason, the complainee shall be notified and afforded the opportunity within 10 days of receipt of notification to replace that individual from among a list of not fewer than four members of the Board of Directors' Standing Hearing Panel. In the event the complainee fails to notify the Director of his or her initial or replacement selections in a timely fashion, the right to do so is waived and the President shall select the Hearing Committee members, whose names shall then be made known to the complainee.

10.2.3.3 Voir Dire of Designated Hearing Committee Members. Within 15 days after receipt of the names of the three designated Hearing Committee members, the complainee may submit in writing, to the Director, a request to question designated Hearing Committee members with respect to potential conflict of interest. Upon receipt of such written request, the Director shall convene by telephone conference call, or otherwise, a formal opportunity for such questioning by the complainee or the complainee's attorney. Legal Counsel for the Association shall preside at such voir dire, shall be the sole judge of the propriety and pertinency of questions posed, and shall be the sole judge with respect to the fitness of designated Hearing Committee members to serve. Failure by the complainee to timely submit a request shall constitute a waiver of the privilege to conduct voir dire.

10.2.3.4 Designation of Chair of Hearing Committee. The President shall designate one of the three Hearing Committee members to serve as Chair. The Chair of the Hearing Committee and Legal Counsel for the Association shall assure proper observance of these Rules and Procedures at the formal hearing.

10.2.4 Documents and Witnesses

10.2.4.1 Committee. At least 30 days prior to the scheduled date of the formal hearing, the Ethics Committee shall provide the complainee and the Hearing Committee with copies of all documents and other evidence, and the names of all witnesses that may be offered by the Committee in its case in chief.

10.2.4.2 Complainee. At least 15 days prior to the scheduled date of the formal hearing, the complainee shall provide the Ethics Committee and the Hearing Committee with copies of all documents and other evidence, and the names of all witnesses that may be offered by the complainee.

10.2.4.3 Rebuttal Documents and Witnesses. At least five days prior to the scheduled date of the formal hearing, the Committee shall provide the complainee and the Hearing Committee with copies of all documents and other evidence, and the names of all witnesses that may be offered in rebuttal.

10.2.4.4 Audiotapes, Videotapes, and Similar Data Compilations. Audiotapes, videotapes, and similar data compilations are admissible at the formal hearing, provided usable copies of such items, together with a transcription thereof, are provided in a timely fashion pursuant to the provisions of this section.

10.2.4.5 Failure to Provide Documents, Other Evidence, and Names of Witnesses in a Timely Fashion in Advance of the Formal Hearing. Failure to provide copies of a document or other evidence or the name of a witness in a timely fashion and consistent with this section and these Rules and Procedures is grounds for excluding such document, other evidence, or witness from evidence at the formal hearing, unless good cause for the omission and a lack of prejudice to the other side can be shown.

10.2.5 Conduct of the Formal Hearing

10.2.5.1 Presiding Officers

10.2.5.1.1 The Chair of the Hearing Committee, assisted by Legal Counsel for the Association, shall preside at the hearing.

10.2.5.1.2 Legal Counsel for the Association shall be present to advise on matters of procedure and admission of evidence, and shall represent neither the Committee nor the complainee at the formal hearing.

10.2.5.2 Legal Representation of the Complainee and Committee

10.2.5.2.1 Complainee. The complainee may choose, at complainee's own expense, to be represented by a licensed attorney.

10.2.5.2.2 Committee. The Chair of the Ethics Committee presents the Committee's case. However, the Committee may choose to have legal counsel present its case.

10.2.5.3 Rules of Evidence. Formal rules of evidence shall not apply. All evidence that is relevant and reliable, as determined for the Hearing Committee by Legal Counsel for the Association, shall be admissible.

10.2.5.4 Rights of the Complainee and the Committee. Consistent with these Rules and Procedures, the complainee and the Committee shall have the right to present witnesses, documents, and other evidence, to cross-examine witnesses, and to object to the introduction of evidence.

10.2.5.5 Burden of Proof. The Ethics Committee shall bear the burden to prove the charges by a preponderance of the evidence.

10.2.6 Decision of the Hearing Committee. The decision shall be by a simple majority vote. Within 30 days of the conclusion of the hearing, the Hearing Committee shall submit in writing to the Board of Directors, through the Ethics Committee, its decision and the rationale for that decision. The Hearing Committee may decide to:

10.2.6.1 adopt the Committee's recommendation to the Board of Directors.

10.2.6.2 recommend to the Board of directors a lesser sanction, with or without directives; or

10.2.6.3 determine that the charges must be dismissed.

10.2.7 Notice to the Complainee and the Ethics Committee. Within 15 days of receipt of the Hearing Committee's decision, a copy of the decision shall be provided to the complainee and the Ethics Committee. If the Hearing Committee determines that the charges must be dismissed, the Ethics Committee will implement this as the final adjudication.

10.3 Proceedings Before the Board of Directors

10.3.1 Referral to Board of Directors. If the Hearing Committee recommends that the complainee be dropped from membership or otherwise disciplined, the matter will be referred to the Board of Directors. In due course, the Ethics Office shall provide the appeals materials to the Board, including a copy of the Hearing Committee's decision, the complainee's timely response, if any, pursuant to Subsection 10.3.2 of this part, the Ethics Committee's timely response, if any, pursuant to Subsection 10.3.3 of this part, and the record.

10.3.2 Complainee Response. Within 30 days from receipt of the Hearing Committee's decision, the complainee shall file a written response, if any, with the Board of Directors, through the Ethics Committee. A copy of the complainee's written response shall be retained by the Chair of the Ethics Committee.

10.3.3 Ethics Committee Response. If the complainee files a written response, within 15 days from its receipt, the Ethics Committee shall prepare a written statement, if any, and provide a copy to the complainee.

10.3.4 Action by the Board of Directors. Within 60 days of receipt of the recommendation of the Hearing Committee (or of the Ethics Committee if no hearing was held), together with any timely responses thereto and the record, the Board of Directors will consider these materials, and will take action as follows:

10.3.4.1 Adopt. The Board of Directors shall adopt the recommendation, unless by majority vote it finds grounds for nonacceptance, as set forth in Subsection 10.3.4.2.

10.3.4.2 Grounds for Nonacceptance. Only the following shall constitute grounds for nonacceptance of the recommendation by the Board:

10.3.4.2.1 Incorrect Application of Ethical Standard(s). The Ethics Code of the Association was incorrectly applied; or

10.3.4.2.2 Erroneous Findings of Fact. The findings of fact were clearly erroneous; or

10.3.4.2.3 Procedural Errors. The procedures used were in serious and substantial violation of the Bylaws of the Association and/or these Rules and Procedures; or

10.3.4.2.4 Excessive Sanction or Stipulations. The disciplinary sanction or directives recommended are grossly excessive in light of all the circumstances.

10.3.4.3 Consequences of Nonacceptance. If the Board of Directors finds grounds for nonacceptance, it shall refer the case back to the Ethics Committee. In its discretion, the Ethics Committee may return the matter for rehearing before a newly constituted Hearing Committee or may continue investigation and/or readjudicate the matter at the Committee level.

10.4 Notification. If the Board of Directors does not adopt the recommendation, it shall notify the Ethics Committee in writing why the decision was not accepted, citing the applicable ground(s) for nonacceptance under Subsection 10.3.4.2 of this part.

10.5 Rehearing.   If a rehearing is instituted the procedures of this part shall apply. Unless any of the following is offered by the complainee, none shall be part of the record before the second Hearing Committee: the original Hearing Committee's report; the complainee or Ethics Committee's written statements made pursuant to Subsections 10.3.2 and 10.3.3 of this part; and the Board of Directors' rationale for nonacceptance of the original Hearing Committee's recommendation. If the complainee offers any portion of any of the foregoing documents as evidence in the rehearing, the Committee may introduce any portion or all of any of all of them.

References

Adkins, D. C. (1952). Proceedings of the sixteenth annual business meeting of the American Psychological Association, Inc., Washington, DC. *American Psychologist, 7*, 645–670.

American Psychological Association, Committee on Scientific and Professional Ethics. (1947). Report of the Committee on Scientific and Professional Ethics. *American Psychologist, 2*, 488–490.

American Psychological Association. (1953a). *Ethical standards of psychologists*. Washington, DC: Author.

American Psychological Association. (1953b). *Ethical standards of psychologists: A summary of ethical principles*. Washington, DC: Author.

American Psychological Association, Committee on Ethical Standards of Psychologists. (1958). Standards of ethical behavior for psychologists. Report of the Committee on Ethical Standards of Psychologists. *American Psychologist, 13*, 266–271.

American Psychological Association. (1959). Ethical standards of psychologists. *American Psychologist, 14*(6), 279–282.

American Psychological Association. (1963). Ethical standards of psychologists. *American Psychologist, 18*, 56–60.

American Psychological Association. (1968). Ethical standards of psychologists. *American Psychologist, 23*, 357–361.

American Psychological Association. (1972). *Ethical standards of psychologists*. Washington, DC: Author.

American Psychological Association, Ad Hoc Committee on Ethical Standards in Psychological Research. (1973). *Ethical principles in the conduct of research with human participants*. Washington, DC: Author.

American Psychological Association. (1979). *Ethical standards of psychologists*. Washington, DC: Author.

American Psychological Association. (1981). Ethical principles of psychologists. *American Psychologist, 36*, 633–638.

American Psychological Association. (1985). *Standards for educational and psychological tests*. Washington, DC: Author.

American Psychological Association. (1987a). General guidelines for providers of psychological services. *American Psychologist, 42*, 712–723.

American Psychological Association, Ethics Committee. (1987b). Report of the Ethics Committee: 1986. *American Psychologist, 42*, 730–734.

American Psychological Association, Ethics Committee. (1988). Report of the Ethics Committee: 1987. *American Psychologist, 43*, 564–572.

American Psychological Association. (1990). Ethical principles of psychologists (amended June 2, 1989). *American Psychologist, 45*, 390–395.

American Psychological Association. (1992a). Ethical principles of psychologists and code of conduct. *American Psychologist, 47*, 1597–1611.

American Psychological Association, Ethics Committee. (1992b). Rules and procedures. *American Psychologist, 47*, 1612–1628.

American Psychological Association. (1993a). *Guidelines for ethical conduct in the care and use of animals.* Washington, DC: Author.

American Psychological Association. (1993b). Guidelines for providers of psychological services to ethnic, linguistic, and culturally diverse populations. *American Psychologist, 48*, 45–48.

American Psychological Association. (1993c). Record keeping guidelines. *American Psychologist, 48*, 308–310.

American Psychological Association. (1994). Guidelines for child custody evaluations in divorce proceedings. *American Psychologist, 49*, 677–680.

Anastasi, A. (1955). Proceedings of the sixty-third annual business meeting of the American Psychological Association, Inc., San Francisco, California. *American Psychologist, 10*, 695–726.

APA continues to refine its ethics code. (1992, May). *APA Monitor*, pp. 38–42.

APA Ethics code draft. (1991, June). *APA Monitor*, pp. 30–35.

Carter, L. F. (1958). Proceedings of the sixty-sixth annual business meeting of the American Psychological Association, Inc. *American Psychologist, 13*, 691–710.

Conger, J. J. (1978). Proceedings of the incorporated American Psychological Association for the year 1977: Minutes of the annual meeting of the Council of Representatives. *American Psychologist, 33*, 544–572.

Ethical principles revised. (1990, June). *APA Monitor*, pp. 28–32.

Ethical standards of psychologists. (1977, March). *APA Monitor*, pp. 22–23.

Ethics Committee issues newly approved statements on ads, "canned" columns. (1993, September). *APA Monitor*, p. 51.

FTC consent order is published in its entirety. (1993, March). *APA Monitor*, p. 8.

Haas, L., & Malouf, J. (1989). *Keeping up the good work: A practitioner's guide to mental health ethics.* Sarasota, FL: Professional Resource Exchange.

Hobbs, N. (1948). The development of a code of ethical standards for psychology. *American Psychologist, 3*, 80–84.

Hobbs, N. (1954). Proceedings of the sixty-second annual business meeting of the American Psychological Association, Inc., New York, New York. *American Psychologist, 9*, 719–748.

Holtzman, W. H. (1979). The IUPS project on professional ethics and conduct. *International Journal of Psychology, 14*(2), 107–109.

Keith-Spiegel, P., & Koocher, G. (1985). *Ethics in psychology.* New York: Random House.

Kitchener, K. (1984). Intuition, critical evaluation and ethical principles: The foundation for ethical decisions in counseling psychology. *The Counseling Psychologist, 12*(3), 43–55.

McKeachie, W. J. (1972). Proceedings of the American Psychological Association, Inc. for the year 1971: Minutes of the annual meeting of the Council of Representatives. *American Psychologist, 27*, 268–299.

McKeachie, W. J. (1973). Proceedings of the American Psychological Association, Inc. for the year 1972: Minutes of the annual meeting of the Council of Representatives. *American Psychologist, 28*, 297–325.

Nagy, T. F. (1988, August). *Revision of the ethical principles of psychologists: APA Task Force's second annual progress report*. Paper presented at the Annual Convention of the American Psychological Association, Atlanta, GA.

Nagy, T. F. (1989, August). *Revision of the ethical principles of psychologists: APA Task Force's progress report—three years later and ready for review*. Paper presented at the Annual Convention of the American Psychological Association, New Orleans, LA.

Nagy, T. F. (1994). The ethical principles of psychologists and code of conduct (1994 revision). In R. J. Corsini (Ed.), *Encyclopedia of psychology (rev. ed.): Vol. 1* (pp. 504–508). New York: Wiley.

National Institutes of Health. (1985). *Guide for the care and use of laboratory animals*. (NIH Publication No. 86-23). Washington, DC: U.S. Department of Health and Human Services.

National Institutes of Health. (1986). *Public Health Service policy on humane care and use of laboratory animals*. Bethesda, MA: Office for Protection from Research Risks, U.S. Department of Health and Human Services.

National Institutes of Health. (1988). *The institutional administrator's manual for laboratory animal care and use*. (NIH Publication No. 88-2959). Bethesda, MD: Office for Protection from Research Risks, U.S. Department of Health and Human Services.

National Institutes of Health. (1993). *Institutional Review Board guidebook*. Washington, DC: U.S. Department of Health and Human Services.

Newman, E. B. (1965). Proceedings of the seventy-third annual business meeting of the American Psychological Association, Inc. *American Psychologist, 20*, 1028–1053.

Nolan, J., & Nolan-Haley, J. (1990). *Black's law dictionary* (6th ed.). St. Paul, MN: West Publishing.

Olson, W. C. (1940). Proceedings of the forty-eighth annual business meeting of the American Psychological Association, Inc., Pennsylvania State College, September 4, 5, 6, 7, 1940. *Psychological Bulletin, 37*, 699–741.

Peak, H. (1947). Proceedings of the fifty-fifth annual business meeting of the American Psychological Association, Inc., Detroit, Michigan. *American Psychologist, 2*, 468–510.

Title 9 C.F.R. Chapter 1, Subchapter A—Animal Welfare, Parts 1, 2, 3 (1992).

Tymchuk, A. (1982). Strategies for resolving value dilemmas. *American Behavioral Scientists, 26*(2), 159–175.

Tymchuk, A. (1986). Guidelines for ethical decision making. *Canadian Psychology, 27*, 36–43.

White v. the North Carolina State Board of Examiners of Practicing Psychologists, 8810SC1137 North Carolina Court of Appeals, Wake County No. 86-CVS-8131 (Feb. 6, 1990).

Wickline v. California, 228 Cal. 661 (Cal. App. 1986).

Wilson v. Blue Cross of Southern California, 270 Cal. 876 (Cal. App. 2d 1990).

Index

About the Authors

Mathilda B. Canter received her PhD from Arizona State University in 1965 and has been in independent practice as a clinical and consulting psychologist in Phoenix, Arizona since completing her postdoctoral internship. Long active in professional affairs on local, state, and national levels, Canter has served as Chair of the American Psychological Association (APA) Ethics Committee and of the subcommittee that shepherded the current APA Ethics Code through to its adoption. A member of the APA Board of Directors, Canter is a past president of the APA Division of Psychotherapy, served for 10 years on the Arizona State Board of Psychologist Examiners, including terms as Secretary and Chair, and has served on the Board of the Association of State and Provincial Psychology Boards (ASPPB). She is also a Distinguished Practitioner of the National Academies of Practice. The APA Divisions of Psychotherapy and Independent Practice and the ASPPB have honored Canter for her contributions to professional psychology.

Bruce E. Bennett is the Executive Director of the American Psychological Association Insurance Trust and a former member of the APA Board of Directors. He was instrumental in the drafting and passage of the new APA Ethical Principles of Psychologists and Code of Conduct. Bennett is a past president of the Illinois Psychological Association and served for many years as the Executive Director and Health Service Consultant to the Illinois Psychological Association. Prior to his relocation to the Washington, DC area, Bennett served on numerous committees of the APA and committees of the American Bar Association and the Illinois State Bar Association. Bennett's areas of expertise include professional liability and risk management, marketing and promotion of psychological services, ethics, and malpractice insurance issues. He is a coeditor of the APA monograph *Professional Liability and Risk Management.*

Stanley E. Jones completed his PhD in clinical psychology at the University of Florida at Gainesville. He worked several years in a mental health center based in Bronson, Florida and then moved to a private practice in Orlando, Florida. After 11 years of practice in Orlando, Jones accepted the position as Director of the APA Ethics Office, where he has served since July 1990. During his years in Florida, Jones was active in the Florida Psychological Association, serving in several positions, including President and Ethics Chair. In APA work, he was the Federal Advocacy Coordinator from Florida (1987–1990), served as the APA Liaison to the Champus Mental Health Advisory Panel (1988), and was elected to the APA Council of Representatives from Florida. In 1989, he was named Outstanding Psychologist of the Year in Florida.

Thomas F. Nagy received his PhD from the University of Illinois at Champaign-Urbana in 1972. He joined the staff at Loyola University in Chicago the

253

same year, beginning a diverse career that includes independent practice, consulting, and teaching. Currently, he is in independent practice in Palo Alto, California and is also affiliated with the Department of Psychiatry at Stanford University School of Medicine. Nagy has been active in the area of professional ethics since 1980, having chaired the Ethics Committee of the Illinois Psychological Association and served on ethics committees of the California and the American Psychological Associations. He chaired the original Task Force for the Revision of the *Ethical Principles of Psychology* and served on the Revision Comments Subcommittee from 1989 through 1992. As a part of his interest in consumer awareness of psychological issues, he consults regularly with students and patients, and he also provides consultation and workshop presentations for attorneys, educators, and institutions.